CONTINUING CRISIS
IN AMERICAN POLITICS

CONTINUING CRISIS
IN AMERICAN POLITICS

Edited by Marian D. Irish

Robert G. McCloskey

Robert J. Harris

Paul T. David

Stephen K. Bailey

Clinton Rossiter

Alpheus Thomas Mason

Morton Grodzins

Arthur Smithies

PRENTICE-HALL, INC., *Englewood Cliffs, N.J.*

A SPECTRUM BOOK

Preface

In the spring of 1962, the Department of Government at Florida State University sponsored a series of public lectures which brought to the campus a group of distinguished scholars representing diverse approaches to political science current in leading American universities. The frame of reference was made broad and flexible so that each lecturer might choose and develop a specific topic within his own area of specialization in American government.

As Head of the Department of Government at Florida State University it was my happy assignment to act as chairman of the lecture series and editor of these collected essays. On behalf of my colleagues in the Department of Government, I thank all of the lecturers for affording the students at Florida State University an exciting intellectual experience. Also on behalf of the Department of Government, I extend particular thanks to Paul Reynolds, Dean of the College of Arts and Sciences, whose educational values reflected in the University budget secured initial support for this visiting company of scholars.

The introduction to the essays was written in the *Bibliothek* of the University of Bonn. I am grateful to Professor Fritz T. Epstein, Managing Editor of the German Editorial Group for the publication of *Akten zur deutschen auswärtigen Politik 1918–45*, who obtained permission for me to work in the *Gastdozenten Zimmer* that overlooks the Rhine River. My personal gratitude goes also to Elke Frank, Assistant Professor of Government at Florida State University, who took time from her own research in archives of the German Foreign Office to read the introduction in manuscript. And I acknowledge with genuine appreciation the enthusiastic encouragement and continuing patience of James Murray, Social Science editor at Prentice-Hall, Inc.

M. D. I.

Table of Contents

INTRODUCTION   I

Marian D. Irish, Professor of Government, Florida State University

THE AMERICAN IDEOLOGY   10

Robert G. McCloskey, Professor of Government, Harvard University

The problem of definition. The nature of American ideology. The literature of American political thought. American political institutions. American political behavior.

THE INDIVIDUAL AND HIS RIGHTS: THE NATIONALIZATION
OF CIVIL LIBERTIES   26

Robert J. Harris, Professor of Political Science, Vanderbilt University

The constitutional guarantees. Judicial protection. The Bill of Rights and the Fourteenth Amendment: the Palko rule. Some practical applications. The preferred position.

THE CHANGING POLITICAL PARTIES   47

Paul T. David, Professor of Political Science, University of Virginia

Changes latent in the party system. A more competitive party system? Competition, cohesion, and centralization. Leadership problems: *Ins versus Outs*. Problems of party and campaign finance. Nationalizing tendencies in congressional politics. From the traditional to the rational.

IS CONGRESS THE OLD FRONTIER?   67

Stephen K. Bailey, Dean, Maxwell Graduate School of Citizenship and Public Affairs

Congress and the President: Old and New Frontiers. What Congress attempts to defend. The common frontier of Congress and the President. The agenda of congressional introspection.

PRESIDENT AND CONGRESS IN THE 1960'S   86

Clinton Rossiter, John L. Senior Professor of American Institutions, Cornell University

Constitutional separation of powers: the mystery of American government. The powers and functions of our "irresponsible" executive. The functions and powers of our "responsible" legislature. Executive-legislative relations: cooperation in contention. New factors in the equation of cooperation. Presidential ascendancy. Presidential "liberalism" and congressional "conservatism." The road ahead.

CONSTITUTIONAL LIMITATIONS IN A WORLD
OF CONTINUING CRISIS   109

Alpheus Thomas Mason, McCormick Professor of Jurisprudence, Princeton University

Judicial review: the sober second thought of the community. The Constitution: instrument of rights and limitations. Judicial restraint and new limitations in World War II. Judicial behavior in the Cold War. The Court's peculiar responsibility. Voting and the crucial preliminaries.

LOCAL STRENGTH IN THE AMERICAN FEDERAL SYSTEM:
THE MOBILIZATION OF PUBLIC-PRIVATE INFLUENCE   132

Morton Grodzins, Professor of Political Science, The University of Chicago

The mixture of public and private business. Private groups doing public business. Public business for private gain. Public officers and the public-private mixture. The public role of private groups. The strength of the mobilized community front. Variations in local influence. Conclusions.

THE EVOLUTION OF UNITED STATES FOREIGN
ECONOMIC POLICY   153

Arthur Smithies, Nathaniel Ropes Professor of Economics, Harvard University

Economic policy in American foreign policy. The United States and Western Europe. The United States and economically underdeveloped countries. The Free World and the Communist Bloc. The United States in the world economy.

CONTINUING CRISIS
IN AMERICAN POLITICS

INTRODUCTION

Marian D. Irish

This collection of essays constitutes an interpretative analysis of the changing values, institutions, roles, and strategies that are giving new dimensions to the American political system. The essays do not profess to be purely informative, wholly objective, or always dispassionate. Each is written by one whose authority stems from long experience in solid and systematic scholarship. Though the authors do not share identical values, all are committed to a realistic analysis of the politics of American democracy. Each incorporates ideas into his concept of reality; for American political behavior, like any other facet of human behavior, can only be assessed within the context of ideas. All are dedicated to the democratic process in politics and, despite their critical commentary and professional concern on many points, the over-all impression is pride in the American tradition.

Since the eight essays were first delivered as lectures, some passages are more eloquent than scholars usually think suitable to their written works. The editor believes, however, that it is good for scholars sometimes to profess, and so the spoken words are left to liven the printed text. The style of each essay befits the materials and methods of its author. Robert Harris and Alpheus T. Mason, for example, pursue a traditional legalistic approach.

MARIAN D. IRISH *is Professor and Head of the Department of Government at Florida State University where she has been a member of the faculty since 1933. She has contributed numerous articles to the professional journals and law reviews and is co-author with James Prothro of* The Politics of American Democracy *(1962).*

Since, to them, "the law is what the judges say it is," both authors incorporate the rhetoric of the Supreme Court into much of their text. They employ the ancient words and phrases of the Justices as "the comfortable words" of the American tradition. On the other hand, the essay of Morton Grodzins, whose research was mainly in field surveys, reflects the easy colloquialism of the local Chamber of Commerce, the Rotary, the City Fathers, and politicians, all of whom carry on the private-public business. The style of Arthur Smithies, a political economist who has frequently served as consultant to the inner circles of decision-makers, has the terseness and persuasiveness of an official paper.

Seven of the eight essays are fully footnoted. The footnotes are important clues to how the author went about his work, where he collected his data, and what methods he used in supporting his hypothesis. The *Suggestions for Further Reading* at the end of each chapter, in addition to the many titles in the footnotes, give the reader opportunity to pursue in depth the problems sketched in the essays. The literature of American government and politics is obviously voluminous. Any listing, short of the Library of Congress catalogue, is highly selective. Because our eight authors hold to various viewpoints and pursue different methods in political science, the sum of their suggestions covers a broad spectrum of source materials: the classics in political theory, biographies and memoirs, scholarly monographs, professional journals, law reviews, newspapers and news weeklies, government documents of all kinds, and survey research including field notes, case studies, opinion polls, and election returns.

An increasing number of political scientists are inclined to be critical, even scornful, of the traditional approaches to political science. They insist upon exact methodology; they prefer problems which lend themselves to observation, quantification, testing, and empirical verification; they shy away from historical materials and concentrate on contemporary data. Behavioral scholars are more likely to draw from the several disciplines of social science, especially from psychology and sociology, and to buttress their techniques with statistical methods and mathematical models. Two of our essays illustrate different aspects of behavioral political science: the studies of voting behavior and election results with which Paul David supports his hypothesis of changing character of political parties; and the case studies of specific situations which Morton Grodzins uses to confute some of the conventional wisdom on federalism and to show how "local is as local does."

The political behaviorists have attempted to develop systematic political theory based on propositions validated by empirical analysis. They have tended to be quantitative in their methods, using sampling and the structured interview among other new techniques. Concentrating on what *is*, they are likely to be indifferent to what *was* and skeptical of what *ought to be*. They have sharply challenged the writings of those who lean on history; and they have been even more acidulous about "political philosophers" who deal with ideologues and normative theory. Emmette Redford, taking cognizance of this schism in the political science profession, has counselled a middle ground for the discipline: a *may be* at the juncture of *is* and *ought to be*.[1]

These essays represent both traditional and behavioral approaches to political science, yet all the authors move toward the middle ground which Redford has in mind. In the first essay, on *The American Ideology*, Robert McCloskey, though traditional in his use of historical materials, recognizes and is conditioned by new studies in political behavior. At the outset, he points out that students of political thought are no longer blessedly free to talk about "agreement on fundamentals" as the indispensable condition of American democracy. The easy assumptions of yesterday have been dispelled by recent empirical studies. Hence he narrows his own conjectures on values to a minority of the American population, to the subculture of American leadership that may be influenced by, and that may in turn influence, an American ideology. He assiduously avoids the controversial issue of *consensus* in the principles of American government. He looks for ideology, not only in the literature of political thought, but also in political institutions and in political behavior.

To be realistic in political science, we must study government in action. Government in action invariably means institutions in transition, new policies emerging, and the balance of power ever shifting. Decision-making never takes place in a situation *de novo*. The input for policy, which is the nucleus of politics, involves cultural, economic, social, and legal factors which constrain the institutions, role-players, and processes in any government. To understand the context of current political action one must be aware of the past which determined the present. Clinton Rossiter, who is obviously much alive to "the problems of a convulsive world and a runaway technology," deliberately keeps in close touch with history as he examines *President and Congress in the 1960's* in terms of "politics, horse-trading, rules, customs, and morality." Alpheus T. Mason, whose essay *Constitutional Limitations in a World of Continuing Crisis* suggested a title for the whole collection of essays, also prefers the historical perspective for a comprehensive view of the Supreme Court in action. For Rossiter and Mason the historical imperative is central to decision-making, at the juncture of *is* and *ought to be*.

---

[1] Emmette Redford, "Reflections on a Discipline," LV *American Political Science Review* (December 1961), 755–762.

These essays do not purport to be a complete and exhaustive investigation of the American political system as it *was*, *is*, or *may be*. For the most part, emphasis is upon transition—between *was* and *is*, between *is* and *may be*. From different standpoints, each author views the government in action as a complex process of decision-making. It is presupposed that readers are generally acquainted with the constitutional background and formal structure of American government; hence the authors spend little time on historical exposition or institutional description. Institutions are broadly conceived as both official and unofficial agencies of government, public policy-makers at work. Thus McCloskey's "ideologues" are political activists ·politicians, lobbyists, official party leaders, and others, who seek to preserve or change values in the American tradition.

Decision-making in any political system occurs simultaneously at many different stages and in many different ways. One's choice of party affiliation is an important decision; every election is an important decision—indeed, these are primary decisions which vitally affect all decision-making by the official agencies of the government. When Congress passes a bill (or fails to), when the President takes a stand on a pressing issue (or fails to), when the Court hands down a decision (or refuses to review)—all such decisions have widespread repercussions on the whole American system. Paul David brings us new data on shifts in party membership and changes in voting behavior, especially in the southern states, which may predicate an entirely new sequence of official decisions, particularly in Congress. Bailey and Rossiter offer new insights into congressional and presidential decision-making. Harris and Mason discuss various political repercussions of recent judicial decisions.

All of the authors are concerned with functional interrelationships. Paul David comments upon "the relationships between competition, cohesions, and centralizations in the party system" and suggests some implications of these relationships. Both Stephen Bailey and Clinton Rossiter are concerned with the working relations between Congress and the President as they meet the urgent issues that confound the country in the 1960's. Bailey buttresses his convictions with empirical observations on how Congress works today. Rossiter views the contemporary in the light of the "pressures of history." Morton Grodzins points up the peculiar relationships that operate between public and private groups at all levels in the federal system. The reader may find some overlapping in these essays, but one cannot expect neat compartmentalization of powers and functions in any realistic study of government in action.

The hierarchial relationships are generally complicated in any political system, but especially so in a federal system. The constitutional relationships among the national government, the states, and the local governments in the United States have always been fraught with dissension. In his essay *Local Strength in the American Federal System*, Grodzins tries an exciting new perspective. Observing national and local politics at work in specific situations, he finds that public-private influence at the local level has been mobilized quite successfully for the purpose of influencing national programs. "The two planes of government are not adversaries. They serve the same people for the same ends."

All of the essayists observe an increasing centralization in American politics and government. Paul David notes that "campaigning by the candidates for President and Vice President has clearly become more national in scope" and finds also a "marked change in the relationships of national party leaders to the congressional compaigns." The subtitle of Robert Harris' essay is self-explanatory—*The Nationalization of Civil Liberties*. A native southerner, teaching constitutional law in a southern university, his personal viewpoint is unequivocal on the ante bellum issue of states' rights: "If the Court is to perform effectively one of its high functions in the maintenance of civil rights, it would do well to discard outmoded and unwarranted theories of dual federalism and a hypersensitive respect for state legislatures and state courts in favor of individual rights."

Representation—the relationship between the legislator and the mass electorate of his constituency—remains the unsolved problem of modern democracy. Although the United States has had long experience with constitutional forms of democratic government, malrepresentation in Congress and in all fifty states has become almost incredibly acute. The American system of representation was established when the majority of the people were farmers or lived in rural areas. The single-member constituency was a fairly equitable basis for representation as long as the majority of voters had similar interests. Today, however, rural constituents everywhere continue to hold the balance of legislative power, despite the fact that a majority of the population now lives in urban or suburban areas, and their interests are highly diversified. On March 26, 1962, the Supreme Court took dramatic cognizance of the rotten-boroughs situation and in *Baker v Carr* decided that voters might go into federal courts to seek relief from discriminatory apportionment of legislative seats. Both Harris and Mason discuss the case within its legal and judicial frame of reference. As to its political import, Bailey foresees immediate consequences in congressional reapportionment as well as reapportionment in the state legislatures: "Probably no Supreme Court decision since *Brown v Topeka* is more fraught with consequence for our political system."

Changing roles is a theme that runs through most of the essays. Robert Harris' essay on nationalization of civil rights and Alpheus T. Mason's essay on constitutional limitations both trace the changing roles of the Supreme Court. In the early period of Franklin Roosevelt's administration the Court's constituency was the conservative business community; with changing times the Court yielded its protection of economic interests; "new-old subjects of judicial guardianship emerged" (preachers, prisoners, pamphleteers, and the like); and the Court became champion of minority rights. *Baker v Carr* establishes still another role for the Court—defender of majority representation. Paul David's essay, *The Changing Political Parties* ("from the traditional to the rational"), draws attention to the regular weekly congressional leadership meetings at the White House, a major innovation in partisan politics that has almost escaped the notice of political scientists, probably because the practice has never been formalized in legislation. In the essays of Stephen Bailey and Clinton Rossiter, institutional dynamics are made to seem kaleidoscopic, roles changing and interchanging, as a succession of presidents from Roosevelt to Kennedy strive with each session of Congress to grapple with vast problems of defense, economic well-being and social welfare.

In an analysis of government in action that posits policy as the nucleus of politics, the functions of government are not considered separately from the agencies that perform them. Every essay treats some aspect of current policy-making. The essays generally are concerned with decision-making within American government; all recognizing, however, the influence of world affairs upon domestic issues. In a world of continuing crisis, national security is paramount in all policies. Arthur Smithies' essay discusses economic policy as a key instrument of American foreign policy, probing deep into problems of contemporary international politics. The Smithies essay takes a hard look at the external side of both input and output: the ideas, interests, and policies of Western Europe, the Communist bloc, and the economically under-developed countries; how their behavior affects what we can plan and how our plans can affect their behavior toward us. The essay considers some possible tactics and practical strategy for meeting continuing crises in world affairs, but always in terms of alternatives, with no single or easy prescription. Having had much experience in public planning, the author is impelled to warn us of the hazard of meeting this year's crisis with last year's plan, next year's crisis with this year's plan.

American government is an old subject in political science; in fact, the Constitution of the United States is the oldest written document of its kind governing a modern state. Stephen Bailey reminds us that Congress is an

"Old Frontier"; Congress has been in business since 1789. The Supreme Court has been exercising judicial review since 1803, in *Marbury v Madison*. It is virtually impossible to produce a study of American government that is both scholarly and wholly novel; as in all facets of human expression the obvious and even the trite is more likely to be accurate than the dashingly different. If we think of government in terms of "forms" and "framework," "structure" and "design," "checks" and "balances," then the study of American government remains old stuff. But if we change our metaphor so that government becomes man writ large and government in action becomes political behavior, then the facets of our study are multiple and ever new. As Harold Lasswell long ago pointed out, who gets what in American politics and how and why are fascinating problems for investigation, the more so because *who, what, why,* and *how* are ever-changing variables that occur in constantly different combinations.

Only two of our essayists, Paul David and Morton Grodzins, can be called political behaviorists within the professional connation, but all of them are avowedly aware not only of the official and legal norms that constitute traditional political science, but also of the many other activities of individual and group behavior that influence public policy. Thus, Robert Harris, who is perhaps the most legalistic of the group, concludes that "in the pluralistic society of the second half of the twentieth century, government is not the only enemy of individual rights and perhaps not even the most important." He is deeply disturbed by the activities of private groups and associations which, more often than the governments, attempt to suppress freedom of conscience and expression.

Government in action is never at a standstill; policy-making is an inexorably continuous process. At the point of decision-making, values are of crucial importance in determining strategy. Objectives and goals for every course of action reflect the values of decision-makers and the impact of every decision is either to preserve or to change the status quo. In either case, value judgments enter into the decision; and just as alternative courses of action involve varying assessments of values, so changes in values result in changing roles in government, changing strategies in politics, new customs, and new laws: the present is simultaneously past and future. The problem for the political scientist concerned for the output (and it is usually sterile scholarship which lacks such concern) is how to engage in political evaluation in a sophisticated way.

The traditional political philosopher has been inclined to appraise the relative merits of different political systems or different ideologies on the basis of a priori judgments. A scientific conclusion cannot be reached, however, until the empirical data is sufficient to show how the institutions actually work, what in fact is required to put ideologies into operation, and what effect the arrangements will have upon the participants. On the other hand, if we wait for all the data to be collected, for all the detailed studies to cover every aspect of even one system, we are not likely to produce any significant major works in the foreseeable future. And yet we cannot ignore the obvious and overwhelming facts, that political systems do exist, do operate, and do affect the lives of all the peoples. Robert Dahl suggests[2] that "empirical science had better find a place for speculation." The natural sciences have left open the door to imagination in scholarship; in the same manner, contemporary political science might profit if its methods of empirical inquiry are illuminated by some vision of the road ahead. Move we must; and preferably in the direction we believe will best take us where we want to go.

It is in this spirit that Stephen Bailey conceives the creative role of political science: "The quintessential business of students of public affairs is to interrelate selected propositions of history, social science, and moral philosphy in such a way as to promote benevolent rationality in the formulation and execution of public policy." Not all of the essayists, of course, accept this proposition; some, notably the behaviorists, have tried to maintain neutrality and detachment, avoiding both metaphysical and prescriptive statements. All of them, however, have brought values into their investigations and most of them, in considering what *may be* the politics of American democracy, have felt free to express their own values.

The McCloskey essay on American ideology perhaps proceeds the most cautiously in delineating values. From the perspective of intellectual history, the author finds a continuing "ambivalence" in the American tradition: "It is characteristic of the American mind . . . to hold contradictory ideas simultaneously without bothering to resolve the potential conflict between them." Several of the essayists voice concern about the current "Radical Right" and the implications it may have for individual freedoms. Professor McCloskey, however, is not greatly perturbed; he has perceived the rise and decline of similar political enthusiasm in American history. He puts his trust in the "pragmatic spirit" which is "perhaps our only really basic quality of mind." Professor Harris, whose investigation was mostly confined to court cases, is somewhat less sanguine. He fervently hopes that the Court and Congress will be more vigorous in exercising their separate responsibilities in the protection of civil rights. He remarks, however, that "the record of the

---

[2] Robert Dahl, "The Behavioral Approach in Political Science: Epitaph for a Monument to a Successful Protest," LV *American Political Science Review* (December 1961) 763–772.

federal government with respect to basic substantive and procedural liberties is far better than that of the states."

"To keep all of us free"—this is the last line from Dean Bailey's essay on Congress. Here is "the common frontier" where all of the essayists, and the editor, stand. It is a value judgment which all of us share—whether we look at what *was*, *is*, or *may be*. This, we believe, is the primary goal of the American government in action.

THE AMERICAN IDEOLOGY

Robert G. McCloskey

THE PROBLEM OF DEFINITION

The title of this essay presents certain obvious difficulties that must be faced at the outset. The first is the problem of definition, and it will be solved in the Humpty-Dumpty tradition by an autocratic act of will. What I mean by "ideology" is an explicit body of political conviction rising to some reasonably advanced level of generality and abstraction. An "ideologue" then, to borrow an ugly but useful term, is a man whose political choices are influenced to some degree by such a body of doctrine. He need not be a political philosopher: the level of abstraction in question is far more modest than that. Concretely, one man may oppose federal medical care for the aged because he feels that his taxes are too high and that he does not want to pay new ones; another may oppose it because he feels it is bad for individual initiative to augment such governmental activities further. The latter is thinking ideo-

ROBERT G. McCLOSKEY *has been a member of the faculty of Harvard University since 1948 and is now Chairman of the Department of Government. Except for a brief experience as administrative assistant to the governor of Michigan in 1944–45, he has stuck to his academic last, contributing frequently to the professional journals and law reviews, and writing several major works on American government, including* American Conservatism in the Age of Enterprise (*1950*) *and* The American Supreme Court (*1960*).

logically; the former is not. The latter is not necessarily superior. He is simply different, whether for better or for worse.

The second difficulty is a graver one and cannot be handled so cavalierly: there may be some reason to doubt that the title refers to a real thing, even if the above definition is accepted, and even if we apply the rather generous standards of reality that normally prevail in the social sciences. The doubt can be expressed in two rhetorical questions: do Americans in significant number and degree think ideologically? And if they do, do they agree enough about what they think to justify the definite article in the title. In short, is there any warrant for using either the word "ideology" or the word "the" in conjunction with it?

Unfortunately these are not the conventional, perfunctory misgivings expressed by the essayist as a ritual observance before he reaches what he regards as the meaty part of his discourse. They are palpable doubts that might threaten to prevent the discourse altogether. A few short years ago they could perhaps have been waived, or overridden by a dogmatic, intuitive assertion. One man's belief that there was a widely shared ideology under-lying American politics was just as good as the next man's conviction that there was not: neither had much hard data to use against the other, and the discussion could proceed comfortably on the basis of either assumption. The student of political thought was blessedly free to talk, as he traditionally had, about the "political values of America" and about "agreement on funda-mentals" as the indispensable condition of American democracy.

But today that freedom has been, if not lost, at least considerably at-tenuated and modified. The students of public opinion have begun to ask questions and find answers that render impossible the easy assumptions of yesterday. For example, Campbell et al. in The American Voter[1] have presented evidence to suggest that only a very small proportion of Americans cherish ideas about politics that are coherent enough to be called "ideology." For another example, Professors Prothro and Grigg in their study of Ann Arbor and Tallahassee were unable to confirm the hoary hypothesis that there is a consensus on fundamental democratic values among Americans, and in fact their evidence suggested pretty strongly that disagreement rather than agree-ment was the American mode.[2] V. O. Key, in his magisterial treatment of Public Opinion and American Democracy,[3] further develops both of these insights

---

[1] Angus Campbell et al., The American Voter (New York: John Wiley and Sons, Inc., 1960).

[2] J. W. Prothro and C. M. Grigg, "Fundamental Principles of Democracy: Bases of Agreement and Disagreement," Journal of Politics, XXII (1960), 276–94.

[3] (New York: Alfred A. Knopf, Inc., 1961).

with his usual combination of caution, reliability, and charm. I concur with Robert Dahl[4] that no would-be analyst of "the American mind" can hereafter reckon without this accumulating evidence. The analyst may be able to get around it; he may be able to explain it away and somehow restore the old axioms to their ancient status. But he cannot ignore it unless he simply prefers the never-never-land of his own imagining to any real world that might impair the shining image. And as the evidence piles up further, the possibility of retrieving the old canons of faith may become thinner and thinner.

Meanwhile however, it seems that at least one escape hatch has been left partly ajar. There is some reason to believe, or at any rate to hypothesize, that there is a small group in the population whose members can be identified as "ideologues." This group includes, as Key says, "politicians, lobbyists, officials, party leaders, and influentials"—in short the "political activists of the society." This group, he suggests, constitutes a kind of "political sub-culture" and "perhaps within this group are to be found in high degree those beliefs, values, habits of action, and modes of political belief that give the political system its distinctive characteristics."[5] The idea is that this "elite" (I use the term with neither pejorative nor complimentary intentions) contains the "carriers" of the political culture and that the mass of the people thus engage in "ideology by proxy." Perhaps ideology does play an important part in determining the character of American government, but it is the ideology of this leadership group that plays the part, not the broad political convictions of people in general.

This hypothesis is in some ways more satisfactory to the student of intellectual history than the traditional assumptions about democratic principles and the mass mind. Both Campbell and Key have collected illustrations of the mass mind in action on questions of political ideology: for example, the college graduate who "when asked what she meant by calling herself a 'liberalist' replied that she liked *both* of the parties."[6] But most of us could draw similar anecdotes from our own experience, and it has always been hard to reconcile such scraps of data with the contention that "the American mind" as a whole has a coherent view about abstract questions of political value. If we hypothesize, with Key, that Americans in general have habits and attitudes of political significance and that the explicit ideology is

---

[4] "The Behavioral Approach in Political Science: Epitaph for a Monument to a Successful Protest," *American Political Science Review*, LV (1961), 771.

[5] *Op. cit.*, p. 51.

[6] Campbell *et al.*, *op. cit.*, p. 232.

"carried" by an influential minority, this difficulty is diminished. Moreover, the traditional materials of American political thought may then begin to have a more plausible relevance to American political behavior. It is most doubtful that the "liberalist" coed just cited could have been greatly affected in her thinking by Jefferson's First Inaugural Address or South Carolina's Ordinance of Nullification. But it is within belief that some of those in the circles of leadership may have a dim understanding of those pronouncements and have been influenced by them. The effect of these modern investigations of the popular mind may be to make it easier than before to talk relevantly about the nature of American ideology.

Suppose then we do narrow our field of discussion to that minority of the American population who can be called ideologues. By assumption and definition we have now disposed of the problem of whether the word "ideology" is permissible. We are talking now only about those to whom the term *does* fairly apply. But there remains the other problem: whether we can speak of "the" American ideology even among this restricted group, and whether we can find in the group the consensus on fundamental political values that political theorists so hunger for. The evidence on this point is very scanty. Prothro and Grigg did find a somewhat higher degree of agreement on some supposedly democratic values as they moved up the educational scale in Ann Arbor and Tallahassee, but the trend was not consistent and on most issues the replies fell far short of unanimity. Herbert McClosky *et al.*[7] seemed to find smaller agreement among leaders than among followers, but their questions were directed to more or less current political issues, not to underlying ideological premises; questions of the latter sort might have changed the picture. Stouffer found "civic leaders" more attached than people in general to such a traditional democratic value as freedom of expression, but some of the answers even from these leaders were intolerant enough to leave doubt that any firm consensus exists.[8] Key offers an educated guess that political activists may share something resembling a common understanding about the rules of the game, but warns that more evidence is necessary before we can be confident even about this.

Both the data that we do have and the data we do not have could provide an opening for this essay. On the one hand the evidence permits (without, of course, proving) the assumption that the American ideology is limited to and

[7] "Issue Conflict and Consensus Among Party Leaders and Followers," *American Political Science Review*, LIV (1960), 406–27.

[8] Samuel A. Stouffer, *Communism, Conformity, and Civil Liberties* (New York: Doubleday and Co., Inc., 1955).

carried by a subculture of leaders. This makes it possible to indulge the further assumption that ideas expressed in the literature of American political thought bear some resemblance to the American ideology, as we have now defined it. Congressman Doe and Senator Roe may be intellectually inferior to John Adams and James Madison, but in their tendencies of thought they represent a lower form, not a wholly different species. We cannot impute Hamilton's specific thoughts to them, but we can believe that they have thoughts about the ideological matters that engaged Hamilton, that there may be some kinship between their ways of thought and the ways of other articulate Americans past and present. In short, the uncertain state of the evidence about this leadership group allows us some freedom to speculate about its character, using the literature as one of the clues, but also drawing on any other resource that may seem plausibly relevant. These speculations may be modified or displaced in the fullness of the years by the weight of contrary data. But one who is grateful for an opportunity when he sees it will waste no time in slipping through the breach.

THE NATURE OF AMERICAN IDEOLOGY

I would like therefore to offer a conjecture (I hesitate to call it a hypothesis) about the nature of the ideology of this group, whose convictions and habits of mind may play a decisive part in setting the tone of American government. The key word, I suggest, is "ambivalence." That is to say, it is characteristic of the American mind, insofar as this group represents it, to hold contra- dictory ideas simultaneously without bothering to resolve the potential conflict between them. I do not simply mean what Madison meant in the 10th Federalist—that there are some who believe in one principle and some who believe in another, and that the conflict between these persons of varying belief is often either compromised or left undecided. This may often be true, but it is not the heart of the matter. Many—perhaps most—of the persons in this group maintain a set of dualistic political values, and the ideology of the typical American "ideologue" is not therefore a consistent body of dogmas tending in the same direction, but a conglomerate of ideas which may be and often are logically inconsistent. Such a state of irresolution about the most fundamental and important articles of political faith would be intolerable to the dogmatic rationalist—to the "logical Frenchman" of folklore, for example. No doubt there have been and are Americans who also are vexed by incertitude and feel driven to seek out and dissipate the potential contra- dictions in their minds—John Calhoun was one of these. But most Americans, even those who are relatively thoughtful and articulate, seem to feel no such compulsion. They are able to believe both in majority rule and minority rights, both in conformity and in freedom, both in federalism and in centralization. Logically, they should either choose between these values or seek the basis for an accommodation between them. It may be rational to believe in both majority rule and minority rights and to a qualified view of each idea—majority rule with *these* reservations, minority rights with *those* reservations. But this is not the way Americans have approached such matters. We have tended instead to hold the two ideas in suspension and have largely ignored the logical difficulties inherent in such doublethink.

This conjecture has an obvious bearing on that traditional question about an American ideological consensus. There may be in fact, among the leadership group we are considering, some tacitly shared understandings about the rules of the game, a pattern of behavior that reflects wide agreement on procedures. But beyond that it may be meaningless to ask whether the members of the group agree with each other about fundamental political values, because they may not even agree with themselves about such values, much less with one another. Perhaps this helps explain the otherwise curious tendency of people to contradict themselves when subjected to public opinion surveys—those who want taxes cut even if it means putting off some important things that need to be done but who also support various kinds of foreign involvement that would obviously make tax cuts quite impossible; or the large number in the Prothro-Grigg sample who professed a belief in majority rule, but also believed that only the well-informed should be allowed to vote in a city referendum. To speak of agreement on fundamental political values among people with such ambivalent propensities may be to indulge the prepossessions of the viewer. Quite possibly the leadership group would display a lower rate of self-contradiction, especially on specific issue questions, because of a greater alertness to the implications of a given answer. But on questions involving root political values, the incidence of irresolution would probably still be very high.

By way of supporting this generalization about the nature of American ideology, let us examine three categories of American political phenomena: the political literature, institutions, and behavior of America. All are in part a reflection of its ideology. Such phenomena as institutions and behavior may be influenced by other factors: an institution may develop a life of its own and may, in fact, be the cause of ideology as well as its effect; behavior, even among the articulate minority, may be a function of habit or interests rather than ideological premises. The question of what weights should be assigned to these various causal elements is a very important one, but for the moment I leave it aside. It is enough if we can assume that ideology plays some inceptive part in our governmental arrangements and our political behavior. Insofar as that is the case, a doubly-explanatory relationship can be discerned: the institutions and the behavior provide us with a key to the nature of the ideology, and the ideology thus understood helps to account for the institutions and the behavior.

THE LITERATURE OF AMERICAN POLITICAL THOUGHT

The literature of American political thought is thickly strewn with evidence of ambivalence about fundamental values that may be attributed to the American mind. Jefferson is such a perfect case that it is almost unfair to cite him, but his stature and his impact on our politics have been so great that it would be quite impossible to leave him out of account. As Merrill Peterson has recently reminded us,[9] he has been invoked on each side of almost every question that American politics has been concerned with. His admirers as well as his critics have endlessly sought the "real" Jefferson in the welter of pronouncements and actions that he bequeathed to us, only to be confounded by the protean quality of the man. His first inaugural address is the text of a mind divided within itself.[10] "The will of the majority," he tells us, "is in all cases to prevail" *but* "the minority possess their equal rights which equal law must protect"; "the support of the state governments in all their rights" *but* "the preservation of the general government in its whole constitutional vigor"; and so on. He is of course aware that these generalities are, on the face, contradictory, so he informs us that he is in each instance "stating the general principle, but not all its limitations." The listener is to infer that Jefferson could resolve the paradoxes if he had time to do so, but the truth is that he never did have the time to spare. The vast body of his writings and the long record of his political career seem to compound the paradoxes rather than dispose of them. Did he believe in absolute majority rule or in minority rights? In state autonomy or in national authority? Jefferson's answer seems to be that in both cases he believed in both values, and similar dualisms are encountered almost everywhere we turn as we try to assess his essential quality.

But Jefferson, it might be said, has always been a special case, a man of such extraordinary qualities that no general insights about *homo Americanus*

---

[9] Merrill D. Peterson, *The Jefferson Image in the American Mind* (New York: Oxford University Press, Inc., 1960).

[10] Henry S. Commager, ed., *Documents of American History* (New York: Appleton-Century-Crofts, 1949).

can be drawn from observing him. On the contrary, he has been enshrined in our political pantheon precisely because he so faithfully mirrored the various and conflicting wills-to-believe that we recognize in ourselves. However, it is true that one swallow, even such a swallow as this, will not make a summer. So let us consider his rival and sometime friend, John Adams. Parrington put him "midway between Hamilton and Jefferson,"[11] and there is some validity in this categorization. There are differences in emphasis among the trio—these dualistic values are not always kept in perfect balance. Yet the dualisms are there in the mind of Adams, too. Did he believe in rule by the wise, rich, and well-born, or in rule by the many? Both, he tells us in the *Defence*,[12] and he offers us an executive who will stand between these contending forces, preventing both from triumphing, preventing in short the resolution of the contradiction between them. Parrington thought him a turncoat because as a youth he had espoused the rights of man, while as an old man he defended the rights of property, but this is to misconceive the nature of his thought. For Adams, young or old, both values had a place in his ethic, neither was displaced by the other.

With Hamilton, to round out that troika, the case becomes a little harder; one might escape making it by arguing that he was in fact atypical. He had a lawyer-like tendency in political disputation to state the position he took as strongly as possible so that the ambivalences he might feel were often overborne in the heat of the moment. His statement, in such a moment, that the people "is a great beast" has frequently been cited as the outcry of an antirepublican dogmatist. But in the famous letter to Edward Carrington he says on his "private faith and honor as a man" that he is "affectionately attached to the republican theory"; then in the next breath admits to some misgivings as to whether that theory is "consistent with that stability and order in government which are essential to public strength and to private security and happiness." If we believe him when he tells Carrington that he is speaking "the real language of [his] heart,"[13] we must accept a Hamilton who, like Jefferson and Adams, held conflicting political values and who had left the basic conflicts unresolved.

I do not contend that such dualisms are never resolved, that the typical

[11] Vernon L. Parrington, *Main Currents in American Thought*, Vol. I (New York: Harcourt, Brace & World, Inc., 1930), 307.

[12] *The Defence of the Constitutions of Government of the United States of America* (*1787–1788*), in Charles F. Adams, ed., *The Life and Works of John Adams* (Boston: Little, Brown & Co., 1851), Vol. VI.

[13] Benjamin F. Wright, ed., *A Source Book of American Political Theory* (New York: The Macmillan Company, 1929), pp. 303–04.

American leader perversely continues to hold them in suspension in the face of circumstances that call imperatively for a choice. On the contrary, we have been able to maintain this ambivalence about fundamental values largely because the pressure of circumstance has seldom been so stringent, because we have usually enjoyed a measure of leeway granted to few other nations in world history. In our comparatively rare moments of great crisis, some choices have become mandatory and then they have been made. Lincoln's insistence on the preservation of the Union at all costs became in his mind such a fundamental principle, allowing for no modification or exception. But it is worth noting that even this idea emerged slowly in his thinking and became fully explicit only when secession forced the decision upon him. Before that and even for a time afterward, the primacy of this value was not apparent in what he did and said, any more than it was apparent among Northerners in general. Before that he was the very proto-type of the American political leader, content to live with contradictory values in the hope that the logical dilemma need never be faced.

The so-called reactionary enlightenment among some Southern thinkers in the pre-Civil War years did involve some dogmatic choices between hitherto incompatible beliefs. George Fitzhugh was not ambivalent about such questions as the equality of man; Calhoun made his decision between majority rule and minority rights in unequivocal favor of the latter. But again we have a case of extraordinary circumstances producing an atypical result among men of a very special temper. It is significant that the intellectual movement in which they participated established no tradition: Fitzhugh had been almost forgotten until comparatively recent times when he was rediscovered by scholarly antiquarians; Calhoun's reputation as a statesman was so great that he himself could never be forgotten, but his concept of absolute minority rights has not been viable, even in the South, except with respect to one issue. And surely it is noteworthy that the issues of the war itself became in time so blurred in the national memory that the conflict could become, by a rather wonderful paradox, a symbol of national unity. To quote Oscar Handlin:

The war was transmuted from the bitter conflict it had been into an episode of high adventure. Every base element vanished; only nobility remained, as if those who survived could thus banish the guilt of having failed those who died. Above all, if the war were to bind Americans in national unity, both sides had to seem right. There could be no villains, only heroes.[14]

---

[14] "The Civil War as Symbol and as Actuality," *The Massachusetts Review*, III (1961), 135.

That is the heart of the matter. Not that there was some right and some wrong on both sides, but that both sides were right. That characteristic American illogicality was untenable for a brief time while the cannons were still firing and during the bitterness of reconstruction. But it could reassert itself later when Confederates and Yankees began to celebrate Decoration Day together.

As I run down the list of articulate Americans who have been influential in political affairs, I find ambivalence wherever I turn. What of Theodore Roosevelt, for example? He is conventionally thought of as the exponent of regulated bigness as against Wilson's preference for restoring small-unit competition. But even on this matter Roosevelt was equivocal. And on what might be thought of as the more fundamental questions of democratic value, he was also firmly on record in support of both sides "exploding," as Richard Hofstadter has said, "in every direction at once."[15] He sometimes professed to fear the influence of the soulless, irresponsible plutocrats, yet he assailed the muckrakers for their exposés of business-government alliances. He was chronically worried about the dangers of populistic radicalism, yet, in his Bull Moose "Confession of Faith" in 1912, he came out for the unqualified right of the people to rule, even to overrule judicial decisions that were contrary to the popular will. These dizzy leaps from one trapeze to another might be set down to mere opportunism, rather than to inner conflict of beliefs; and opportunism may indeed have played its part. But he was, I think, too moral a person to assume consciously a position at odds with his fundamental values. The point—a convenient one for him—was that he had two sets of fundamental values, so that in a given political context he could choose either one. And the fact that so many of our articulate leaders have been likewise richly endowed lends color to my conjecture that ambivalence is characteristic of the American political temper.

AMERICAN POLITICAL INSTITUTIONS

The coloring is reinforced when we turn away from what American political activists have said and consider the political institutions they have helped to shape and have lived with. Take the presidency, for example. Certain of the Founding Fathers—James Wilson, Gouverneur Morris, and perhaps Hamilton—hoped to establish an executive with broad powers resembling those described by John Locke under the heading of the "prerogative."

[15] Richard Hofstadter, *The American Political Tradition and the Men Who Made It* (New York: Alfred A. Knopf, Inc., 1948), p. 225.

However, the nation had recently undergone some vivid experiences involving the royal governors and George III himself, experiences that fostered a deep suspicion of executive authority. Nor was this conflict of opinion resolved by the enactment of Article II of the Constitution. A political power play put the Constitution over and Article II along with it, but no clearcut image of democratic leadership was embodied either in the Constitutional language or in the thinking of those who influenced the development of the office.

In truth no such image has developed in the years that have followed. Is the presidency meant to be a position of creative leadership such as that described by James Burns in his evaluation of Franklin Roosevelt?[16] Does our ideology presuppose that the President will, like Jackson, mold the environment of public opinion, and "lead" in the literal sense of the word? Or is it expected that he will, like Eisenhower, follow public opinion and embody it, rather than try to control it? Either conception of the Presidency may be defensible in terms of one facet or another of the American tradition. As Myrdal has remarked, Americans seem to believe in leadership on the one hand and to resist it on the other.[17] We are prone to use the word "leadership" like an incantation. The impression is that any problem—slum clearance, juvenile delinquency, or the atom bomb—will be solved if we can only get the right leadership to go to work on it. But we are equally quick to condemn as "dictatorship" (once it would have been "monarchy") any attempt to step in and provide the leadership we seemed to be calling for. In short, the passivity of a Coolidge or the activism of Franklin Roosevelt in his first hundred days are both consonant with the institution that history has shaped; for that institution reflects the divided political mind of America.

Or take the Congress, which must surely be one of the most curious repositories of paradox that ingenious political man has yet devised. This was an agency set up to express the will of American democracy, and we might legitimately expect that the institution would reflect the nation's answer to the eternal democratic question about majority rule versus minority rights. But it gives us no such answer, unless the failure to provide one is a kind of answer in itself. In the first place, as everyone knows, the very creation of the two houses involved a contradiction: the House was dedicated to the proposition that the majority must rule; the Senate, to the idea that minority rights are sacrosanct. But it goes far beyond that. Within each of the two

---

[16] James M. Burns, *Roosevelt: The Lion and the Fox* (New York: Harcourt, Brace & World, Inc., 1956).

[17] Gunnar Myrdal, *An American Dilemma* (New York: Harper & Row, Publishers, 1944), p. 709.

houses we find the same contradiction embodied. Consider, for example, the Senate's famous filibuster tradition. Under the present rule, the vote of two-thirds of the Senators present is necessary to halt debate and no limit at all can be imposed on debate on a motion to change the rules. Thus the minority enjoys, theoretically, an absolute power to frustrate the will of the majority. But on the other hand, there is no real doubt that a majority vote of the Senate could kill the filibuster rule tomorrow—including the rule that purportedly forbids cloture on a rules change. The Constitution gives each house the right to determine its own rules and that right is lodged in the majority of the Senate. So what we have here is not a choice between majority rule and minority rights, not even (in theory) a compromise between them, but an absolute representation of both ideas.

A similar paradox is mirrored in the procedures of the House. We hear much nowadays about the Rules Committee and its power to prevent the majority from expressing itself, a power analogous to that of a filibustering minority in the Senate. Yet a discharge petition signed by a majority of the House can at any time wrest a bill from the Committee's grasp and thus over-ride the minority. Again we see the idea of majority rule and the idea of minority rights existing side by side. In practice, of course, in both Senate and House the two ideas are often compromised. The minority refrains from exercising its theoretically absolute veto unless the issue seems really vital to minority interests; in return for such self-restraint the majority does not invoke its own absolute power to override. But apparently there is symbolic value in maintaining the formal existence of the essential paradox. It comforts those who believe in both majority rule and minority rights and have never bothered to choose between them.

Or take finally the Constitution itself. The more one ponders the ancient cliché that the Constitution was a "bundle of compromises," the less satisfactory that seems as a description of what happened in 1787. Rather, the Constitution can be understood as a bundle of unresolved contradictions. The contradictions led, of course, to ultimate compromises in practice. But that is very different from saying that they were written into the Constitution. Does the Supreme Court, for example, have the power to say the last word about the validity of a legislative act, the power of judicial review? Certainly it does, and our constitutional history resounds with declarations that this is the case. Yet Congress has the impeachment power and the power over appellate jurisdiction, either one of which is enough to destroy the authority of the Court at a single stroke. So it would appear that the judiciary is both omnipotent and subservient to the legislative will. Did the Constitution seek to create a unified national government, or a league of sovereign states?

Professor Crosskey on the one hand and Senator Thurmond on the other, the answer is again "both," or at any rate both ideas are tolerably plain in the document. Does the Constitution ordain the separation of powers? Surely the Framers thought it did. Yet the powers are also mingled in a variety of ways as every schoolboy knows, and the Congress can, if it really wants to, impinge on both the executive and judiciary unmercifully.

In short, the institutions of American government, like the spokesmen previously discussed, display a pervasive ambivalence about the most fundamental questions of political value. It seems reasonable then to suppose that the very existence of such self-contradictory governmental forms is further testimony to the thought processes of the men who have fostered them. Indeed, the institutions may be a more reliable clue to underlying ideology than the explicit statements about it. For institutions are a form of action, and there is truth in the old saw that actions speak louder than words. Senator Roe may say he believes in majority rule; Congressman Doe may say he believes in the indefeasible rights of the minority. But when we see the former accept an institutional arrangement that qualifies the majority principle; and the latter agree to an arrangement that involves majority control—we may wonder whether their statements reflect the truth of the matter after all.

AMERICAN POLITICAL BEHAVIOR

These observations are also relevant to my final body of evidence to support the conjecture I have advanced. I suggest that the essential ambivalence of the American political mind is further reflected in certain peculiarities of American political behavior. Here, as before, my choice of illustration will have to be selective, but the examples are not chosen tendentiously.

The phenomenon of behavior that I am specifically interested in is a recent one, commonly called "McCarthyism." We have had a tendency in our political history to indulge in brief frenzies of anger, intolerance, or reform, those frenzies being followed almost invariably by a cooling of tempers and a return to the status quo. Instances of this tendency abound in American history; one thinks of the Alien and Sedition Acts period, of the Progressive Era, of the Red Scare following the first World War. In each case the initial excitement was considerable; in each case the excitement died down almost as suddenly as it had arisen. I choose McCarthyism because it is the most recent complete example of such a phenomenon, and because none of the explanations of its rise and fall that I have seen appears wholly satisfactory.

The basic explanation may be found in the propensity of the American political mind that I have been urging. McCarthyism directly or indirectly involved some of the primary-value dualisms of the American tradition. Take, for example, the question of the rule of law. In one sense Americans seem to be almost intoxicated with the wine of legalism. No other country has ever assigned courts the power we have assigned them. The public opinion polls regularly reveal that the judge is the most respected of our fellow citizens. We venerate the Constitution. Yet at the same time, one of the most striking things to foreigners who come here is the strain of lawlessness in our character. Every crisis in American history—some of them very mild crises—has seen demands that the rule of law be abrogated, has revealed a certain impatience with legal forms. No other civilized nation has had a record of lynching and mob violence comparable to ours.

Or take our attitude toward learning, toward education. Since the time of Jefferson, we have had a faith in the beneficence of education that is almost touching. We have dreamed of education for all; we have multiplied colleges and universities as no other nation has. Every other hamlet in the Midwestern states boasts a college, a monument to our national belief that, to put it in Platonic terms, knowledge is virtue. Yet on the other hand there is a parallel tradition that distrusts book-learning, that exalts the school of hard knocks. The comic, halfwitted professor of Hollywood's imagining is the symbol of our counter image. The state legislature of any state is at once proud of its great public university yet suspicious that it is a hotbed of subversives and impractical dreamers.

Or take, for one further dualism, the twin values of respectability and rebelliousness. Most of us are impressed by the spectacle of solid, affluent, silk-hat respectability. But at the same time there is a streak of the derisive in most of us. We take a certain pleasure in seeing the silk hat knocked off with a snowball, in seeing respectability challenged and defied.

The initial success of McCarthy and his movement may be explained by his appeal to one side of ideology. His evident contempt for the rule of law, his assault on education and especially on the ivy-covered institutions of the Eastern seaboard, his raffish irreverence toward such symbols of respectability as Dean Acheson, *The New York Times*, and the Army—all this struck a responsive chord in American breasts. The observer recognized one side of his own value system in these qualities and was drawn to the movement thereby.

That was the initial reaction. But as the Senator ran his course, something else began to be apparent. This man was not, like most of us, ambivalent about these values. He really meant it. His contempt for the rule of law was not matched by a parallel regard for it. His hostility toward education and related values was single-minded. He was interested not merely in knocking off the silk hat of respectability, but the head as well. And at that point his support, especially among political activists,[18] began to recede. Their regard for the rule of law, for education, for the ikons of respectability asserted itself and neutralized their initial attraction to his standard. He was a man with his mind made up who was trying vainly to appeal to an audience which had not made up its mind and felt no compulsion to do so.

No doubt other examples of the rise and decline of political enthusiasms in America can also be explained in these terms. This hypothesis about the character of American ideology might illuminate other common incidents of our political behavior. The apparent ease with which statesmen like Burton Wheeler or Tom Watson move from progressivism to the extremes of reaction, for example, may suggest that an ambivalence in basic values has been present from the first.

Space is too short to permit exploration of these possibilities and others that a further consideration of our political behavior might suggest. Suffice it to argue that our reaction to such phenomena as McCarthyism is consistent with the thesis I have advanced. The literature of American political thought, our political institutions, and our political behavior all indicate that our ideology may be a conglomerate of mutually inconsistent beliefs. If so, it may be idle to seek for "the" American tradition, for a "consensus" in any usual sense of the word. Perhaps our only really basic quality of mind is the pragmatic spirit that can tolerate such a state of affairs and build an enduring polity upon it.

Suggestions for Further Reading

Becker, Carl, *The Declaration of Independence* (New York: Alfred A. Knopf, Inc., 1942).
Boorstin, Daniel, *The Genius of American Politics* (Chicago: University of Chicago Press, 1953).
Gabriel, Ralph Henry, *The Course of American Democratic Thought* (New York: The Ronald Press Company, 1940).
Goldman, Eric F., *Rendezvous with Destiny* (New York: Alfred A. Knopf, Inc., 1952).
Hartz, Louis, *The Liberal Tradition in America* (New York: Harcourt, Brace & World, Inc., 1955).
Hofstadter, Richard, *The Age of Reform* (New York: Alfred A. Knopf, Inc., 1955).
Mason, Alpheus T., ed., *Free Government in the Making: Readings in American Political Thought* (New York: Oxford University Press, Inc., 1949).

---

[18] Unhappily, the citizenry in general seem to have been largely unaffected by such misgivings. See G. D. Wiebe, "The Army McCarthy Hearings and the Public Conscience," *Public Opinion Quarterly*, XXII (1958–59), 490.

McCloskey, Robert G., *American Conservatism in the Age of Enterprise* (Cambridge: Harvard University Press, 1950).

———, *The American Supreme Court* (Chicago: University of Chicago Press, 1960).

Parrington, Vernon L., *Main Currents in American Thought* (New York: Harcourt, Brace & World, Inc., 1956).

Rossiter, Clinton, *Conservatism in America* (New York: Alfred A. Knopf, Inc., 1955).

Smith, J. Allen, *The Spirit of American Government* (New York, 1912).

THE INDIVIDUAL
AND HIS RIGHTS
The Nationalization
of Civil Liberties

Robert J. Harris

THE CONSTITUTIONAL GUARANTEES

A central article of faith of the American political religion is the intrinsic worth and dignity of the individual person endowed with natural and inalienable rights under the sanction of the "Laws of Nature and Nature's God." Implicit in this creed are two assumptions: first, the individual is a moral and political unit; second, rights exist guaranteed by a higher law both of nature and of a written constitution, and the ensuing function of government is to protect these rights. In the Declaration of Independence Jefferson distilled volumes of ancient, medieval, and modern political philosophy into a few sentences when he declared that

. . . *all men are created equal, that they are endowed by their Creator with certain unalienable Rights, that among these are Life, Liberty, and the pursuit of Happiness. That to secure these rights, Governments are instituted among Men, deriving their just*

ROBERT J. HARRIS, *Professor of Political Science at Vanderbilt University, was a student of Edward S. Corwin at Princeton University. He collaborated with Professor Corwin in* Constitution of the United States: Analysis and Interpretation *(1953): a phrase-by-phrase analysis of the Constitution, fully annotated with Supreme Court decisions 1789–1952. From a legal standpoint, this is probably the most useful single reference volume to the changing Constitution. He is the author of* The Quest for Equality: The Constitution, Congress and the Supreme Court *(1960) and* The Judicial Power of the United States *(1940).*

powers from the consent of the governed. That whenever any Form of Government be-
comes destructive of these ends it is the Right of the People to alter or to abolish it, and
to institute new Government, laying its foundation on such form, as to them shall seem
most likely to effect their Safety and Happiness.[1]

In confirmation of these ideas the Revolutionary Fathers drafted constitutions in specially chosen conventions and placed limitations on the governments established by written guarantees of individual rights. Such in itself
was a novelty, and it may well be that the greatest political contribution of
the American Revolution was the Constitutional Convention. Thomas
Paine, who was something of a crude genius, reached a wise conclusion when
he observed that constitutional government is limited government and that
any exercise of governmental power beyond the limits of the constitution is
the exercise of power without right. In this argument Paine is describing
the effect of early American constitutions and expressing the implicit views
of their framers on the necessity of constitutional limitations. The men of
1776 were not content to confide the sole care of basic rights to "the Laws of
Nature and Nature's God." In this respect the celebrated Virginia Declaration of Rights of 1776 is very important because of its substance and
its subsequent influence, as the earliest American bill of rights, upon the
constitutions of other states and the first eight amendments to the Constitution of the United States. In it we find the recurrent themes of the
natural liberty and equality of all men, inalienable rights, government by
the consent of the governed for the benefit and protection of the people,
separation of powers, and free and frequent elections. Here, too, we encounter the familiar procedural guarantees to persons accused of crime,
condemnation of general search warrants, support of freedom of religion and
the press, the subordination of the military to the civil power, and echoes of
Magna Carta in the section forbidding the deprivation of a person's liberty
"except by the law of the land or the judgment of his peers."[2]

Specific guarantees in American bills of rights are the result of political
speculation and practical experience. Indeed, much of English and American
natural rights philosophy is a blend of theory and experience. In such a
sense freedom of speech and the press was regarded both as an intrinsic good

---

[1] *The Rights of Man*, in Howard Fast, ed., *The Selected Work of Thomas Paine* (New York:
Duell, Sloan, & Pearce, Inc., 1945), pp. 124–25. On this point see also, Charles H.
McIlwain, *Constitutionalism, Ancient and Modern*, revised edition (Ithaca, New York:
Cornell University Press, 1947), pp. 2, 14.

[2] Francis N. Thorpe, ed., *The Federal and State Constitutions, Colonial Charters and Other
Organic Laws* (Washington, 1909), Vol. 7, pp. 3812–14.

and as a practical necessity for the maintenance of free government. Hence, Milton in the *Areopagitica* argues that to kill a book is almost to kill a man, because "a good Booke is the pretious lifeblood of a master spirit,"[3] but also that the knowledge of vice is necessary to virtue and the scrutiny of error to the confirmation of truth. As a printer, Benjamin Franklin knew the utility of freedom of thought and expression more than most of his contemporaries. In his view, without "Freedom of Thought there could be no such Thing as Wisdom; and no such Thing as publick Liberty, without Freedom of Speech."[4] In a similar way the other substantive freedoms of the First Amendment—freedom of religion, separation of church and state, and the rights of assembly and petition—are grounded on abstract and practical bases. "The Church of Christ needs no aid of government to bring men to the true profession of faith," Roger Williams declared. Indeed, according to him, freedom of conscience, expression, and assembly is one of the principal means for "the" propagating and spreading of the gospel of the son of God."[5]

The more dramatic nature of the great substantive rights of freedom of conscience, expression, religion, and assembly and the ringing defenses of them by men like Milton, Williams, Jefferson, Mill, and Holmes, have done much to obscure the importance of procedural rights as guaranteed by American constitutions in specific detail and in the broad generalities of privileges and immunities of citizens of the United States, due process of law, and the equal protection of the laws. Yet the great procedural rights of habeas corpus, to privacy against unreasonable searches and seizures, to a speedy public trial with confrontation and cross-examination of hostile witnesses, and against self-incrimination, not to mention others, go to the very essence of freedom. Justice Frankfurter noted the importance of procedure when he stated that "The history of American freedom is, in no small measure, the history of procedure."[6] The statesmen of the eighteenth century who formed the Bill of Rights were alert to the necessities of procedure and its relationship to liberty, with the result that by far the larger portion of the Bill of Rights is devoted to procedural guarantees.

---

[3] John Milton, *Complete Poetry and Selected Prose*, Modern Library ed. (New York: Modern Library, Inc., 1950), pp. 681, 692.

[4] Quoted in Clinton Rossiter, *Seedtime of the Republic* (New York: Harcourt, Brace & World, Inc., 1953), p. 299. For one of the best justifications of freedom of thought and expression on utilitarian grounds see John Stuart Mill's *Essay on Liberty and other Essays*, Modern Readers' Series (New York: The Macmillan Company, 1926).

[5] Rossiter, *op. cit.*, pp. 197–98.

[6] Concurring opinion in *Malinski v New York*, 324 U.S. 401, 414 (1945).

JUDICIAL PROTECTION

It is obviously one thing to write guarantees of rights into a constitution and another to enforce them. The one is to proclaim an ideal, to state a dream; the other is to fulfill it. In large measure, but not exclusively, the American Constitution confides the protection of individual rights to the judiciary. Accordingly, the history of constitutional guarantees in the United States has been uneven and sporadic, dependent upon the fortuity, sometimes planned, of law suits presented to the courts by private litigants and upon the ambivalence of judges in reconciling the competing claims of liberty and authority.

In this connection it is necessary to state for the benefit of those not inducted into the mysteries of constitutional law that the federal courts hear and decide only justiciable cases and controversies between adverse litigants with real interests and that even then they avoid the constitutional issue and dispose of the case on some other basis if that is possible, or on the narrowest constitutional issues if it is not.[7] Hence, when the Supreme Court dismissed the issue of legislative malapportionment as a political question until 1962,[8] it converted the right of representation which was regarded as fundamental by the men of 1776 into an imperfect right and contradicted the Court's own ruling that among the privileges and immunities of federal citizenship is the right of a qualified citizen to vote and have his vote counted the way he cast it.[9] Whenever, indeed, the Court avoids or postpones the decision of constitutional issues for any of the reasons contained in the elaborate ritual of judicial review, it is contracting the efficacy of individual rights, and to a degree the rights themselves. If the rights of individual persons are a central theme of the American Constitution and judical review is the prime agent for enforcing them, it is perhaps time for the Court and its observers to study and assess the impact of judicially imposed limitations upon judicial review and the viability of constitutional limitations.[10]

Because the enforcement of individual rights depends in large part upon private litigants to present issues for judicial determination, the time and

[7] On this point see Edward S. Corwin, ed., *The Constitution of the United States, Analysis and Interpretation* (Washington, 1953), pp. 538–62, and the cases cited therein.

[8] *Colegrove v Green*, 328 U.S. 549 (1946); *South v Peters*, 339 U.S. 276 (1950); and *Baker v Carr* (Decided March 26, 1962) reversing *Colegrove v Green*.

[9] *United States v Classic*, 313 U.S. 299 (1941).

[10] On this point see Charles L. Black, *The People and the Court: Judicial Review in a Democracy* (New York: The Macmillan Company, 1960).

manner of presenting constitutional questions is important. In this context we may note that the Supreme Court decided very few cases involving freedom of expression prior to the first World War[11] or of freedom of religion prior to the 1930's[12] when the Jehovah's Witnesses took their place alongside whiskey and milk as a major ingredient in constitutional law. Such a result is not a tribute to governmental or individual toleration of political and religious dissent. On the contrary, the history of the Alien and Sedition Laws, the suppression of dissent during the Civil War, and private and state harassment of the Abolitionists and the Mormons are ample testimony of the virus of ignorance and intolerance. What happened was that free speech issues did not reach the Supreme Court at all with respect to the Sedition Act, and that issues respecting freedom of speech and the press during the Civil War were decided as questions involving the suspension of the writ of habeas corpus.[13]

Much depends, too, upon the selection of cases and the manner of their preparation and presentation. Without arguing that the result would have been different, anyone studying some of the cases involving racial discrimination prior to 1938 must conclude that the cases were poorly prepared and inadequately presented so that constitutional rights were decided in part by default.[14] It would be a gross error to attribute exclusively the changed tenor of civil rights decisions since the *Scottsboro* cases of the 1930's[15] to the timely selection of litigation and the careful presentation of cases by the American Civil Liberties Union or the National Association for the Advancement of Colored People. Nevertheless, these and other organizations contributed significantly in ways that cannot be precisely measured to constitutional change and the advancement of civil rights through astute planning of legal tactics and strategy.[16]

---

[11] See *e.g.*, *Robertson v Baldwin*, 165 U.S. 275 (1897); *Davis v Massachusetts*, 167 U.S. 43 (1897); *Patterson v Colorado*, 205 U.S. 454 (1907); *Gompers v Bucks Stove and Range Co.*, 221 U.S. 418 (1911); *Fox v Washington*, 236 U.S. 273 (1915).

[12] See *Reynolds v United States*, 98 U.S. 145 (1897); *Bradfield v Roberts*, 175 U.S. 291 (1899); *Davis v Beason*, 133 U.S. 333 (1890).

[13] *Ex parte Milligan*, 4 Wallace 2 (1866).

[14] *Cumming v Board of Education*, 175 U.S. 528 (1899), is a good example.

[15] *Powell v Alabama*, 287 U.S. 45 (1932); *Norris v Alabama*, 294 U.S. 587 (1935).

[16] For an account of the role of the NAACP in the restrictive covenant cases see Clement E. Vose, *Caucasians Only: The Supreme Court, the NAACP, and Restrictive Covenant Cases* (Berkeley: University of California Press, 1959). See also the records compiled in trial courts and briefs filed before the Supreme Court in *Sweatt v Painter*, 339 U.S. 629 (1950), and *Brown v Topeka Board of Education*, 347 U.S. 483 (1954), and the *Public School Segregation Cases*, collectively.

Added to the vagaries of chance and the calendar in the disposition of cases are the ambiguities, inconsistencies, and uncertainties of judicial decisions affecting individual rights. These are well illustrated in cases involving the incorporation of the Bill of Rights of the Constitution into the Fourteenth Amendment, the interpretation of the freedoms of the First Amendment, and particularly freedom of expression, and the scope of the guarantee against unreasonable searches and seizures.

THE BILL OF RIGHTS AND THE FOURTEENTH AMENDMENT: THE PALKO RULE

Long before the ratification of the Fourteenth Amendment the Supreme Court had held that the limitations of the Bill of Rights applied only to the federal government and did not in any way operate against the states.[17] In a succession of cases between 1876 and 1925, the Court held that the Fourteenth Amendment did not require the states to provide trial by jury in civil or criminal cases, indictment by grand jury, confrontation of witnesses, or to protect a defendant against self-incrimination.[18] In some instances, too, the Court pronounced dicta to the effect that none of the first ten Amendments applied to the states and that the guarantee of freedom of speech did not limit state action.[19]

In *Gitlow v New York* (1925), the Court began the gradual process of selective inclusion of specific guarantees of the Bill of Rights into the Fourteenth Amendment. By 1937 it had incorporated the First Amendment freedoms of speech, press, religion, and assembly, without any particular rationale.[20] That was provided by *Palko v Connecticut* in 1937.[21] Here the Court sustained the authority of Connecticut to appeal a conviction of a defendant of second degree murder on errors of law, obtain a reversal, and then try him again on the same indictment and obtain a conviction of murder in the first degree. However, Justice Cardozo expressly avoided a ruling that other kinds of

---

[17] *Barron v Baltimore*, 7 Peters 243 (1833).

[18] *Walker v Sauvinet*, 92 U.S. 90 (1876); *Maxwell v Dow*, 176 U.S. 581 (1900); *Hurtado v California*, 110 U.S. 516 (1884); *West v Louisiana*, 194 U.S. 258 (1904).

[19] *Spies v Illinois*, 123 U.S. 13 (1887); *Brown v New Jersey*, 175 U.S. 172 (1899); *Prudential Life Insurance Co. v Cheek*, 259 U.S. 530 (1922).

[20] *Gitlow v New York*, 268 U.S. 252 (1925); *Near v Minnesota*, 283 U.S. 697 (1931); *Hamilton v University of California*, 293 U.S. 245 (1934); *Pierce v Society of Sisters*, 268 U.S. 510 (1925); *De Jonge v Oregon*, 299 U.S. 553 (1937).

[21] 302 U.S. 319 (1937).

double jeopardy would be consistent with due process of law. In rationalizing this decision the Court formulated general principles governing the selective inclusion and exclusion of specific guarantees of the Bill of Rights into or from the Fourteenth Amendment.

Speaking in the *Palko* case for an all but unanimous Court, Justice Cardozo distinguished between those rights which are "of the very essence of a scheme of ordered liberty," the abolition of which would violate "a principle of justice so rooted in the traditions and conscience of our people as to be ranked as fundamental," and those which "may have value and are important." The Court went on to speak of those rights without which "neither liberty nor justice would exist," and of those "fundamental principles of liberty and justice which lie at the base of all our civil and political institutions."

Such concepts are obviously rather pure natural law, and therein lies both their strength and weakness: the superiority of right and justice to all law and government, and the subjective nature of all higher law doctrines. Hence there has rarely been unanimous agreement among the Justices or constitutional scholars with respect to fundamental rights and merely valuable or important rights. For many years the first Justice Harlan, usually as a minority of one, contended that all the guarantees of the first eight Amendments were carried over into the Fourteenth either as privileges and immunities of citizens of the United States or essential elements of due process of law.[22] Since the *Palko* case a sharp and sometimes bitter dispute has raged within the Court over selective incorporation of some rights as opposed to the inclusion of the whole Bill of Rights.[23]

Of more importance than the ruling in the *Adamson* case—which reaffirmed *Twining v New Jersey* (1908), that the right against self-incrimination is not so essential to ordered liberty as to be an element of due process of law—are the opinions of Justices Frankfurter and Black, the one concurring, the other in dissent.[24] Justice Frankfurter rejected both the selective inclusion of some rights into the Fourteenth Amendment as too subjective and the inclusion of all as too impractical and unrealistic. He suggested instead that natural law had "a much better meaning and justification" as a basis for the determination of rights than selections of legal forms from the Bill of Rights, "even though they have the sanction of the eighteenth century." Moreover, he argued, the Fourteenth Amendment "neither comprehends the specific

---

[22] *Hurtado v California,* 110 U.S. 516 (1884); *Maxwell v Dow,* 176 U.S. 581 (1900); *Patterson v Colorado,* 205 U.S. 454 (1907); *Twining v New Jersey,* 211 U.S. 78 (1908).

[23] *Adamson v California,* 332 U.S. 46 (1947).

[24] 211 U.S. 78 (1908).

means by which the founders deemed it appropriate to restrict the federal government, nor is it confined to them. The Due Process Clause of the Fourteenth Amendment has an independent potency, precisely as does the Due Process Clause of the Fifth Amendment in relation to the Federal Government."

Justice Black, whose outlook on rights generally needs the support of natural law concepts more than do the outlooks of most of the Justices, was not impressed either by Justice Reed's opinion of the Court or Justice Frankfurter's concurrence in the *Adamson* case. Seizing upon what he regarded as subjective natural law elements of each, he indicated that as between the selective process of the *Palko* decision and the exclusion of the whole Bill of Rights from the Fourteenth Amendment, he would choose the former. But rather than accept either he would follow what he regarded as the original purpose of the Fourteenth Amendment; namely, the extension of the complete protection to the people of all of the Bill of Rights against state action. In his view, the incorporation of the Bill of Rights into the Fourteenth Amendment would have the advantage of providing greater protection to individual rights than the *Palko* rule and at the same time avoid the danger of "the natural-law due-process" formula's licensing the Court "to roam at large in the broad expanses of policy and morals and to trespass, all too freely, on the legislative domain of the states as well as the Federal Government."

A few months before the decision in the *Adamson* case, the Supreme Court was presented with similar problems by *Louisiana ex rel. Francis v Resweber*.[25] Willie Francis had been convicted of murder and sentenced to die in Louisiana's portable electric chair in St. Martin Parish. At the appointed time of the execution, Francis was strapped in the chair and the current turned on, but due to mechanical difficulties an amount of current insufficient to kill him passed through Francis' body. The state supreme court refused to intervene to prevent a second attempt at electrocution, and Francis appealed to the Supreme Court of the United States on the ground that a second attempt at electrocution would place him twice in jeopardy of life and limb and inflict cruel and unusual punishment in violation of the Fifth and Eighth Amendments as carried over into the Fourteenth. Because no opinion in the case was supported by a majority of the Court, it is difficult to say conclusively and precisely what was decided. Justice Reed prepared the opinion of the Court, in which Chief Justice Vinson and Justices Black and Jackson joined, and assumed for the purposes of the case, but without so

[25] 329 U.S. 459 (1947).

deciding, that the guarantees against double jeopardy in the sense of double punishment and against cruel and unusual punishments are incorporated into the Fourteenth Amendment. Although these Justices found double punishment by the same jurisdiction for the same offense abhorrent, they could find neither double jeopardy nor cruel and unusual punishment in a second attempt to execute Francis, largely because they regarded the mechanical failure of the chair as accidental rather than as a planned attempt at prolonged torture. After a discourse on the Bill of Rights and due process of law in which he apparently assumed that due process of law forbids cruel and unusual punishments, Justice Frankfurter reached a similar conclusion. In a dissent, in which Justices Douglas, Murphy, and Rutledge joined, Justice Burton found the taking of life by "unnecessarily cruel means" shocking to the "most fundamental instincts of civilized man," and any further attempt to take Francis' life a cruel and unusual punishment.

Two other cases pertaining to the Bill of Rights and the Fourteenth Amendment are worthy of notice. In *Wolf v Colorado* (1949) and *Mapp v Ohio* (1961), the Court was concerned with unreasonable searches and seizures by state officials and the admissibility of evidence so obtained to procure convictions in state courts.[26] All the Justices agreed that the right to privacy against unreasonable searches and seizures is basic in a free society, but there agreement ended. As spokesman for the majority in the *Wolf* case, Justice Frankfurter restated his view that due process of law is independent of the Bill of Rights as "a compendious expression of all those rights" which courts must enforce because they are basic to a free society. "But basic rights do not become petrified as of any one time, even though, as a matter of human experience, some may not too rhetorically be called eternal verities. It is of the very nature of a free society to advance in its standards of what is deemed reasonable and right. Representing as it does a living principle, due process is not confined within a permanent catalog of what may at a given time be deemed the limits or the essentials of fundamental rights." Hence, to Justice Frankfurter, "the real clue to the problem confronting the judiciary in the application of the Due Process Clause is not to ask where the line is once and for all to be drawn but to recognize that it is for the Court to draw it by the gradual and empiric process of inclusion and exclusion." Having said all this, Justice Frankfurter went on to rule that even though due process of law prohibits unreasonable searches and seizures, it does not require state courts to suppress evidence so obtained, partly because of practice in a

[26] 338 U.S. 25 (1949); 367 U.S. 643 (1961).

majority of the states and in ten jurisdictions in the United Kingdom and the British Commonwealth of Nations, and partly because of the availability of other remedies against unreasonable searches and seizures.

To reach this conclusion it was necessary to construe *Weeks v United States* (1914),[27] which renders inadmissible in the federal courts any evidence obtained by unreasonable search and seizure, as a mere rule of evidence devised by the Supreme Court in the absence of an act of Congress rather than as a mandate of the Fourth Amendment. In a brief opinion Justice Black reiterated his earlier views concerning the whole absorption of the Bill of Rights by the Fourteenth Amendment and concurred in the result. Justice Murphy, joined by Justices Douglas and Rutledge in dissent, could not accept the elimination of what they regarded as the most effective sanction against illegal searches and seizures for other remedies which were in their view illusory or the denigration of the *Weeks* rule to a judicial expedient. The closeness of the decision and the vigor of the dissents in *Wolf v Colorado* foreshadowed its possible subsequent reversal with respect to the admissibility of evidence illegally obtained. The reversal came twelve years later in *Mapp v Ohio* where the Court held that the states, like the federal government, cannot partake of the forbidden fruit of illegal searches and seizures.

In the process of nationalizing individual rights from *Gitlow v New York* in 1925 to *Mapp v Ohio* in 1961, majority and dissenting judges advanced a number of propositions. Prior to 1925 a majority of the Court appears to have accepted and followed, with a few possible exceptions, the rule that none of the guarantees of the Bill of Rights as such is incorporated into the Constitution by the Fourteenth Amendment. During a portion of this period the first Justice Harlan stood alone in proclaiming that all such guarantees were carried over intact, and after 1946 Justices Black, Douglas, Murphy, and Rutledge (the latter two until their deaths in 1949) supported this contention. Twelve years after the Court began the nationalization of the Bill of Rights, Justice Cardozo, speaking for the Court, rationalized previous decisions and stated the selective-inclusion rule on the basis of the formula of ordered liberty and the conscience of a free people. Justice Frankfurter enunciated his own formula, which has had some support from other Justices, to the effect that due process of law is independent of the Bill of Rights insofar as it does not include all of them, but does include all rights basic to a free society regardless of whether they are guaranteed by the first eight Amendments. Such a view is at the same time broader and narrower than that of

[27] 232 U.S. 383 (1914).

complete incorporation. It is broader in that it protects some procedural rights not guaranteed in specific detail in the Constitution, narrower in that it does exclude some constitutional guarantees.

The view that due process of law may command more than the specific guarantees was neither new nor original with Justice Frankfurter. Long ago the Court refused to define due process of law specifically in favor of applying it to individual cases through the "gradual process of judicial inclusion and exclusion as the cases presented shall require, with the reasoning on which such decisions may be founded."[28] Ever since it has included specific details not mentioned in the Constitution within due process of law, such as freedom of contract in substantive due process[29] and the prohibition of coerced confessions in procedural cases,[30] even though the latter may be condemned through a combination of the guarantees against unreasonable searches and seizures and self-incrimination.[31] Moreover, a view of due process of law, or of the Fourteenth Amendment generally which transcends the more specific limits of the Bill of Rights, is consistent with the incorporation theory as exemplified by the cases involving coerced confessions either through police brutality or prolonged questioning of a suspect by relays of police officers.

All these tests of the Fourteenth Amendment have their strengths and their infirmities. Complete incorporation, at the outset at least, is more exact and more certain and, in cases involving the right to counsel and against self-incrimination, more consistent with the protection of basic rights as well. Yet historically and practically it is difficult to envisage indictment by grand jury as distinguished from a bill of information or the common law jury of twelve and the necessity of unanimity instead of a smaller jury or a majority verdict as a desecration of constitutional altars. It is equally difficult to contend that such guarantees would obstruct the administration of justice in the states. The *Palko* formula of selective inclusion and exclusion presents the disadvantage of judicial subjectivity as noted by Justice Frankfurter in the *Adamson* case, and his formula is at least equally open to the same objection of subjectivity as Justice Black was quick to note in the same case.

---

[28] *Davidson v New Orleans*, 96 U.S. 97, 104 (1878).

[29] *Lochner v New York*, 198 U.S. 45 (1905), for example.

[30] *Brown v Mississippi*, 297 U.S. 278 (1936); *Chambers v Florida*, 309 U.S. 227 (1940) among others.

[31] In an entirely different context such a connection was made in *Boyd v United States*, 116 U.S. 616 (1886).

SOME PRACTICAL APPLICATIONS

The *Palko* rule in its subsequent triumph over its competitors has been re-
peated with varying nuances. Thus, such concepts as "the very essence of a
scheme of ordered liberty" and "hardship so acute and shocking that our
policy will not endure it" become rights "basic to our free society," "conduct
that shocks the conscience," or "decencies of civilized conduct." Despite
Justice Frankfurter's protests that such terms are capable of empirical and
scientific definition and application, as opposed to the ad hoc or episodic
decision of particular cases unrelated to previous decisions, the litigated cases
are demonstrations to the contrary. *Wolf v Colorado* (1949), *Rochin v California*
(1952), *Irvine v California* (1954), and *Breithaupt v Abram* (1957) illustrate the
confusion which can ensue in the practical applications of lofty principles.[32]

A review of the facts of these cases, some of which are not pleasant, is
necessary to illustrate the confusion following *Wolf v Colorado*. The *Wolf* case,
as noted earlier, wrote into the Fourteenth Amendment the principle underlying the Fourth Amendment that the right to privacy as basic to a free
society is protected against unreasonable searches and seizures, but the
Court did not apply the federal rule that illegally obtained evidence is
inadmissible in subsequent prosecutions. Justice Black concurred; Justices
Douglas, Murphy, and Rutledge dissented. In this case, which was decided
without reference to the particular facts, a deputy sheriff and others went
into a physician's office without a search warrant, seized his appointment
book, interrogated some of the patients whose names were listed in it, and
used this evidence and the book to convict him.

In the *Rochin* case, three deputy sheriffs of Los Angeles County entered
Rochin's house through an open door and then forced open the door to his
bedroom. They found him partly dressed sitting on the side of the bed near a
"night stand" on which they saw two capsules. When asked about them
Rochin seized them and put them in his mouth. A struggle then ensued, but
the throat was quicker than the hand, and Rochin was taken to a hospital.
There his stomach was pumped, the two capsules containing morphine were
recovered, and Rochin was tried and convicted on the evidence thus obtained. As spokesman for the Court, Justice Frankfurter found the conduct
shocking to conscience and too close to the methods of the rack and the
screw to comport with due process. Hence, the conviction was reversed, not
on the basis of an unreasonable search and seizure which would have been

[32] 338 U.S. 25 (1949); 342 U.S. 465 (1952); 347 U.S. 128 (1954); 352 U.S. 432 (1957).

difficult under the *Wolf* rule, but on the basis of the inadmissibility of coerced confession. Justice Black concurred in the result, but he preferred to rest the decision upon the guarantee against self-incrimination on the basis of his dissent in the *Adamson* case. Justice Douglas preferred to rest the judgment on this basis and the *Weeks* rule which he had supported in the *Wolf* case.

Two years later in *Irvine v California* the Court was confronted with another problem respecting unreasonable searches and seizures. Police officers had made a key to fit Irvine's door, entered his house, installed a microphone in his bedroom closet, and set up a listening post in a neighboring garage where officers listened to his and his wife's conversations in relays. Subsequently, using their key they went into Irvine's house and, in the course of arresting him, conducted a search. As a result of these efforts sufficient evidence was obtained to convict Irvine of bookmaking. The Supreme Court affirmed the conviction on the basis of the *Wolf* rule in an opinion by Justice Jackson in which only Chief Justice Warren and Justices Reed and Minton joined. In a separate concurrence Justice Clark stated his adherence to the *Wolf* rule solely on the basis of *stare decisis* and criticized the ad hoc approach whereby convictions are reversed when five Justices are sufficiently revolted by police action to react in ways that influence the conduct of the police in no way. Justice Frankfurter, joined by Justice Burton, dissented on the ground that *Wolf v Colorado* did not mean that evidence in every unreasonable search and seizure could be admitted, but only when it was obtained in ways that are not shocking to the conscience. Here, the conviction was obtained by methods and in circumstances "which offend elementary standards of justice." In a separate dissent, Justice Douglas reiterated his earlier views as already outlined. Apparently Justice Black did not participate in the decision.

Like *Rochin v California*, *Breithaupt v Abram* involves the extraction of substances from the human body. While driving a pickup truck on a road in New Mexico, Breithaupt collided with an automobile. Three of its occupants were killed and Breithaupt was seriously injured. A pint whiskey bottle, nearly empty, was found in the glove compartment of his truck. While he was still unconscious at a hospital, a state patrolman detected the odor of liquor on his breath and requested a physician to take a sample of Breithaupt's blood. The sample was taken, analyzed, and found to contain enough alcohol to cause Breithaupt to be under the influence of intoxicating liquor as defined by state law. On this evidence he was convicted of involuntary manslaughter and sentenced to imprisonment. Subsequently, he unsuccessfully sought a writ of habeas corpus from the state courts for release on the basis of the involuntary blood test and the decision in *Rochin v California*. A majority of the Court, speaking by Justice Clark, sustained the conviction, because it found nothing brutal or offensive in the taking of a sample of blood when done by a nurse under the protective eye of a physician. The Court cited the commonplace nature of the ritual of blood tests in the armed forces, college entrance tests, and blood donations, and noted that the absence of conscious consent by Breithaupt did not necessarily render the taking unlawful. Chief Justice Warren, joined by Justices Douglas and Black in dissent, could find no difference between the taking of a sample of blood from a man who could not protest and the forcible invasion of the stomach of a man who could. Justice Douglas, joined by Justice Black in a separate dissent, placed even greater emphasis upon the sanctity of the human body than the opinion of the Chief Justice. With all these inconstancies of the judges and the inconsistencies of decisions it is perhaps just as well that the admissibility rule in *Wolf v Colorado* was reversed in *Mapp v Ohio*.

THE PREFERRED POSITION

In *Palko v Connecticut* Justice Cardozo had referred to freedom of thought and speech as "the matrix, the indispensable condition, of nearly every other form of freedom," so that when the Court construed liberty to be more than mere physical restraint, it included "liberty of the mind as well as liberty of action." Decisions interpreting the basic right of liberty of conscience and freedom of expression as restraints upon all governments present their share of tests, standards, inconsistencies, and internal contradictions. In some instances, the Court has followed the preferred-position principle whereby the usual presumption of the validity of statutes is reversed in reviewing legislation adversely affecting the freedoms of the First Amendment.[33] In others, it has applied the rational-basis test whereby the constitutionality is not only assumed beyond all reasonable doubt, but is sustained if the Court believes that a rational man could find facts to justify the statute.[34] In some cases the Court has employed the test of clear and present danger to sustain or invalidate statutes regulating or suppressing expression;[35] in others it has

---

[33] As applied to the First Amendment, the preferred position formula originated in a footnote by Justice Stone to an opinion in *United States v Carolene Products Co.*, 304 U.S. 144, 152 (1938). It was applied to invalidate a statute involving freedom of speech in *Thomas v Collins*, 323 U.S. 516 (1945), and to one involving freedom of religion in *West Virginia Board of Education v Barnette*, 319 U.S. 624 (1943). For a full discussion of the principle and a dispute among the Justices about it, see *Kovacs v Cooper*, 336 U.S. 77 (1949).

[34] See for example, *Minersville School District v Gobitis*, 310 U.S. 586 (1940) for freedom of religion; *American Communications Association v Douds*, 339 U.S. 382 (1950); *Kovacs v Cooper*, 336 U.S. 77 (1949), for freedom of speech.

[35] *Schenck v United States*, 249 U.S. 47 (1919); *Thomas v Collins*, 323 U.S. 516 (1945).

used the evil or dangerous tendency test for the same purpose;[36] and in 1950 it devised what has been called the "clear and probable danger" test to disguise the evil tendency standard and make it more respectable.[37] Within entirely different contexts there have emerged such concepts as "fighting words" which can be suppressed,[38] and the Blackstonian limitation against previous restraint to prevent the suppression of a newspaper,[39] but not to protect a motion picture from the censor.[40]

These concepts are not only very general, but the clear and present danger test in particular can be used either as a criterion for determining the applicability of a valid statute to a conviction under it or as a test of the validity of the statute to put a man in jail or to keep him out.[41] Added to the clash of rhetoric in majority, concurring, and dissenting opinions in efforts to apply or reconcile competing doctrines are the differences encountered between decisions applying the First Amendment directly to the federal government and indirectly to the states by way of the Fourteenth Amendment.

In his dissent in *Gitlow v New York* (1925), Justice Holmes indicated that the authority of the states to regulate speech under the Fourteenth Amendment could be "accepted with a somewhat larger latitude of interpretation than is allowed to Congress by the sweeping language that governs, or ought to govern, the laws of the United States." Twenty-seven years later Justice Jackson, dissenting in *Beauharnais v Illinois*,[42] suggested that the "liberty" protected by the Fourteenth Amendment against state action is different from the "freedom" protected by the First Amendment in its context of federal powers and functions and that the principles underlying the right of free expression and not the First Amendment freedom was what had been incorporated into due process of law. The result, he concluded, was that the states are less limited by the right of freedom of expression than the federal government. In support of his argument for a double standard for the nation and the states, Justice Jackson pointed to the disparity of their functions and duties with respect to such freedom. He thought that protection of personal reputation and preservation of local tranquility, were primarily

---

[36] *Gitlow v New York*, 268 U.S. 652 (1925).
[37] *Dennis v United States*, 341 U.S. 494 (1951).
[38] *Chaplinsky v New Hampshire*, 315 U.S. 568 (1942); *Feiner v New York*, 340 U.S. 315 (1951).
[39] *Near v Minnesota*, 283 U.S. 697 (1931).
[40] *Times Film Corporation v Chicago*, 366 U.S. 431 (1961).
[41] *Schenck v United States*, 249 U.S. 47 (1919); *Herndon v Lowry*, 301 U.S. 242 (1937).
[42] 343 U.S. 250, 252 (1952).

the responsibility of the states. Therefore, the states should have greater latitude in the enactment of libel laws than Congress.

Justice Jackson's ideas were reiterated and modified by Justice Harlan in *Roth v United States* (1957).[43] In balancing the interests of free expression against other interests, the Court "should keep in the forefront the question of whether these interests are state or federal," because the validity of a limitation upon free expression must, to a large extent, "depend on whether that government has, under the Constitution, a direct substantive interest, that is the power to act, in the particular areas involved." Thus, the federal government's concern for national security would place it under fewer restrictions of free expression than the states, whereas the states' primary interest with morals would place them under less rigid restrictions in regulating obscenity in which the federal interest is attenuated. Moreover, in his view, the dangers of federal censorship are greater than anything the states may do. Within this context a book which circulates freely in one state may be suppressed as obscene in another. So long as some states are free to suppress *Lady Chatterley's Lover* and others are free to resist censorship, the dangers are less than those in a federal uniform standard. Such diversity may be neither wise nor desirable, but it is acceptable, whereas federal censorship which would prevent everyone from reading D. H. Lawrence would be "intolerable, and violative of both the letter and spirit of the First Amendment."

Justice Harlan's double standard for the federal government and the states with respect to freedom of expression is an outgrowth of the dual standards suggested by Justices Holmes and Jackson. It is also a substantial modification of them. The dualism of Holmes and Jackson, if the latter's views are taken generally instead of being confined to criminal libel, differentiate applications of the First Amendment almost exclusively on federal-state grounds. The argument of Justice Harlan is founded to a large degree upon the more relevant basis of function, and in some ways upon the extent of the dangers implicit in federal or state controls. A majority of the Court, needless to say, has never expressly accepted double standards of freedom of expression as a limit upon the Nation or the states, nor has it accepted the views advanced by Holmes and Jackson that the Fourteenth Amendment has not literally incorporated the command of the First Amendment against abridgement of freedom of speech and the press. However, beneath the inconsistencies of multiple opinions and the ambiguities of rival doctrines and concepts a

[43] 354 U.S. 476 (1957).

pattern of differentiation on the basis of function and perhaps on federalism does emerge.

If we look at what the Court has done we are struck at once by the failure of the Court ever to invalidate an act of Congress as an unconstitutional abridgement of freedom of speech or the press in contrast to the great number of state statutes and local ordinances so invalidated. The preferred-position doctrine has never been applied to the federal government; it has been used only against the states. When the clear and present danger test has been used in federal cases, it has been invoked as a justification for the exercise of power and not as a limitation upon it, and more often than not the standard applied to federal legislation affecting expression has been the bad tendency test, or its white-collar version, the clear and probable danger test.[44] These phenomena can be partially explained by changes in the composition of the Court, the fortuities of the calendar, and the planning of legal strategy and tactics. But these factors are only partially influential and are not the most significant in making for a differentiation in the construction of federal and state powers over expression.

The most important factors in the Court's balancing of the rival claims of liberty and authority in cases involving freedom of expression are the magnitude of the public interests involved and the pertinence which regulation bears to the protection of these interests. Such considerations tend to favor federal rather than state power in imposing restraints upon expression. Few would deny that the public interest in national security against internal subversion or external attack is greater than that of a municipality in keeping its streets free of litter in the form of handbills distributed by the Jehovah's Witnesses or of a state in compelling children to raise chubby little hands in salute of the flag.[45] With respect to these and comparable matters the decisions vary.

In cases dealing with subversion the Court has sustained statutes which go far toward denying Communists freedom of expression just as John Milton would have suppressed Popery and that "which is impious or evil absolutely either against faith or manners."[46] In *Dennis v United States* (1951) the Court sustained the Smith Act which makes it unlawful to advocate, advise, or

---

[44] *Schenck v United States*, 249 U.S. 47 (1919); *Abrams v United States*, 250 U.S. 616 (1919); *Dennis v United States*, 341 U.S. 404 (1951); *Communist Party of the United States v Subversive Activities Control Board*, 367 U.S. 1 (1961).

[45] *Lovell v Griffin*, 303 U.S. 444 (1938); *West Virginia Board of Education v Barnette*, 319 U.S. 624 (1943).

[46] *Op. cit.*, p. 721.

teach the necessity or desirability of overthrowing any government in the United States by force and violence, to organize groups for so doing, to become a member of such groups knowingly, or to conspire to commit any of these acts.[47] Although the Court spoke of clear and present danger, it adopted the formula of Judge Learned Hand in the Circuit Court of Appeals of the measure of "the gravity of the 'evil,' discounted by its improbability," and actually applied the bad tendency test of the *Gitlow* case on the ground that in the light of the substantial interest of the United States it need not wait until the *putsch* is about to be executed before taking action to suppress the danger.

Throughout the opinion of the majority and the concurring opinion of Justice Jackson in the *Dennis* case there is the recurrent theme of paramount national interests. Referring to the clear and present danger test as applied to subversion, Justice Jackson said, "When the issue is criminality of a hot-headed speech on a street corner, or circulation of a few incendiary pamphlets, or parading by some zealots behind a red flag, or refusal of a handful of school children to salute our flag, it is not beyond the capacity of the judicial process to gather, comprehend, and weigh the necessary materials for decision whether it is a clear and present danger of a substantive evil or a harmless letting off of steam. It is not a prophecy, for the danger in such cases has matured by the time of trial or it was never present."[48]

In contrast to the *Dennis* case, and others sustaining federal legislation punishing subversion, most of the state cases affect the matters which Justice Jackson mentioned under the head of "harmless letting off of steam" or less, and in these cases the clear and present danger test emerges as an effective impediment to state and local control of thought and expression. A good example is *Thomas v Collins* (1945) in which the Supreme Court invalidated the conviction of a labor union official for making a speech under a Texas statute which required persons soliciting memberships in labor unions to register with the secretary of state in advance.[49] In so doing the Court laid perhaps its greatest stress upon the combined principles of preferred position and clear and present danger. As spokesman for the Court in a case marked by multiple opinions, Justice Rutledge referred to "the preferred place" given

---

[47] 341 U.S. 494 (1951).

[48] *Ibid.*, 568. In *Uphaus v Wyman*, 360 U.S. 72 (1959), the Supreme Court recognized the right of the state to protect itself against subversion without disturbing the holding in *Pennsylvania v Nelson*, 350 U.S. 497 (1956), that because of the paramount interest of Congress in matters affecting national security, the Smith Act supersedes similar state legislation.

[49] 323 U.S. 516 (1945).

"to the great, the indispensable democratic freedoms secured by the First Amendment" which gives these liberties "a sanctity and a sanction not permitting dubious intrusions." Accordingly, any restriction of these freedoms "must be justified by clear public interest, threatened not doubtfully or remotely, but by clear and present danger . . . only the gravest abuses, endangering paramount interests, give occasion for permissible limitation." Or, as Justice Douglas said in another case, there must be "a clear and present danger of a serious substantive evil that rises far above public inconvenience, annoyance, or unrest."[50]

A double standard in the application of the limitations of freedom of expression has some merits. The magnitude of the interests confided to the care of the federal government, the greater insulation of national officials and even Congress against ephemeral local passions and distempers, and the greater vigilante perspective of state and local governments all support an argument for a greater power in the federal government than in the states with respect to controls over thought and expression within their respective areas of authority. Moreover, the greater professionalization of federal officials and the dissipation of pressure as it is spread over a broad territorial area corroborate Madison's formula in the celebrated tenth of the *Federalist Papers* in which he proposed to prevent one faction or a combination of factions from controlling the government for their own interests by dispersing power over a broad area in a representative republic.

Despite any congressional encroachments upon basic liberties in the past or the excessive zeal sometimes displayed by federal law enforcement agencies to the detriment of basic rights, the record of the federal government with respect to basic substantive and procedural liberties is far better than that of the states. Moreover, as Professor Burgess declaimed a long time ago, "civil liberty is national in its origin and sanction."[51] If the Court is to perform effectively one of its high functions in the maintenance of civil rights, it would do well to discard outmoded and unwarranted theories of dual federalism and a hypersensitive respect for state legislatures and state courts in favor of individual rights. To do so would not only be consistent with the practical course of the Court's decisions but also in accord with the results of four years of civil strife, the underlying purpose of the Fourteenth Amendment, and almost a century of subsequent experience.

Even so, the judiciary is not and cannot be the only instrument of govern-

[50] *Terminiello v Chicago*, 337 U.S. 1, 4 (1949).
[51] John W. Burgess, *Political Science and Comparative Constitutional Law* (Boston, 1890), Vol. 1, p. 225.

ment for the protection of basic rights. The Bill of Rights and the Fourteenth Amendment limit only governmental action, but in the pluralistic society of the second half of the Twentieth Century, government is not the only potential enemy of individual rights and perhaps not even the most important. Groups and associations which attempt to suppress freedom of conscience and expression through the control of the curriculum and text-books in the public schools, the intimidation of college faculties, and the destruction of the people's faith in their churches or political leadership in the name of patriotism or national security pose grave threats both to civil liberty and national security. As Justice Jackson stated in 1943 "If there is any fixed star in our constitutional constellation it is that no official, high or petty, can prescribe what shall be orthodox in politics, nationalism, religion or other matters of opinion or force citizens to confess by word or act their faith therein."[52] What Justice Jackson says of officials is equally applicable to private groups in their efforts to control any except their own members and sometimes to control them. However, the protection of individual rights against group action, social pressure, and economic reprisals is a task for Congress with its broad delegation of ample powers and not for the Courts. Both the legislature and the judiciary have their separate responsibilities for the protection of civil rights, and unless they exercise them we further corroborate Mark Twain's dictum that "It is by the goodness of God that in our country we have three unspeakably precious things: freedom of speech, freedom of conscience, and the prudence never to practice either of them."[53]

Suggestions for Further Reading

Barth, Alan, *The Price of Liberty* (New York: The Viking Press, Inc., 1961).

Cushman, Robert E., *Civil Liberties in the United States* (Ithaca, New York: Cornell University Press, 1956).

Fellman, David, *The Defendant's Rights* (New York: Holt, Rinehart & Winston, Inc., 1958).

Harris, Robert J., *The Quest for Equality* (Baton Rouge, La.: Louisiana State University Press, 1961).

Konvitz, Milton R., *Fundamental Liberties of a Free People* (Ithaca, New York: Cornell University Press, 1957).

[52] *West Virginia Board of Education v Barnette*, 319 U.S. 624, 642 (1943).

[53] S. Clemens, *Following the Equator*, Vol. 1, p. 198 (New York: Harper & Row, Publishers, 1903); quoted by Justice Douglas, dissenting in *Scales v United States*, 367 U.S. 203, 263–264 (1961).

Mason, Alpheus T., *The Supreme Court from Taft to Warren* (Baton Rouge, Louisiana: Louisiana State University Press, 1958).

Pritchett, C. Herman, *Civil Liberties and the Vinson Court* (Chicago: University of Chicago Press, 1954).

Roche, John P., *Courts and Rights, The American Judiciary in Action* (New York: Random House, Inc., 1961).

Spicer, George W., *The Supreme Court and Fundamental Freedoms* (New York: Appleton-Century-Crofts, 1959).

THE CHANGING
POLITICAL PARTIES

Paul T. David

CHANGES LATENT IN THE PARTY SYSTEM

Viewed retrospectively, the eight years of the Eisenhower administration were something of an interregnum in the evolution of the political parties. Some innovative changes occurred that seemed of moderate importance at the time, but mostly it was a period of catching up. The Republicans shook off their out-party reluctance to embrace programs that had long since had the support of overwhelming majorities of the American people. To some extent, at least, they abandoned what Julius Turner and Ivan Hinderaker have identified as the "self-destructive tendencies in the minority major party."[1] The Democrats, out of power in the White House for the first time

PAUL T. DAVID *is Professor of Political Science at the University of Virginia. He has had a varied career in governmental as well as academic posts. He was associated with The Brookings Institution 1950–1960, where he organized and directed a series of major studies of party politics. He was one of the authors of the report of the American Political Science Association,* Toward a More Responsible Two-Party System *(1950); and principal author and editor of* Presidential Nominating Politics in 1952 *(5 vols.). His most recent publications, all with Ralph Eisenberg, are* Devaluation of the Urban and Suburban Vote *(2 vols., 1962) and* State Legislative Redistricting: Major Issues in the Wake of Judicial Decision *(1962).*

[1] Julius Turner, "Responsible Parties: A Dissent from the Floor," *American Political Science Review*, XLV, March 1951, at pp. 151–52; Ivan Hinderaker, *Party Politics* (New York: Holt, Rinehart & Winston, Inc., 1956), pp. 634–36. The quoted phrase is Hinderaker's.

in twenty years, discovered that even in defeat they could retain most of their New Deal and Fair Deal party followings, and they made some progress in dealing with the problems of how to operate when in the opposition.

But during six of the eight Eisenhower years, the Democrats held ostensible majorities in both houses of Congress while out of power in the administration. The period was one of almost unprecedented ambiguity in regard to partisan responsibility for the conduct of the government. Neither party could develop much of a sense of direction, and there was no strong impulse to deal firmly with the party institutions.

With the advent of the Kennedy administration, the situation changed. President Kennedy is clearly a party leader, and he is trying hard to give his party a strong lead. He may be in office for the full eight years allowed under the Twenty-second Amendment, and he can hope to retain partisan majorities in both houses of Congress throughout all or most of his administration. Accordingly, this may be an eight-year period in which considerations of party responsibility will be given a renewed emphasis.

It is the general purpose of this essay to note some of the more important kinds of change existing and latent within the parties, and to explore their potential consequences.

Specifically, the objectives are as follows:

First, to discuss whether the American political parties are becoming more competitive with each other, and whether there is a rising level of competitive tension within the party system.

Second, to comment briefly on the relationships between competition, cohesion, and centralization in the party system, and to suggest some of the implications of these relationships.

Third, to consider the consequences of party competition for the organization of party leadership, the requirements of party finance, and the development of nationalizing tendencies in congressional politics.

A MORE COMPETITIVE PARTY SYSTEM?

In a review of contemporary politics in 1961, it was my conclusion that "the party system as a whole now occupies what is probably the most highly competitive position it has ever reached in national politics."[2] This conclusion was based on such factors as the following:

—the scale, scope, and nature of the national campaigns of 1960;

[2] Paul T. David *et al.*, *The Presidential Election and Transition 1960–61* (Washington, D. C.: The Brookings Institution, 1961), p. 339.

—the number of states in which the election was fought hard to a close outcome in presidential, congressional, and state elections;

—the speed with which the professionals and the party organizations in each party turned to preparations for the 1962 campaigns;

—the number of close votes in Congress on major items in the President's legislative program;

—the evident disposition of the administration to sharpen issues in Congress in preparation for future election campaigns;

—the aggressive character of the leadership that has come to the top in each of the national parties.

These signs, however, may be more persuasive than probative; and the future remains uncertain. We would like to know whether the 1960 elections were merely the highest point of a competitive tension that will recede until 1964 or 1968; and also whether the long-term drift toward a more competitive situation that has been evident for a generation will continue, despite the fluctuations that may be related to the circumstances of particular election years.

On the short-term side, there were indications early in 1962 that the Republican Party might do poorly in the 1962 elections, contrary to the historical experience in which the party out of power has usually gained seats in Congress in midterm elections.[3] The Republican Party also has been engaged in an unusual amount of soul-searching over its internal problems; but the kind of ferment that is in process suggests that the Party will eventually recover strongly even if its competitive fortunes become worse before they become better.[4]

[3] The most specific evidence came from the Gallup Poll, which from April 1961 to March 1962 was reporting that voter preferences for the Democratic party were at a level indicating Democratic gains in the 1962 elections. In March 1962, the apparent split in the two-party vote for Congress was placed at Democratic, 61 per cent; Republican, 39. George Gallup, "GOP Lag in Congress Races Indicated," *Washington Post and Times Herald*, Mar. 25, 1962.

On February 24, 1962, Republican Chairman Miller told a closed meeting of Republicans that "continued stress" on adverse public opinion polls would "undermine the enthusiasm of the rank-and-file," and that the party should not "succumb to the psychological warfare of the Democrats." *Congressional Quarterly Weekly Report*, XX, Mar. 2, 1962, p. 361.

[4] Robert C. Albright, "Republicans Fretting Over Future of Party," *Washington Post and Times Herald*, Mar. 4, 1962; "Self-Analysis by GOP Brings Gleams of Hope," *ibid.*, Mar. 5, 1962.

The longer-term aspect of the problem of interparty competition is obviously the more important for students of the party system; and an opinion that projects past trends into the future needs to be supported by some long-term interpretation of party history. Such a view could begin by noting the political events of 1896, when a Republican sweep elected William McKinley president.

The election of 1896 is generally credited with a restructuring of political affiliations that endured for more than a generation. The South became the solidly Democratic South. It is all too often forgotten that twenty northern states became so solidly Republican that they could reasonably have been called the "solid North." The period was the high point of a sectional political alignment, and the low point in the effectiveness of the competitive relationship between the Democratic and Republican parties, both nationally and in most states.

These relationships were changed by the realignments that occurred in 1928, 1932, and 1936. The Democratic Party replaced the Republican as the party with a majority following; and whereas the former Republican majority had been sectional, the Democratic majority was national. By 1940, the Republican Party had begun to recover, but a new cleavage line had been established between the parties. Though the South was still solid and still Democratic, in most of the nation, and especially in the central urban and industrial areas from Massachusetts to California, the parties were again competitive in state-wide elections. The cleavage line within the electorate, moreover, essentially followed social and economic divisions in the states where the parties were competitive.[5]

The broad effect of these changes is apparent in the election returns when they are arranged to show the relative amounts of one-party voting by states, taking first the period from 1896 to 1927 and second the period from 1928 to 1956. This has been done in a tabulation of the voting in presidential and gubernatorial elections, giving each state its percentage weight in the electoral college as follows:

---

[5] For a fuller statement, see Paul T. David, Ralph M. Goldman, and Richard C. Bain, *The Politics of National Party Conventions* (Washington, D. C.: The Brookings Institution, 1960), chap. 3; paperback ed., chap. 2.

	Period of 1896 to 1927		Period of 1928 to 1956	
Categories of States[a]	President	Governor[b]	President	Governor
One-party Republican	50.0%	35.1%	1.5%	7.5%
Two-party Leaning Republican	10.7	10.5	23.1	18.4
Two-party Uncertain	10.3	16.4	23.4	33.0
One-party Leaning Democratic	4.9	12.3	40.2	14.0
One-party Democratic	24.1	25.7	11.8	27.1
	100.0	100.0	100.0	100.0

[a] States were classified in the one-party category when the party concerned was victorious in 80 per cent or more of the elections during the period; as leaning to one party when the party was victorious in 60 to 79.9 per cent of the elections; and as uncertain when neither party won more than 60 per cent of the time. These tabulations were originally made by Richard C. Bain for a paper by Paul T. David, "Intensity of Inter-Party Competition and the Problem of Party Realignment," presented at the annual meeting of the American Political Science Association, September 1957.
[b] Based on the period 1901–27.

In presidential voting, as these figures show, most of the states were solidly for one party or the other in the earlier period, while in the recent period, the solidly Republican states had almost disappeared and there had been major inroads in the solidly Democratic states, coupled with a great increase in the number of states leaning toward the Democratic Party. In gubernatorial elections, the shifts were somewhat different. The shrinkage in Republican areas was reflected mainly in an increase in the competitive areas; and the solid South was still solid in electing Democratic governors.

In recent years, the partisan attachments of the electorate have been remarkably stable in most parts of the country. Throughout the Eisenhower period, apparently about 60 per cent of the voters continued to consider themselves Democrats. In a "normal" election, however, it has been computed that the Democratic share would be no more than 54 per cent, because many Democrats are habitual nonvoters. This relatively narrow Democratic vote, moreover, consists of a lopsided majority in the South, and a 49 per cent *minority* outside the South.[6]

It would be easier to predict that the two national parties will continue

[6] Philip E. Converse, Angus Campbell, Warren E. Miller, Donald E. Stokes, "Stability and Change in 1960: A Reinstating Election," *American Political Science Review*, LV, June 1961, pp. 269–80; Donald E. Stokes, "1960 and the Problem of Deviating Elections," paper presented at annual meeting of the American Political Science Association, September 1961.

to become more competitive if some increase could be predicted in the Republican Party's share in the southern vote. On this, the Party's shortage of effective candidates is one of its most serious problems. As recently as 1960, it offered no candidate for Congress in 62 of the 106 congressional districts in the eleven one-time Confederate states. But in the more than forty districts where it offered candidates, it polled 26.5 per cent of the vote in 1948, 27.4 in 1952, 38.0 in 1956, and 37.8 in 1960. In recent years, seven of these districts sent Republican members to Congress. The Republican vote in many of the other districts is high enough to fall within striking range of a majority whenever the Party is again in a favorable position nationally in a presidential election.

Republican prospects in the South—and the prospects for a two-party system in the southern region—were substantially improved by the Supreme Court's decision of March 26, 1962, in the Tennessee reapportionment case, *Baker v Carr*. The new Republicans of the South have been concentrated in the most under-represented urban and suburban areas. If given fair representation, they seem certain to expand their beachheads in southern state legislatures and in Congress. Attractive candidates developed through these opportunities could in turn do much to expand the Party's following throughout the South. On the other hand, liberal Democrats of the southern cities, also under-represented in previous districting arrangements, will be able to increase their weight in southern Democratic Party affairs. Where this happens on a sufficient scale, conservative southern Democrats may find their inclination to shift to the Republican Party somewhat increased.

By a coincidence that is not entirely accidental, the effects of the Tennessee case are coming at the same time that major efforts to increase Negro registration and voting in the South are reaching fruition. If the increased Negro vote materializes, the new Negro voters may help to maintain Democratic Party majorities in presidential elections, while engaging in split-ticket voting locally on the basis of the characteristics of the candidates locally available. Obviously these are complex processes, but they seem more likely to increase competition between the parties in the end than to reduce it; and in time they will certainly change the nature of the Democratic Party in the South and in Congress.[7]

In other parts of the country, substantial revisions of the political map are also in prospect as a result of the redistricting activity impelled by judicial action. The rapidly growing suburban areas and smaller cities will be the major beneficiaries. The Republican Party will lose representation in some

[7] Louis E. Lomax, "The Kennedy's Move In On Dixie," *Harper's*, May 1962, pp. 27–33.

northern rural areas, but may achieve offsetting gains in big city suburbs. More important, however, opportunities for new political leadership may emerge in both parties from the new political units where population growth and economic activity are greatest.

In most of the states, neither party can any longer anticipate a permanent monopoly in the statewide elections for governor, for senator, and for President. In these states, the long-term outlook continues to point toward a rising level of competitive tension. The readjustments resulting from *Baker v Carr* and from other contemporary changes are likely to enhance the tension rather than to lessen it.

COMPETITION, COHESION, AND CENTRALIZATION

Politicians of both parties are undoubtedly like many businessmen in their preference for monopolistic situations in which benefits accrue with a minimum of risk and uncertainty. Situations of this kind have been so common that the normal thinking of party strategists seems often to run in terms of how to develop or maintain a monopoly, rather than in terms of how to be competitive if it is necessary to compete.

The logic of competitive success is different from the logic of monopolistic success. Monopolistic success usually turns on the exploitation of some built-in strategic advantage. Competitive success requires continuous attention to such factors as effective leadership, adequate campaign resources, and attractive programs and candidates.

We can suppose, therefore, that if the competitive tension within the party system continues to rise during the years ahead, there will be a growing disposition to deal with the institutional problems that affect party leadership, campaign finance, the development of party programs, and the selection of party candidates. Conversely, if the tension sags and there is some kind of return to a less competitive party system, then the prospects for any form of innovative change in dealing with these problems would be poor.

The basic competition in politics today, however, is not between the Republican and Democratic Parties as such, but rather between the Republican Party and the majority wing of the Democratic Party, with a third force of southern Democrats who sometimes vote with one party sometimes with the other, while generally also pursuing some special objectives of their own. The one-party Democrats will continue to be a confusing influence in Congress and elsewhere as long as they survive, but they are not likely to reduce materially the pressures of competition between the major parties in the states outside the South and in the nation as a whole.

If this is true, the theoretical relationships among competition, cohesion, and centralization in the party system may become increasingly important. Cohesion within the competing elements is a normal product of competition in any competitive system. Cohesion need not extend to a complete identity of points of view or objectives. What it does extend to generally is a program of cooperative action on whatever is deemed most essential for success in the competitive struggle. In the party system, those elements of each party that carry the burden of competition with the other party tend to become increasingly cohesive. This applies not only in the case of campaign efforts, but also to the party task of governing when the party is in power—to the extent that party success in the activities of governing is deemed essential for party success in the next electoral competition.[8]

Centralization is in turn a product of the cohesion that is induced by competition. For success in the competition, the executive functions of centralized communication, policy leadership, and strategical decision all take on an obvious importance. Under conditions of competition and cohesion, there is not much objection to a centralization of such executive functions and there may be a strong desire to achieve it. In such cases, centralization is not so much imposed from above, as supported from below. This is especially the case when institutions of majority rule make possible a choice among alternative sources of leadership; in this case, the chosen leadership can be instructed to maintain discipline and apply such sanctions as may be feasible in dealing with dissident minorities who are found to be trading with the enemy.

There are many areas of American politics in which we might conduct a search for the centralizing tendencies of party competition, examine their nature, and consider their effects. Within the limited scope of this essay, the search will be devoted to areas previously suggested: party leadership, party finance, and some aspects of congressional politics.

LEADERSHIP PROBLEMS: INS VERSUS OUTS

Within the last century, the President has been gaining stature in his own party. The solid base of the President's power is found in his position as the nation's leader in a dangerous world. Often he must rise above party; but most students hold that it is not safe to rise too far—a capable President must continuously make certain that his partisan troops are still with him.

[8] Relationships between competition and cohesion have been noted by many analysts, but see particularly Robert T. Golembiewski, "A Taxonomic Approach to State Political Party Strength, *Western Political Quarterly*, XI, September 1958, pp. 494–513.

The evolution of the President's role as party leader has not been traced in adequate detail. Most scholars have given more attention to his role as leader of the legislature. Under modern conditions Congress cannot function effectively unless the President provides the legislative agenda. Even the Republican Party now accepts this; during the Eisenhower administration, many Republicans also came to feel rather strongly that when the President is functioning as legislative leader, he must also act visibly as the leader of his party if the basis is to be laid for partisan success in the congressional elections that are always just around the corner.

The President's connection with the party machinery and party functioning involves a series of problems on which there has been much controversy. It is also an area in which change in the norms of our political culture has come late and probably remains incomplete. Presidents had been renominated in national party conventions for a century before an incumbent President appeared in person to accept renomination, as Franklin Roosevelt did in 1936. It is generally accepted that the President may name the chairman of his national party committee, but this is not a responsibility of great antiquity. Presidential involvements in campaigns and elections have developed intermittently through a trial-and-error process, with every innovative precedent under attack, but generally with some net increment of presidential influence when the dust had settled.

The President's combined role as party leader and legislative leader took on new importance on at least one occasion, however, with a minimum of fanfare. This was the meeting held at the White House on Monday morning, November 15, 1937; those present included President Roosevelt, Vice President Garner, Speaker Bankhead, Senate Majority Leader Barkley, and House Majority Leader Rayburn. This was not the first time this group had met, but it was the first time that they met with an intention to meet once a week, with a fixed membership constituted on an *ex officio* basis. This was the beginning of the regular weekly congressional leadership meetings at the White House—meetings that have continued through the successive administrations of Presidents Roosevelt, Truman, Eisenhower, and Kennedy. If those present had been formally designated "The Legislative Cabinet," and if the meetings had been initiated by an Act of Congress, they would have attracted immediate attention as a major innovation in American constitutional practice. As it was, even the White House press corps remained unaware for some years that the leadership meetings were different from the many other meetings at the White House that continued to involve members of Congress.

There is still much less than a full realization among political scientists that the American government now contains a collegial body, constituted on a partisan basis at the highest political level, that regularly concerns itself with the forward program of the party in power, with special reference to those program elements involving legislation, appropriations, and congressional action. Political scientists as eminent as Edward S. Corwin and Charles S. Hyneman, apparently unaware of what already existed, continued to advocate the creation of a presidential legislative council in books published long after 1937.[9] The true importance of the leadership meetings was probably first noticed by the Committee on Political Parties in its report entitled *Toward a More Responsible Two-Party System*, published in 1950.[10]

Out-party difficulties in developing a leadership that can compete for public attention have long been obvious, but only under the competitive pressures of recent years has there been any strong impulse to do something about it. Two leading precedents were provided by the Democrats while out of power between 1953 and 1961. One was Adlai Stevenson's demonstration of the potentialities inherent in the out-party titular leadership under modern conditions; his performance as Party spokesman and chief campaigner was especially noteworthy during the midterm campaign of 1954. The second precedent was the creation of the Democratic Advisory Council as an instrument of collective leadership for the presidential wing of the out-party between 1956 and 1960. Although the Council was boycotted by the congressional leaders, it provided an influential voice for majority elements in the Party. It also regularly brought together most of those who were most concerned over the succession in the Party nomination in 1960. By the end of 1959, all the Party's leading contenders for the presidential

---

[9] Edward S. Corwin, *The President, Office and Powers 1781–1957*, 4th rev. ed. (New York: New York University Press, 1957), pp. 297–305; Charles S. Hyneman, *Bureaucracy in a Democracy* (New York: Harper & Row, 1950), pp. 571–79. Corwin in 1957 was still repeating the proposal of his first edition in 1940; in the 1957 edition, he refers to the leadership meetings of the Eisenhower administration, but the description is less than fully accurate and makes no reference to the prior practice of the Roosevelt and Truman administrations.

[10] David, Goldman, and Bain, *op. cit.*, pp. 67–68. It has since been discovered that the origin and continuity of the meetings can be documented for the initial years from the appointment books in the Roosevelt Library at Hyde Park.

Because of a considerable strain in the relationships between President Roosevelt and Vice President Garner between 1937 and 1940, the meetings began experimentally and with no certainty that they could be continued indefinitely. The problem was resolved in part by the fact that Garner absented himself from Washington for long periods; but when in Washington, he continued to attend as long as he was Vice President. The meetings seem to have been suggested initially by Mr. Rayburn, and were an attempt to improve procedures for consultation after the difficulties engendered by the Supreme Court proposal of 1937.

nomination of 1960 except Senate Majority Leader Lyndon Johnson had accepted membership on the Council.[11]

Both precedents just mentioned were actively debated in the Republican Party as it went through its leadership crisis on leaving office in 1961. For a brief interval, it appeared that former Vice President Nixon would accept major responsibilities as the Party's new titular leader. Instead, he seems to have abandoned the role, apparently having concluded that he would be committed to a hopeless race in 1964 if he functioned actively in the titular leadership in the meantime.

Discussions of alternative patterns of collective leadership resulted in agreement that the Party's congressional leaders and the national Party chairman would hold weekly meetings (while Congress is in session), after which the leaders make their views public through a television show—the so-called Ev and Charlie show.[12] Later, plans for an "All-Republican Conference" were developed, and six senators and six representatives were designated to draft a statement of Republican principles, with staff service provided by the Republican National Committee.[13]

In all these efforts, the prize at stake is the opportunity to influence the development of the party image. The symbolism of program intentions can provide clues to whether the party is being merely defensive, or whether it is indeed actively developing alternatives to the programs advocated by the party in power. For much of this, the real payoff is the party's voting record in Congress. This is always likely to be more conservative than the party's next candidate for President might desire. Yet if leadership structures are devised in which the presidential wing of the out-party can be more effective, some influence may be exerted on the party's congressional leaders and on the party's legislative record.

PROBLEMS OF PARTY AND CAMPAIGN FINANCE

A student of party finance recently commented that "The experience of 1960 suggests that a critical point is being reached in which financial necessities may bring on substantial changes in American party organization."[14] The

---

[11] On the long-term evolution of out-party leadership, see David, Goldman, and Bain, *op. cit.*, chap. 5; paperback ed., chap. 4.

[12] Thruston B. Morton, "Leadership Problems in the Opposition Party," in David *et al.*, chap. 11; see also pp. 327–28, 333–34.

[13] *Congressional Quarterly Weekly Report*, XX, Mar. 2, 1962, p. 361.

[14] Herbert E. Alexander, "Financing the Parties and Campaigns," in David *et al.*, *op. cit.*, pp. 116–49, at 145. The 1960 and related data summarized hereafter are mainly from this source.

1960 campaign was undoubtedly the most expensive ever. Expenditures by political committees operating nationally were about $25 million, an increase of 46 per cent from 1956. Total campaign costs at all levels have been estimated at $140 million in 1952, $155 million in 1956, and $175 million in 1960. These amounts do not include the estimated $15 to $20 million expenditures of the radio and television networks in providing coverage of the conventions and campaigns in 1960; nor do they include the free advertising valued at $12 million that was contributed by the major media, including newspapers, in the effort to encourage citizens to contribute campaign funds to the candidates and parties of their choice.

Both parties maintained fund-raising organizations during the 1960 campaign that were somewhat more effective than those of prior years, and most of the money expended was in the till before it was committed. Both parties nonetheless came out of the campaign with substantial deficits. The Republican deficit at the national level was a relatively manageable $700 thousand. The Democratic National Committee found itself in debt to the extent of $3.82 million, an amount large enough to be embarrassing even in victory, one that would have been catastrophic in defeat.

The 1960 experience again made it clear that the parties remain much too dependent on large contributors, who are fewer than formerly, and that the parties are not adequately organized to reach the mass of potential small contributors. Over 40 per cent of the gross receipts of the committees operating nationally came from the 5300 individuals who contributed $500 or more, for an average of about $1600 each. Only 95 persons seem to have given over $10,000. Between the unfavorable publicity that attends large contributions and effect of the tax laws on gifts over $3000, the wealthy Americans who formerly contributed $100 thousand or more to a single campaign are a vanishing race.[15]

At the other end of the spectrum, the Survey Research Center reported that whereas only 4 per cent of the voters made any political contribution in 1952, 10 per cent did so in 1956 and 11.5 in 1960. Despite this response to the advertising campaign for small contributions, the amounts actually reaching national party headquarters remained small. Most local party organizations failed to organize adequately to solicit small contributions on a door-to-door basis in the neighborhoods. Those that did needed the money so much that they were reluctant to pass on any substantial share to the state and national party committees.

[15] On the special impact of the tax laws, see Alexander Heard, *The Costs of Democracy* (Chapel Hill: The University of North Carolina Press, 1960), pp. 213, 348–50.

In 1961, both parties faced the problem of financing current operations while trying to pay off their campaign debts of 1960. The Republicans spent $2.7 million on current operations at the national level, but were able to raise only $2.3 million in contributions, with the result that the Party's indebtedness increased by $0.4 million.[16] The Democrats spent something like $1.3 million in 1961 on the current operations of the national committee and the two congressional campaign committees, but took in a total of $4.2 million at party headquarters and were thus able to apply about $2.9 million to reduction of indebtedness, bringing the debt down to about $0.9 million at the end of 1961.[17]

Both parties continued to rely heavily on national fund-raising dinners, but state quota systems took on new importance. The state quotas are amounts levied on the state party organizations for the support of national party operations. In the Republican Party, state quota systems have provided much of the routine support of national party operations for many years; little has been revealed, however, concerning the details of which states pay up regularly and which do not. In the Democratic Party, state assessments for the four-year period from 1957 to 1960 inclusive totaled $4.4 million, of which $2.8 million had been paid by May of 1960. Of the 54 states and territories, only six had paid in full; such major states as New York and Illinois were near the foot of the list in relative performance.[18]

The new managers of the Democratic Party succeeded in securing agreement on state quotas for 1961 at a level much higher than the scale previously in effect. The four largest states—New York, Pennsylvania, Illinois, and California—each agreed to pay an assessment of $250 thousand, and each promptly did so. By the end of 1961, payments on state quotas for the year had apparently reached about three-quarters of the total amount assessed for all states. A similar scale of state quotas remained in effect for 1962, in view of the financial requirements of a campaign year.

As the state quotas become heavier and payment becomes more imperative for the state organizations that wish to remain in good standing, the party organizations in the states are under pressure to rationalize their systems of party finance. The pressure exists in any case, because the state organizations face their own problems in financing state and local campaigns in situations of greater party competition. As a result more attention is given to putting various forms of party activity on a membership basis, with regular payments

---

[16] *Congressional Quarterly Weekly Report*, XX, February 16, 1962, p. 263.
[17] *Ibid*. The figures given involve estimates in some cases.
[18] Alexander, *op. cit.*, pp. 135–36.

of dues. More effort is also devoted to patterns of organization that will increase effectiveness in securing annual contributions of $1 to $20 throughout the party rank-and-file.[19]

Greater reliance on contributions of small and moderate size could be facilitated by the changes in tax laws that are under active consideration. The President's Commission on Campaign Costs recommended as follows on April 18, 1962:

That for an experimental period extending over two presidential campaigns:

Political contributors be given a credit against their Federal income tax of 50 per cent of contributions, up to a maximum of $10 in credits per year;

Contributors be permitted, alternatively, to claim the full amount of their contributions as a deduction from taxable income up to a maximum of $1,000 per tax return per year;

The only contributions eligible for these benefits be ones made to a national committee of a party, and to a State political committee designated by such a national committee (provided that no more than one committee per State be designated by a national committee).[20]

One commentator referred to these recommendations as

. . . a political scientists' dream. American parties are the most incoherent on earth; broadening their financial base would weaken their mortgage to the rich, and channelling

---

[19] The Republican National Committee's publication, *Battle Line*, March 28, 1962, carried a full page advertisement for the party's new Sustaining Membership Program, in which Chairman Miller of the national committee and Chairmen Goldwater and Wilson of the two congressional committees urged all to contribute $10 and become sustaining members. It was stated that "This membership should not be in lieu of your normal support for State and Local organizations, but rather an *extra* for National Headquarters operations. Your state will automatically receive full credit toward its national quota for your membership."

The Democratic national committee has been operating a similar $10 sustaining membership scheme for several years. The amounts produced have not been great—$200,000 during the early months of 1961—but are useful in providing routine support for national staff operations. Alexander, *op. cit.*, p. 143.

[20] President's Commission on Campaign Costs, *Financing Presidential Campaigns* (Washington, D.C.: U.S. Government Printing Office, 1962), pp. 4–5. For biographical notes on members of the Commission, see pp. 35–36. The quoted recommendations of the Commission had been foreshadowed in part by an earlier publication of its research director: Herbert E. Alexander, *Tax Incentives for Political Contributions* (Princeton: Citizens Research Foundation, 1961).

An expectation that the Commission would recommend public subsidies for the parties, as earlier advocated by President Kennedy, was not borne out, for reasons indicated in the report, pp. 30–32. On the case for public subsidies and a plan for making them feasible, see Philip M. Stern, "A Cure for Political Fund-raising," *Harper's*, May 1962, pp. 59–63.

the money through central committees (as proposed) should strengthen discipline and national (as opposed to parochial) direction.[21]

The Commission's report was nonetheless heartily welcomed by President Kennedy, who indicated that he would use it as a basis for seeking legislation in due time. The Commission was chaired by Alexander Heard, author of the leading work on party finance, and also included Professor V. O. Key, Jr., of Harvard University. Of the other seven members, four have had extensive experience with fund-raising problems in the higher echelons of the Republican Party, and three in the Democratic. Their recommendations are not likely to be dismissed as impractical by the officers of either political party or by members of Congress. If strong presidential support is forthcoming, major recommendations of the commission may reach enactment in advance of the campaigns of 1964.

NATIONALIZING TENDENCIES IN CONGRESSIONAL POLITICS

For some years, Professor E. E. Schattschneider has been saying in his various writings that Congress is increasingly involved in politics. He means, of course, an increasing involvement in the important varieties of politics: the politics of national issues, of nationally oriented interest groups, of the national parties, and of national campaigns and elections.

The evidence of increasing congressional involvement in presidential and vice-presidential nominations is especially clear. Senators have been gaining in strength as vice-presidential nominees and as potential presidential nominees; the successful nomination of Senator John F. Kennedy brings this progression to a realization. For about thirty years, congressional leaders have been dominant in both parties most of the time as the presiding officers at the national party conventions. This is a complete reversal of the nineteenth century practice under which convention leadership was almost completely divorced from congressional leadership.[22]

For a century, there has been a slow increase in the proportion of senators who attend the party conventions as delegates; 64 of them did so in 1960.[23] The patterns associated with this long-term tendency are highly revealing. Even in the late nineteenth century, when a state had one senator of each

[21] "T.R.B. from Washington," *New Republic*, April 30, 1962, p. 2.
[22] David, Goldman, and Bain, *op. cit.*, Table 4.1 and pp. 64–69.
[23] For the historical statistics, see *ibid.*, Table 14.5, p. 345. The 1960 data were provided by Thomas N. Schroth, Executive Editor of Congressional Quarterly Service.

party—a prima facie case of active party competition—*both* senators were usually present at their respective party conventions as delegates. Conversely, in the states represented by two Republican senators, the integration between state and national politics has been so weak that the senators from these states still usually refrain from active participation in the conventions. The one-party Democratic states occupy an intermediate position in this form of political behavior: the senators from these states have usually attended the Democratic national conventions in recent years, presumably to defend sectional interests.

Members of the House of Representatives, less nationally oriented and less capable of securing prestige recognition from their state party organizations, have not served as convention delegates proportionately as often as senators. But even here there has been marked change; the number of members of the House of Representatives who served in convention delegations (as delegates or alternates) is as follows since 1948:[24]

Year	Democrat	Republican
1948	32	20
1952	56	18
1956	80	39
1960	136	32

In view of the long-term data from the conventions, we can suppose that there may have been a similar long-term increase in the numbers of senators and representatives who have worked in national party campaigns outside the limits of their own states and districts. The data to test this tendency have never been accumulated, although possibly they could be secured from the archives of party speakers' bureaus or from newspaper files.

Campaigning by the candidates for President and Vice President has clearly become more national in scope, reaching the limits of the 50-state type of campaign in 1960. There is a general impression that the ticket-leaders are involved with the local candidates in more states that formerly as they progress from state to state. This is to be expected as more states become competitive, and the various candidates become more dependent on each other for marginal increments of strength in appealing to the voters.

The changing patterns of midterm campaigning are even more striking and suggest marked change in the relationships of national party leaders to the congressional campaigns. For years, Woodrow Wilson was criticized for

[24] *Ibid.*, Table 14.7, p. 347, and Mr. Schroth.

even his mild intervention in the 1918 campaign—an intervention that took the form of a brief press statement in which he expressed a hope for congressional majorities of his own party. But as the Roosevelt and Truman years wore on, there seemed to be increasing activity by the national party leaders in the midterm campaigns.

When President Eisenhower faced the issue for the first time, in 1954, his first inclination was one of withdrawal, following the doctrine of those who had criticized Woodrow Wilson. But after Adlai Stevenson had announced his intention to campaign actively from July to November, 1954, pressures from within the Republican Party brought President Eisenhower to a much more active performance than he had previously contemplated; Vice President Nixon was assigned the duty of campaigning in as many of the critical states as possible.

In 1962 President Kennedy kicked off the midterm campaign on January 20 at a $100-a-plate fund-raising dinner in Washington. Six thousand Democrats were present, including most Democratic members of Congress. He said:

What we are attempting to do tonight is to lay the groundwork for the Congressional campaigns of 1962, and we realize, I think, all the Members of the House and Senate, that history is not with us, that in this century only in 1934, during the periods of the great pre-eminence of the Democratic Party, did the Party in power ever win seats, let alone hold its own. But we believe in 1962 that the Democratic Party, both at home and abroad, is best fitted to lead this country—and therefore we start tonight on the campaigns of 1962.[25]

Later it was indicated that the President would undertake on-the-spot campaigning to assist members of his party in some instances, and that Vice President Lyndon Johnson would be available for active campaigning in at least a dozen states.[26]

[25] From the White House press release as subsequently issued. This was the occasion on which, in a high-spirited moment, the President produced a remarkable parody of portions of his Inaugural address:

. . . we observe tonight not a celebration of freedom but a victory of party, for we have sworn to pay off the same party debt our forebears ran up nearly a year and three months ago. Our deficit will not be paid off in the next hundred days, nor will it be paid off in the first one thousand days, nor in the life of this administration. Nor, perhaps even in our lifetime on this planet, but let us begin—remembering that generosity is not a sign of weakness and that Ambassadors are always subject to Senate confirmation—for if the Democratic party cannot be helped by the many who are poor, it cannot be saved by the few who are rich. So let us begin.

[26] Jack Bell, "Johnson to Campaign in Dozen Key States," *Washington Post and Times Herald*, March 13, 1962.

The dinner at which President Kennedy spoke was a sign of the new centralization of party fund-raising for congressional campaigns. For some years, the Republican National Finance Committee has been in charge of fund-raising for the Party's congressional campaign committees as well as for the National Committee. The Democrats came to this pattern in the spring of 1961 and seem likely to maintain it.

In the entire range of party affairs, centralization may come last and most slowly in the nomination of party candidates for Congress. Even here, however, one of the most respected students of the party system has suggested that "National party leaders in quest of a point of leverage to strengthen their party might well give thought to spending a few hundred thousand dollars a year in drumming up and supporting able House and Senate candidates for seats held by the opposition."[27] Others have suggested that the Republican National Committee needs paid staff workers in every critical congressional district, presumably to perform functions somewhat similar to those of the British constituency agents who are paid from national party funds.[28] So far, however, the national Party authorities seem mainly to have contented themselves with urging the local Party groups to work actively on candidate recruitment, so the Party may secure the kind of candidates for Congress that will enable it to compete more effectively.

The manner in which Richard Nixon was initially recruited to run for Congress in 1946 by a local group of Republican businessmen is well known. The activities of similar groups locally based but nationally oriented are probably becoming more important in the congressional nominating processes of both parties. Apparently they are a natural result of the club movement spreading in suburban politics.[29] They also seem to be a natural result of the increasingly effective interventions of organized labor and of organized business in their political efforts to compete with each other.

FROM THE TRADITIONAL TO THE RATIONAL

In view of the data so far reviewed, the party system of this country may well be moving in some greater degree than formerly from the traditional to the rational. This is a process going on throughout the world in the underdeveloped countries. Most countries seem to be politically underdeveloped,

---

[27] V. O. Key, Jr., *Politics, Parties, and Pressure Groups*, 4th ed. (New York: Thomas Y. Crowell Co., 1958), p. 497.

[28] Roscoe Drummond, "Memo to GOP," *Washington Post and Times Herald*, July 3, 1961.

[29] Stephen A. Mitchell, *Elm Street Politics* (New York: Oceana Publications, Inc., 1959).

and there are times when it is possible to suspect that even the United States belongs in this category.

In a rational world, political philosophers might suppose that political life would be primarily concerned with a politics of issues. That, at least, was the supposition of the Committee on Political Parties in its report of 1950, *Toward a More Responsible Two-Party System*. In the years since that report was published, the system seems to have moved at least slightly in the direction favored by the Committee; and the prospects for a further movement in that direction now seem moderately favorable. If this is indeed the case, the workings of the competitive impulse in politics can be given most of the credit. Minority major parties that seriously seek to become competitive within the two-party system have found it expedient in state after state to develop a strong interest in issues—an interest that is practical and strategic, rather than doctrinaire, but one that nonetheless assists in the education of voter opinion, and that may eventually produce a marked increase in voter turnout—especially in those states where turnout has traditionally been low.

It has been assumed much too often in the one-party states and localities that it is necessary to join the dominant party in order to be politically effective. This may have been true thirty or forty years ago, but it does not seem to be true any longer. The situation has changed to the point where many of the greatest political opportunities of the future are probably now available in minority party situations where the smaller of the two major parties is still greatly outnumbered.[30] The exploitation of these opportunities will require an eye for issues and a willingness to open them up for public debate. The process can be assisted by help from the central party headquarters when the central staffs are sufficiently vigorous and alert, but often it has proceeded even more fully on the strength of local impulses. The game of competitive politics can be initiated at any level, and it is a game in which any number can play. Fortunately it is a game in which all who participate can obtain some reward, and in which it is to the nation's interest for many to be engaged.

Suggestions for Further Reading

Bailey, Stephen K., *The Condition of Our National Political Parties* (New York: The Fund for the Republic, 1959). "An Occasional Paper on the Role of the Political Process in the Free Society."

[30] On the special problems of the Republican party in northern cities where the party organization is moribund or worse, see Robert L. Johnson, "We've Got to Wake Up in the Big Cities," *U.S. News & World Report*, April 23, 1962, pp. 68–70.

David, Paul T., "Comparative State Politics and the Problem of Party Realignment," in Stephen K. Bailey, *et al. Research Frontiers in Politics and Government* (Washington, D. C.: The Brookings Institution, 1955).

Eagleton Institute of Politics, *Cases in Practical Politics* (New York: McGraw-Hill Book Company, Inc.). See especially cases by Francis Carney, John C. Donovan, Bernard Hennessy, Abraham Holtzman, Frank Munger, Kenneth N. Vines, and Philip S. Wilder, Jr.

Heard, Alexander, *The Costs of Democracy* (Garden City: Doubleday & Company, Inc., 1962).

Rossiter, Clinton, *Parties and Politics in America* (Ithaca, New York: Cornell University Press, 1960).

Schattschneider, E. E., *The Semisovereign People* (New York: Holt, Rinehart & Winston, Inc., 1960).

Sindler, Allan P., "Political Parties," in Alan F. Westin, ed., *The Uses of Power* (New York: Harcourt, Brace & World, Inc., 1962).

IS CONGRESS
THE OLD FRONTIER?

Stephen K. Bailey

CONGRESS AND THE PRESIDENT: OLD AND NEW FRONTIERS

The quintessential business of historians is to formulate general propositions about the past.

The quintessential business of scientists—including social scientists—is to formulate general propositions about what is.

The quintessential business of moral philosophers is to formulate general propositions about what ought to be.

The quintessential business of students of public affairs is to interrelate

STEPHEN K. BAILEY *has mixed much practical political experience with his professional political science: he has been staff associate with the first Hoover Commission, Chairman of the Connecticut Democratic State Platform Committee, Administrative Assistant to Senator William Benton, Mayor of Middletown, Connecticut, and President of the Connecticut Association of Towns and Cities. He has taught at Wesleyan University, and guest lectured at Harvard, Oxford, and the University of Pennsylvania. He was Director of the Graduate Program in the Woodrow Wilson School of Public and International Affairs at Princeton 1954–1958. Professor of Political Science at Syracuse University since 1959, he became Dean of the Maxwell Graduate School of Citizenship and Public Affairs in 1961. His book* Congress Makes a Law (1950) *won the Woodrow Wilson Foundation Award of the American Political Science Association as the best publication of the year in American government and democracy. Other books, with co-authors, include* Congress at Work (1952), Government in America (1958), *and* Schoolmen and Politics (1962).

selected propositions of history, social science, and moral philosophy in such a way as to promote benevolent rationality in the formulation and execution of public policy.

It is in the spirit of a student of public affairs that I address myself to the question: Is Congress the Old Frontier?

In chronological terms, Congress is indeed the "Old Frontier." Congress as an institution is almost four times as old as President Kennedy as an individual, and the average age of all congressmen and senators is roughly 20 per cent higher than the age of Mr. Kennedy. Such comparisons are not entirely specious. The age of institutions, and of persons within institutions, is politically significant. In personal terms, age often brings a lowering of energy, a hardening of habits, and a suspicion of either the efficacy or the novelty of recommended change. Institutionally, age tends to deify traditional procedures and to solidify the in-group feelings of institutional leaders. The Constitutional continuity of the Senate and the political continuity of the House are forces of consequence in the continuing tension between the President and the Congress. The Presidency is an historic office, but its incumbents are always new. No matter what the chronological age of the President, he is always dealing with a legislative branch whose leaders have served with many Presidents. Some Chief Executives, such as Roosevelt, Truman, and Kennedy, have attempted to compensate for this ineluctable fact by immersion in historical and biographical literature. But vicarious experience is not the same as direct experience. Exposure to literature is rarely an adequate substitute for experience in office.

In this sense, Congress is inevitably the Old Frontier. Congress is the defensive stockade, not the pioneering scout. It is an old stockade, under the command of seasoned veterans. Its manual of arms is traditional and wily. Its defensive capacity is impressive. And this defensive capacity is directly related to the age, experience, and continuity of the institution and its commanding officers.

This, of course, raises a central question: what is it that the Congressional stockade is attempting to defend? And this presents a sticky problem of analysis. Even a cursory glance at congressional behavior reveals that the national legislature is organized to defend a wide variety of things. Taking a leaf from the notebook of Pendleton Herring, this essay will discuss the congressional defense of ideas, interests, institutions, and individuals.

WHAT CONGRESS ATTEMPTS TO DEFEND

The central *idea* which Congress is designed to defend is human freedom. This point would hardly need elaboration were it not so frequently and tragically forgotten in the mid-twentieth century.

If anything is clear in this fretful age, it is that legislative institutions which gave freedom its birth and meaning have been eroded in power and denigrated in reputation the world around—eroded and denigrated, that is, where they have not been totally destroyed. Necessary as the Gaullist revolution in France may have been, nobody will pretend that the French National Assembly was upgraded in power or influence by the change. The first casualty of wobbly novitiates in the family of nations seems to be their parliaments or assemblies. In the past few years, a half-dozen new nations have abolished the pretense of democracy, and have reverted to rule by tribal chieftains decked out in modern military garb. Scrawled in invisible ink on the walls of the empty parliament buildings are the words, "Parliaments, Go Home."

How short historical memories are! It was a congress of nobles that met at Runnymede to make John Lackland sign Magna Carta. It was a congress of estates called "Parliament" that gradually reduced the prerogatives of the English crown from absolutism to a benign symbol of spiritual and moral unity. It was assemblies of free men which tempered and hamstrung the insolence of appointed Royal Governors during our own colonial days.

Of what does freedom consist, unless it is the atmosphere of human dignity made possible by the existence of representative restraints upon rulers? Benevolent despots have dotted the pages of human history, but like the barking dog who never bites, no one knows when a despot is going to stop being benevolent. And on this score, history is not encouraging.

It was with considerations of this sort in mind that our Founding Fathers, after a brief preamble, began the Constitution of the United States with the words, "All legislative Powers herein granted shall be vested in a Congress of the United States, which shall consist of a Senate and House of Representatives."

That the first Article of the Constitution deals with the Congress is no accident. Congress is first because, living in the long shadow of the Glorious Revolution of 1688 and of its great philosophical defender John Locke, our Founding Fathers fully understood that, although you could have government without a representative assembly, you could not have *free* government without a representative assembly.

Congress defends freedom by asking rude questions; by stubbornly insisting that technology be discussed in terms of its human effects; by eliciting new ideas from old heads; by building a sympathetic bridge between the bewildered citizen and the bureaucracy; by acting as a sensitive register for group interests whose fortunes are indistinguishable from the fortunes of vast numbers of citizens and who have a constitutional right to be heard.

Congress defends freedom by being a prudent provider; by carefully sifting and refining legislative proposals; by compromising and homogenizing raw forces in conflict; by humbling generals and admirals—and, on occasion, even Presidents.

Freedom is neither an old nor a new frontier. It is, for as far ahead as man can see, an eternal frontier. If not constantly cleared and defended it reverts to jungle where wild beasts play out their morbid and sullen dramas. As one of the great institutional forces in the life of modern man dedicated to the perpetuation of freedom, Congress deserves our support and our reverence.

But if Congress exists to defend the idea of freedom, it also exists to defend a range of specific interests, institutions, and individuals in our society. And here there is an obligation to sort out whether the defense of the three remaining terms is always compatible with the defense of the first one. Is the cause of human freedom, looked at in the large, helped or hindered by a preoccupation with the defense of the specific interests, institutions, and individuals which the national legislature is presently designed to serve?

Social science writings on Congress of the past generation are generally agreed on the following propositions:

—that Congress over-represents rural populations as contrasted with big city and suburban populations;[1]

—that Congressional leadership comes, by and large, from one-party areas in the south and middle west;[2]

—that producer interests are more effectively represented in the Congress than consumer interests, and some producer interests more effectively than others;[3]

---

[1] "Suburban Areas Most Underrepresented in the House," *Congressional Quarterly Weekly Report*, February 2, 1962, pp. 153–69. Gordon E. Baker, *Rural Versus Urban Political Power: The Nature and Consequences of Unbalanced Representation* (New York: Doubleday & Company, Inc., 1955). For a statistical analysis of urban and rural congressional districts, see study by Senator Paul H. Douglas (D., Ill.) in 102 *Congressional Record* 5535-74.

[2] In the 87th Congress Southerners chaired 10 of the 16 Senate standing committees; in the House, they held 11 of the 21 chairs. Five of the seven joint committees were chaired by Southerners. See *Congressional Directory; Congressional Quarterly;* and Nicholas A. Masters, "Committee Assignments in the House of Representatives," *The American Political Science Review*, June 1961, pp. 345–57.

[3] See the last chapter of Wilfred E. Binkley, *President and Congress* (New York: Alfred A.

—that Congress often supports the particular interests of parts of the bureaucracy in opposition to the more general designs of the President;[4]
—that the internal workings of the Senate and the House are designed to give special power to and to serve the interests of legislative leaders who are not representative of the nation as a whole or even, on some occasions except under duress, of the Congress itself;[5]
—that on many issues of national importance, the alliance between sections of the two parties in the Congress is more powerful than the alliance represented within the majority party itself.[6]

These propositions can generally be empirically verified, although conceptual fuzziness haunts some of the propositions themselves. It is doubtful that social scientists would long debate the validity of most of these generalizations. The fact is that Congress presently defends a set of interests, institutions, and individuals which are frequently alien to the national interest as viewed by the President. When the President calls his policies in defense of a different amalgam of interests, institutions, and individuals the "New Frontier," it may not be out of place to call the congressional amalgam the "Old Frontier." But in so doing, it is important to be aware that the terms "new" and "old" in this context are invidious, and that there is nothing in social science as social science which gives license to invidiousness. The fact that two branches of our government—both of them representative—do not see eye-to-eye on everything is initially, at least, a matter for analysis, not for

Knopf, Inc., 1947). *The New York Times*, March 16, 1962, pp. 1, 16. "President Submits Message on Consumer Interests," *Congressional Quarterly Weekly Report*, March 16, 1962, p. 435.
[4] J. Leiper Freeman, *The Political Process: Executive Bureau-Congressional Committee Relations* (New York: Doubleday & Company, Inc., 1955).
[5] For an early discussion of this, see Woodrow Wilson's chapter, "The Executive," in his book *Congressional Government; A Study in American Politics*, 2nd ed. (Boston: Houghton Mifflin Company, 1885). Neil MacNeil, "The House Confronts Mr. Kennedy," *Fortune*, January 1962, pp. 70–73 ff. George Goodwin, Jr., "The Seniority System in Congress," *The American Political Science Review*, June 1959, pp. 412–36. Emanuel Celler, "The Seniority Rule in Congress," *Western Political Quarterly*, March 1961, pp. 160–67. James A. Robinson, "The Role of the Rules Committee in the U.S. House of Representatives," *The Midwest Journal of Political Science*, February 1961, pp. 59–69. American Political Science Association, Committee on Political Parties, *Toward A More Responsible Two-Party System* (New York: Holt, Rinehart & Winston, Inc., 1950). Stephen K. Bailey and Howard D. Samuel, *Congress at Work* (New York: Holt, Rinehart & Winston, Inc., 1952). James MacGregor Burns, *Congress on Trial* (New York: Harper & Row, Publishers, 1949).
[6] See William S. White, "Rugged Days for the Majority Leader," *The New York Times Magazine*, July 13, 1949, p. 14 ff. "Conservative Coalition Appeared on 28 Per Cent of Roll Calls," *Congressional Quarterly Weekly Report*, November 3, 1961, pp. 1796–1802. "Extent of North-South Democratic Split Analyzed," *Congressional Quarterly Weekly Report*, November 3, 1961, pp. 1806–10.

alarm or scorn. Furthermore, it is perfectly arguable that the bias of congressional organization and procedure toward certain interests, institutions, and individuals is in fact in the long-range public interest. This may be true either because, in the spirit of the Constitution, the Presidency over-represents other interests, institutions, and individuals, and Congress therefore merely redresses an imbalance; or because it is in the majority's long-run interest to give short-run advantage to the peculiar minority clientele which finds its representative strength in a procedurally ponderous legislative branch.

The present orientation and organization of Congress has been stoutly defended on both these grounds. The moral philosophy behind this defense has been stated or implied in many or all of the following propositions:

—that the maintenance of freedom depends, not upon simple majority rule, but upon the rule of what Calhoun called a *concurrent* majority which can exist only if the intensity of feeling of powerful minorities is given uncommon weight in the determination of public policy;[7]

—that the 90 million American citizens who are rurally oriented would be swamped by an urban and suburban majority if Congress were reorganized to be more faithfully representative of majority interests, and that such a swamping would not be in the public interest;[8]

—that rural dwellers have more character and intelligence than urban dwellers, and character and intelligence need to be over-represented in a free society;[9]

—that the serving of producer interests is automatically in the interest of consumers;[10]

[7] Peter Drucker, "A Key to American Politics: Calhoun's Pluralism," *Review of Politics*, October 1948, pp. 412–26. John C. Calhoun, *A Disquisition on Government*, ed. by C. Gordon Post (New York: Liberal Arts Press, 1953). John Fischer, "Unwritten Rules of American Politics," *Harper's Magazine*, November 1948, pp. 27–36.

[8] Andrew Hacker, "Voice of Ninety Million Americans," *The New York Times Magazine*, March 4, 1962, p. 11ff.

[9] Although the following statement was made over a century ago, the attitude expressed is still widespread among certain rural citizens. "In the hands of moderate and moral farmers liberty was not likely to be lost . . . . The Senate . . . should be representative of the landed interests and its security against the caprice of the motley assemblage of paupers, emigrants, journeymen, manufacturers, and those indefinable classes of inhabitants which a state and a city like ours is calculated to invite . . . . Universal suffrage . . . puts it into the power of the poor and profligate to control the affluent." Statement by delegate to the Constitutional Convention of 1821, as quoted from Nassau Democratic County Committee (Willis Ave., Mineola, New York: 1962). Mimeograph.

[10] Since the late nineteenth century, the laissez-faire ethic has identified the public welfare with the capacity of entrepreneurs to press for the furtherance of their goals. The Smithian argument runs that through the advancement of personal values and desires the nation as a whole prospers. Defenders of this idea have argued that to avoid retarding

—that party neatness would separate America into warring factions of liberals and conservatives and that this nation would, in Acton's phrase, then be no longer sufficiently at one so that it could safely afford to bicker;[11]

—that the electoral college gives such predominant strength in the Presidency to urban minorities in evenly-balanced industrial states that only a Congress which over-represents rural population can save the nation from the parochial importunities of religious, racial, national, and economic minorities in our metropolitan centers—especially in the fields of social welfare and foreign affairs;[12]

—that the experience and power represented in existing congressional leadership is a balance wheel to flighty and ephemeral forces which occasionally find their spokesmen in the Presidency and in junior legislators;[13]

—that the procedural cumbersomeness of the Congress, as represented in such phenomena as the House Rules Committee or the filibuster in the Senate, is a great safeguard against hasty and passionate action which even the advocates of haste might live to regret.[14]

---

industrial growth only minimal government regulation is justified. See, as an almost classic statement of this position, Ray Lyman Wilbur and Arthur Mastick Hyde, *The Hoover Policies* (New York: Charles Scribner's Sons, 1937), p. 297.

[11] Harold Laski argued that the basic beliefs of the English Labor and Conservative Parties were at direct odds with one another; he predicted civil war would result if the Labor Party came to power. Harold J. Laski, *Parliamentary Government in England* (New York: The Viking Press, Inc., 1938). See Ernest S. Griffith, *Congress, Its Contemporary Role*, 3rd ed. (New York: New York University Press, 1961). Ralph K. Huitt, "Democratic Party Leadership in the Senate," *The American Political Science Review*, June 1961, pp. 333–44. Julius Turner, "Responsible Parties: A Dissent from the Floor," *The American Political Science Review*, March 1951, pp. 143–52. Morton Grodzins, "American Political Parties and the American System," *The Western Political Quarterly*, December 1960, pp. 974–98.

[12] For a discussion of the Lodge-Gosset amendment, see "Should Congress Adopt the Pending Plan for Direct Election of the President?" *Congressional Digest*, August 1949. Samuel Krislov, "The Electoral College," *Parliamentary Affairs*, Autumn 1958, pp. 466–74. Lucius Wilmerding, Jr., *The Electoral College* (Newark, New Jersey: Rutgers University Press, 1958). "New Interest Shown in Reform of Electoral System," *Congressional Quarterly Weekly Report*, February 17, 1961, pp. 179–88. David O. Dewey, "Madison's Views on Electoral Reform," *The Western Political Quarterly*, March 1962, pp. 140–45. Anthony Lewis, "The Case Against Electoral Reform," *The Reporter*, December 8, 1960, pp. 31–33. Joseph E. Kallenbach, "Our Electoral College Gerrymander," *Midwest Journal of Political Science*, May 1960, pp. 162–91.

[13] Griffith, *Congress, Its Contemporary Role, op. cit.*

[14] Franklin L. Burdette, *Filibustering in the Senate* (Princeton: Princeton University Press, 1940), p. 9. James A. Robinson, "Decision Making in the House Rules Committee," *Administrative Science Quarterly*, June 1948, pp. 73–86. See *The New York Times*, December 1960-January 1961 on the reorganization fight of the House Rules Committee.

This line of reasoning does not question the proposition that Congress is indeed the "old frontier"; it accepts this reality and concludes, "Thank God!"

On the other side, there are those who view with alarm that what Congress presently represents establishes a critical tension with a more inclusive public interest to the mortal danger of the latter. The propositions of the alarmists can be summarized as follows:

—that in the kind of world we live in, speed is often the handmaiden of prudence; and congressional practice is not friendly to speed;[15]

—that the lack of responsiveness of Congress to the needs of the majority of our people who live in non-rural areas is having the effect of multiplying a series of pathologies in America's great metropolitan centers which can have serious and even disastrous consequences in such fields as housing, education, transportation, and welfare;[16]

—that international problems of diplomacy, trade, and aid are incapable of being solved intelligently by a Congress dominated by parochial and short-term constituent interests;[17]

—that political coalitions cutting across partisan divisions lead to a lack of accountability which both frustrates and enervates a democratic citizenry and makes a mockery of the franchise;[18]

—that th veto power of the southern delegation in the Congress delays

[15] See Stephen K. Bailey, *The Condition of Our National Political Parties* (New York: The Fund for the Republic, 1959). William Y. Elliott, *The Need for Constitutional Reform* (New York: McGraw-Hill Book Company, Inc., 1935). Thomas K. Finletter, *Can Representative Government Do The Job?* (New York: Reynal & Company, Inc., 1945).

[16] Douglas, *Congressional Record, op. cit.* George B. Galloway, *Congressional Reorganization Revisited* (College Park, Maryland: University of Maryland Press, 1956). Senator Joseph S. Clark (D., Pa.) has been an eloquent defender of urban areas: see "To Come to the Aid of Their Cities," *The New York Times Magazine*, April 30, 1961, p. 11; 106 *Congressional Record* 14901; "A Voice for the Cities," *The Nation*, March 7, 1959, pp. 199–200.

[17] Charles O. Lerche, Jr., "Southern Congressmen and the 'New Isolationism,'" *Political Science Quarterly*, September 1960, pp. 321–37. Malcolm E. Jewell, "Evaluating the Decline of Southern Internationalism Through Senatorial Roll Call Votes," *The Journal of Politics*, November 1959, pp. 624–46. Oscar William Perlmutter, "Acheson v. Congress," *The Review of Politics*, January 1960, pp. 5–44. Robert A. Dahl, *Congress and Foreign Policy* (New York: Harcourt, Brace & World, Inc., 1950). Ernest S. Griffith, "The Place of Congress in Foreign Relations," *The Annals*, September 1953, pp. 11–21. David N. Farnsworth, "A Comparison of the Senate and its Foreign Relations Committee on Selected Roll-Call Votes," *The Western Political Quarterly*, March 1961, pp. 168–75.

[18] "Trade Battle Features Unique Lobby Alliance," *Congressional Quarterly Weekly Report*, March 9, 1962, pp. 403–08. Joseph S. Clark, "The Hesitant Senate," *The Atlantic*, March 1962, pp. 55–60. E. E. Schattschneider, *Party Government* (New York: Holt, Rinehart & Winston, Inc., 1942). American Political Science Association, *Toward A More Responsible Two-Party System, op. cit.*

the resolution of racial conflicts, and seriously harms our international image in our struggle with the Communist world;[19]

—that the advantage which Congress presently allows to particular producer interests in our society militates against the interests of the consumer, of labor, and of less powerful producers;[20]

—that the three-way alliances between parts of Congress, parts of the bureaucracy, and special private interests is a constant log-rolling threat to Presidential proposals designed with long-range and majoritarian interests in mind;[21]

—and, finally, that the bickering and conflict between President and Congress fractures our capacity to develop unified and consistent policies at home and abroad at a time when the United States is in mortal danger.[22]

With these fears in mind, alarmists have recommended everything from major constitutional reforms of a parliamentary character to modest changes in congressional procedures and party organization.[23]

But what if one finds himself neither among the sanguine nor the alarmists, but among the fretful? And what if one finds himself more organically-minded than structurally-minded—less enamored of grandiose gimmicks, and more receptive to marginal adjustments? What if one believes that great institutional arrangements change safely and intelligently by increments rather than by revolutions? What if one finds sufficient merit in the arguments both of the defenders and the attackers of Congress in its present form to wish to construct a position which is in effect a synthesis? How, in short, is it possible to enjoy the benefits of a strong and pluralistic legislature without suffer-

[19] "Latest Efforts to Change U. S. Senate's Cloture Rule 22," *The Congressional Digest*, December 1958. See *The New York Times*, April-May 1962 for reports on cloture on debate over literacy qualifications in Federal elections.

[20] Binkley, *President and Congress, op. cit.*

[21] William T. R. Fox, "Representativeness and Efficiency: Dual Problem of Civil-Military Relations," *Political Science Quarterly*, September 1961, pp. 354–66. Freeman, *The Political Process, op. cit.*

[22] Holbert Carroll, *The House of Representatives and Foreign Affairs* (Pittsburgh: University of Pittsburgh Press, 1958). Cecil Craff, *Bipartisan Foreign Policy: Myth or Reality?* (White Plains, New York: Harper & Row, Publishers, 1957). Hubert H. Humphrey, "The Senate in Foreign Policy," *Foreign Affairs*, July 1959, pp. 525–36. Thorsten V. Kalijarvi and Chester E. Merrow, eds., "Congress and Foreign Relations," *The Annals*, September 1953. Finletter, *op. cit.*, Elliot, *op. cit.*

[23] Henry Jones Ford, *The Rise and Growth of American Politics* (New York: The Macmillan Company, 1898). William MacDonald, *A New Constitution for a New America* (New York: B. W. Huebsch, Inc., 1921). Ivan W. Parkins, "Let's Disassemble the House: A Proposal for Reform of Congress," *South Atlantic Quarterly*, Spring 1960, pp. 226–38. Bailey, *op. cit.*, Burns, *op. cit.*

ing inordinately from its disadvantages? How can there be established, not a new frontier or an old frontier, but a common frontier in the face of a wilderness of dangers?

In the first place, it is fair to say that on many vital matters a common frontier has already been established. In vast areas of defense, foreign, economic, and scientific policy Congress in recent years has either deferred to the President, or has worked in close and patriotic understanding with him. This sharing of power—sometimes to the point almost of abdication—has been an inevitable result of the times in which we live. This deserves a brief elaboration.

THE COMMON FRONTIER OF CONGRESS AND THE PRESIDENT

The present era, in public affairs terms, has been marked by two qualities: first, the unending character of crisis; and second, the development of appallingly complex aspects of diplomacy, national defense, economic stability, and scientific technology.

On the matter of crisis, it is a natural tendency of all nature to seek shelter in time of storm. For society, the great psychological shelter is the political leader, the father image, the personified protector. This century has been and is a century of wars and the threat of wars, of economic eruptions and social disruptions. How many human beings have echoed the plaintive and pitiful words of Lord Tennyson?

> *But what am I*
> *An infant crying in the night,*
> *An infant crying for the light,*
> *And with no language but a cry?*[24]

In the repetitive convulsions of this era, is it any wonder that Americans submit to what Clinton Rossiter has called "Constitutional Dictatorship"[25]—that they have sought comfort in the solemn singularity and emergency discretion of the Presidency? Is it any wonder that the Congress itself has sought such comfort? It was a Republican, not a Democratic congressman, who, when the Emergency Banking Act of 1933 was submitted to vote in the Congress without so much as a legislative hearing or even a printed bill, said:

[24] Alfred Tennyson, "In Memoriam A. H. H.," *Poems of Tennyson* (New York: Oxford University Press, 1916), p. 348.
[25] *Constitutional Dictatorship; Crisis Government in Modern Democracies* (Princeton: Princeton University Press, 1948).

Of course it is entirely out of the ordinary to pass legislation in this House that, as far as I know, is not even in print at the time it is offered. The House is burning down and the President of the United States says this is the way to put out the fire. . . . I am going to give the President of the United States his way today. He is the man responsible and we must follow his lead.[26]

But urgencies in economic affairs have been more than matched by the urgencies of our diplomacy and defense. The difficulty for Congress has been that the success of our diplomacy and the posture of our defense are not easily subject to meaningful control by traditional legislative action and surveillance. For all of Woodrow Wilson's genius, his plea for "open covenants openly arrived at" was surely one of the most irresponsible maxims ever coined by a public leader. Diplomacy, if it is to be successful, necessarily involves secrecy and unity of direction. The heart of diplomacy is in the informal probing sessions which precede public pronouncements and ratifications. Constitutionally, diplomacy is properly the job of the Executive, not of a debating society. Senator Fulbright once commented on an attempt by some of his colleagues to draft a congressional resolution on the Berlin crisis:

To force the President [he wisely wrote], *into a negotiating straitjacket or to over-whelm him—and the world—with uncoordinated and perhaps conflicting advice would cause nothing but trouble. The Foreign Relations Committee is available to advise the President, but his is the primary responsibility.*[27]

And just as diplomacy necessarily involves secrecy and unity of direction, so national defense necessitates complex and often secret preparations and swift response. Legislatures are far too cumbersome to manage the national defense in an operational sense. It is the President who is Commander-in-Chief, and his decisions must at times be split-second. If the DEW-line radar spots an intercontinental ballistic missile, the question of how or whether America should retaliate is hardly a matter for extended congressional debate.

In a sense, Congress does have the job of making broad determinations of defense policy. It authorizes expenditures and makes the laws, including appropriations. But it would be unrealistic to suggest that Congress could do these things unaided by the Executive branch.

I remember once talking to the late Senator Brian McMahon—then the

---

[26] *77 Congressional Record* 76.
[27] Fulbright, as quoted in *The New York Times*, March 1, 1959, p. 4.

most knowledgeable man in Congress in the field of atomic energy—about the military budget. "How on earth," he complained, "are we in the Congress supposed to apply intelligent control to matters we can't understand? The whole military picture is too gigantic and too technical for congressional minds to comprehend; and often the basic questions hinge upon information which is withheld because it is 'top secret.' If one or two of us are let in, the rest of the Congress votes on blind faith. What kind of democracy is this?" he concluded.

But the perplexity of Congress ranges far beyond questions of diplomacy and defense. Almost every aspect of America's economic life has become complex beyond belief—as have questions of health, space, resource conservation, and other policy children of a burgeoning science and technology. A few years ago T. Swann Harding noted that it was

. . . up to congressional committees and then to the Congress as a whole to grasp and decide upon the justice of appropriations for such projects as: the use of endocrines to increase egg production; the role of Johne's disease; coccidiosis and worm parasites in cattle production; the production of riboflavin from milk by-products; spot treatment with soil fumigants for the control of root knot nematode on melons; the use of mass releases of Macrocentrus ancylivorus *to control oriental fruit moth injury; and the conversion of lactose into methyl acrylate to be polymerized with butadiene for the production of synthetic rubber.*[28]

And this, of course, was before the days of astronautics. It seems obvious and inevitable that the experts, the scientists, the economists, the agency specialists—the fellows who spend their lifetimes on these matters—have to work in sympathetic cooperation with lay politicians in dealing with such issues if this nation is to survive and prosper.

There are of course some people who believe that Congress has deferred to the executive too abjectly. Amaury de Riencourt, James Burnham, and others have viewed the common frontier between President and Congress as a simple manifestation of the rise of Caesarian government.[29] Their fear seems to be that if, as is likely, the psychological tensions continue, with continuing crises, the American people will become so restive of the bickerings and seeming delays of Congress that they will cling to the President

[28] T. Swann Harding, "The Marriage of Science to Government," *American Journal of Pharmacy*, October 1944, reprinted in U. S. Congress, *Symposium on Congress by Members of Congress and Others*, Joint Committee Print, 79th Congress, 1st Session (Washington: USGPO, 1945), p. 94.
[29] Amaury de Riencourt, *The Coming Caesars* (New York: Coward-McCann, Inc., 1957). James Burnham, *Congress and the American Tradition* (Chicago: Henry Regnery Co., 1959).

alone. This puts Congress in a dilemma: if it cooperates with the President, it fosters Caesarian government; if it squabbles with the President, it dangerously delays or distorts the policy-making process. With this logic, no matter what Congress does, it undermines freedom.

But logic is an uncertain guide to truth. It seems both inevitable and desirable that the Congress should defer and cooperate as it has on many issues of national security, technology, and economic growth and stability. There could have been an intolerable constitutional crisis if Carl Vinson had insisted upon mandating the President and the Secretary of Defense to keep producing B-70's.[30] Similarly, great danger could be done to the American economy if the Congress should see fit not to grant presidential requests, on occasion, to raise the debt limit.

In short, where the dangers to the common frontier are obvious and reasonably immediate, our government has acted with considerable unity and dispatch. Certainly in the face of the most appalling and critical issue of our time—national survival—Congress has not hesitated to appropriate funds requested by the Chief Executive for the military establishment. In fact, it can be argued that the congressional tendency is to go beyond Executive requests in this area—to embarrass the President with appropriations more lavish than he can intelligently spend or than he believes to be prudent. The congressional desire to cooperate on military appropriations has now reached a point where self-generating pressures of a constituent character may in fact be the enemy of flexible and efficient planning by the Pentagon. And the congressional scramble for defense procurement has implications as well for the flexibility of American diplomacy. This deserves careful scrutiny. The issue is not that our level of defense spending is presently too great or that it will or should materially decrease in the foreseeable future. But it would surely be one of the grimmest ironies of history if this nation should become so dependent upon the economic pep pill of defense spending that it found that it could not function without it. George Kennan has wisely pointed out that perfect military posture may be the enemy of perfect diplomatic posture.[31] It may not be easy to lessen international tensions over the years when it is a heightening of tension that keeps military hardware flowing and congressional constituents prosperous.

In any case, the issue is not that Congress has failed to respond to overt

[30] "Showdown Averted on RS-70 Funds," *Congressional Quarterly Weekly Report*, March 23, 1962, pp. 469–70. Roland Evans, Jr., "The Sixth Sense of Carl Vinson," *The Reporter*, April 12, 1962, pp. 25–30. *The New York Times*, March 9, 1962, pp. 14–15; March 22, 1962, p. 1.

[31] This essentially is the position taken in George F. Kennan, *Russia, the Atom and the West* (New York: Harper & Row, Publishers, 1958), pp. 50–65.

needs in such fields as national defense, but that existing congressional organization, procedures, and patterns of representation have tended to foster an unwarranted division between national security policy on the one hand and policies designed to strengthen national freedom, prosperity, and welfare on the other. Many congressional leaders seem unwilling to understand or—if they understand—to admit that domestic questions such as racial inequality, unemployment, slums, inadequate education, and a shocking waste of natural resources, are intimately and inexorably related to the fact and quality of our national survival. Furthermore, in areas of practical diplomacy represented by such words as "trade" and "aid," many legislators seem incapable of sensing the relationship between economic programs on the one hand and the on-going diplomatic and military policies of the United States on the other.

Surely these points do not need extensive elaboration. Little Rock and Montgomery make hot copy for *Pravda* and for the worldwide propaganda machine of international communism. Unemployment at home raises serious questions in the minds of allies, neutrals, and enemies as to the seriousness of America's collective effort and the humaneness of her economic system. The failure to provide adequately stimulating and sufficiently rigorous educational opportunities for America's young people casts a shadow upon the nation's future capacity to withstand the competition of an implacable enemy—an enemy which has put enormous store and resources in education.

In the fields of trade and aid, Congress has been less unresponsive than inconstant. The building of strong alliances with Western Europe, Japan, and the British Commonwealth of Nations, and the bringing of light and hope to the darkness of the underdeveloped world, inevitably involve a series of adjustments and sacrifices on the domestic front. These adjustments and sacrifices are necessary by whatever standards of long-range self-interest the United States wishes to set. But too frequently Congress tends to act and react in relationship to these issues as though they were somehow peripheral rather than central to America's long-range national security and survival.

It is, in short, the seeming incapacity of Congress as presently organized to see our national security as a *total* effort which raises immediate and distressing questions. It gains the nation little to have the most impressive military system on earth if its economic and social life corrodes at home and its diplomatic and commercial activities flap aimlessly abroad. Unless the attack on poverty, discrimination, economic insecurity, and ignorance—at home and abroad—are seen as integral aspects of national security policy, this country will either not survive at all or will survive without meaning.

How can the Congress be brought to this realization? Drastic Constitutional change is neither possible nor desirable. Presidential leadership can do much; more could be done if the President would devote even more of his unusual talents to the selection and support of congressional candidates with a broad view of the world. All citizens could help by contributing more generously and more purposefully to congressional campaigns. Part of the unfair advantage of certain producer groups in the Congress is due to their financial power in determining the level of support and often the outcome of legislative campaigns.[32]

THE AGENDA OF CONGRESSIONAL INTROSPECTION

But a great deal can and should be done by Congress itself. Is it not time that Congress once again examined the equity of its representation, the wholeness of its perspective, and the efficiency of its deliberations? Rules and procedures suitable for the 1920's are not adequate for the 1960's.

If Congress should institute such a study it would undoubtedly find the sympathetic support of concerned citizens throughout the nation. Congress cannot ignore the constituent problems which it is designed to reflect—nor should it. But after the needs of individuals, institutions, and interests from several parts of America have been made vocal, the national legislature has an obligation to create public policies designed to upgrade the national life and to protect the national security viewed in the large and as a whole. This at present it is not well organized to do.

If a new self-study should be undertaken by Congress, it might well be addressed particularly to three important matters:

First, through what device or devices can the House of Representatives be brought into line with the spirit of Article I Section II, and Amendment 14 Section 3 of the Constitution? The former provision mandates representation in the lower House by population; the latter guarantees equal protection of the laws to all citizens. Congressional Districts, excluding statewide districts, now vary in population from under 200 thousand to over a million. If a person lives in a district with a million population, his vote has one-fifth the value of his neighbor's who lives in the smaller district. Fair and equitable districting will not work miracles, but it should at least increase the constitu-

---

[32] Alexander Heard, *The Costs of Democracy* (Chapel Hill, North Carolina: University of North Carolina Press, 1960). "Federal Campaign Financing Studied by Commission," *Congressional Quarterly Weekly Report*, February 23, 1962, pp. 299-301. For excerpts from report of President's Commission on Campaign Costs, see *The New York Times*, April 19, 1962, pp. 1, 20, 21. In 1961 Senator Maurine B. Neuberger (D., Ore.) introduced S. 1555 which provides for federal funds in primary and general campaigns of Congressional and Presidential candidates.

tionality of the House of Representatives and increase the weight of urban and suburban interests in congressional deliberations. On March 26, 1962, the Supreme Court of the United States in an historic decision broke a constitutional and political log jam by deciding in the case of *Baker v Carr*[33] that Federal District Courts had the right to determine whether city voters are unconstitutionally discriminated against in the apportionment of legislative seats.

Probably no Supreme Court decision since *Brown v Topeka* is more fraught with consequence for our political system. More equitable representation within state legislatures as between rural and urban interests may in turn be reflected in the future drawing of congressional district lines. Actually, there is no reason why the Supreme Court's judgment should not be applied at once to inequities among congressional districts themselves.

In any case, this is an item high on the agenda of congressional reform. It would be healthy and refreshing to see Congress itself take the leadership in bringing itself within the spirit of Article I and Amendment 14 of the Constitution.

The second major issue on the agenda of congressional introspection should be a re-examination of existing rules and procedures. Most of these have excellent reasons for being, and undoubtedly should be kept much as they are. But there may well be reason for modifying some rules and procedures in the interest of greater dispatch, and in the interest of majority desires within the Congress itself. This item suggests an agenda all its own.

First, the reasonableness of some of the unanimous consent rules which enable one Representative or Senator to throw a monkey wrench into congressional procedures.

Second, the reasonableness of the rules presently governing unlimited debate in the Senate. This is not to advocate easy devices for assuring immediate cloture on the Senate floor, but surely rules can be devised which would provide for thought-provoking delay, yet not hamstring the ultimate power of the majority to act.

Third, the reasonableness of the seniority system as it presently operates. Certainly, procedural devices can be explored which give due weight to experience but which do not accentuate the risks associated both with senility and political monopoly. It is anomalous that, at this critical point in our history, Otto Passman sits as an effective tollgate keeper on all foreign aid bills going through the United States Congress. Mr. Passman comes from the northeast corner of Louisiana—a part of the United States which is uncom-

---

[33] *Baker v Carr* (1962), 82 S. Ct. 691. For a summary of the Court's decision, see *The New York Times*, March 27, 1962, pp. 1, 18–21.

monly removed from the stream of responsible discourse about America's vital interests in a complex world. It is unfortunate and dangerous that accidents of longevity and geography, rather than demonstrated ability and breadth of view, should determine the quality and nature of congressional leadership.

Fourth, the reasonableness of the committee and subcommittee system itself. No one doubts that a division of labor is needed if Congress is to bring careful and expert lay opinion to bear upon complex issues of public policy. But has this not been carried too far in such areas as appropriations subcommittees? And do not the jurisdictions of the existing committees need redefinition? And may there not be need for strengthened party policy committees which can attempt to relate in a meaningful way the operations and deliberations of separate standing committees to general party and Presidential programs?

Fifth, the reasonableness of existing congressional staffing practices. Are qualifications for committee staffs sufficiently high—especially in such vital areas as scientific and military policy? Are committee staffs distributed equitably between the majority and the minority party? In what areas would it be in the public interest to have the minority party hold the larger number of staff assistants—the Committees on Government Operations, for example?

Sixth, the reasonableness of present congressional practices which impinge directly upon the internal procedures and operations of executive agencies. Some impingements are mandated by the Constitution—Senate approval of key Presidential appointments, for example. But a dangerous tendency has grown up in recent years. Committees and subcommittees and their respective chairmen have issued informal edicts or have prepared legislation the effect of which has been to cut substantially into the administrative discretion of executive managers. These informal edicts and legal interferences should be aired and tested by standards other than those of legislative whim.

Seventh, the reasonableness of hanging on to congressional prerogatives which effectively limit the capacity of the President to take sound actions involving long-range planning, and quick actions involving immediate executive discretion! Reference can be made here, of course, to such examples as the strictures set by the annual appropriations process which limit long-range planning and commitments in the international field, and the cumbersomeness of tax legislation as an anti-cyclical device. Surely it is possible to find ways of maintaining checks upon presidential discretion without denying the discretion itself.

The third main area of congressional introspection should deal with problems of campaign finance and with problems of conflict of interest. Under what duress do Congressmen and Senators feel themselves to be as a result of their dependence upon the generosity of particular individuals or interests in their communities? It is probable that the duress is less than popularly imagined; but this is in part because man is more of a rationalizing than a rational animal. "Good old Joe, who sent a thousand-dollar check for my last campaign, would never put the pressure on me for anything." But good old Joe has established access and a will on the part of the legislator to believe, which makes the hard sell unnecessary. Congress needs to look forthrightly at the problem of uneven advantage in a society based upon ethical pre-suppositions of human equality. It needs to examine even more rigorously the question of personal economic interests of individual legislators, and how the effect of these personal interests can be minimized in the formulation of public policy. To what extent, for example, should the personal economic interests of Congressmen and Senators be officially recorded and publicized?

This agenda is neither exhaustive nor revolutionary, but if seriously pursued it could lead to reforms in the operations of Congress which would permit that impressive institution to serve the citizens of the United States with far greater effectiveness and responsiveness than it does at present.

This generation has a strange mission. In Albert Camus' poetic language, men must forge for themselves "an art of living through times of catastrophe, in order to be reborn, and then to fight openly against the death-instinct which is at work in our time."[34] This is a mission far beyond the realm of politics and representative democracy alone; it is a mission for poets and philosophers, for the prophetic voice of religion and art, for a value-oriented science. But granted representative government by itself is not the good society; it is the condition within which the good society can grow. And in this century, the success of American representative institutions is of universal consequence. To brag about the success of our democracy to date is an irrelevant and dangerous exercise. Good as they have been, our representative institutions are not good enough. Emerson once wrote, "Great men, great nations, have not been boasters or buffoons, but perceivers of the terror of life, and have manned themselves to face it.[35]

Terror we know. If Americans are to man themselves to face it, priority must be given to the rebuilding and strengthening of the national legislature—America's basic institution of freedom. This strengthening must come from within and without. Too much is at stake not to take this task seriously.

Is it not time once again to have a massive reappraisal of congressional

---

[34] Quoted in an interview with Jean Bloch-Michel, "Camus: The Lie and the Quarter Truth," *The Observer* (London), November 17, 1957, p. 16.
[35] Ralph W. Emerson, *Emerson's Works*, Vol. II (London: G. Bell and Sons, 1924), p. 188.

organization and politics—similar to, but going beyond the LaFollette-Monroney Committee of 1945–46? The issue is not that Congress is the old frontier, but that Congress must free itself from those obsolescent myths and practices which keep it from performing effectively the great tasks which history now rests on its shoulders: to relate the particular to the general, to resolve conflict with the majority's interest especially in mind; to keep the bureaucracy and the executive accountable, and, by protecting minority rights, to keep all of us free.

Suggestions for Further Reading

Bailey, Stephen, *Congress Makes a Law: The Story Behind the Employment Act of 1946* (New York: Columbia University Press, 1950).

—— and Howard Samuel, *Congress At Work* (New York: Holt, Rinehart & Winston, Inc., 1952).

Burns, James MacGregor, *Congress on Trial* (New York: Harper & Row, Publishers, 1949).

Carroll, Holbert N., *The House of Representatives and Foreign Affairs* (Pittsburgh: University of Pittsburgh Press, 1958).

Dahl, Robert A., *Congress and Foreign Policy* (New York: Harcourt, Brace & World, Inc., 1950).

Farnsworth, David N., *The Senate Committee on Foreign Relations* (Urbana, Ill.: University of Illinois Press, 1961).

Galloway, George B., *History of the House of Representatives* (New York: Crowell, 1961).

Griffith, Ernest S., *Congress, Its Contemporary Role*, 3rd ed. (New York: New York University Press, 1961).

Wilson, Woodrow, *Congressional Government: A Study in American Politics*, 2nd ed. (Boston, 1885).

Young, Roland, *The American Congress* (New York: Harper & Row, Publishers, 1958).

PRESIDENT AND CONGRESS
IN THE 1960's

Clinton Rossiter

CONSTITUTIONAL SEPARATION OF POWERS: THE MYSTERY
OF AMERICAN GOVERNMENT

The study of government is always and everywhere the study of the dimensions, powers, procedures, and limitations of the instrumentalities that make
and administer public policy. In the United States it is most certainly the
study of all these things, but it is also—perhaps more certainly than it is in
any other country in the world—the study of the relationships among these
instrumentalities. No one can begin to understand the operations of our
extraordinary system of government until he has looked long and hard at
the points of contact, both formal and informal, among the four great organs
established in the Constitution: President, House of Representatives, Senate,
and Supreme Court. This is, perhaps, the most instructive aspect of the
government of the United States, and also the most fascinating.

One element in the fascination that envelops the relationships between
the President and Supreme Court, or House and Senate, or Senate and the

CLINTON ROSSITER *is the John L. Senior Professor of American Institutions at
Cornell University, where he has been a member of the faculty since 1946. He is both
a first-rate historian and a first-rate political scientist.* Seedtime of the Republic
*(1953) was awarded the Bancroft Prize by the American Historical Association and
the Woodrow Wilson Foundation Award by the American Political Science Association,
top recognition in both disciplines. He is also author of* Conservatism in America
(1955) and The American Presidency *(2nd ed. 1960).*

President is a quality that is always present where men are fascinated—whether by women on earth or by stars in the heavens—and that quality is mystery. If the texts and commentaries on comparative government may be believed, the largest single unsolved mystery in the whole realm of political science is the success we have had in governing ourselves according to the frugal, subtle, and exasperating directions of the Constitution of 1787. Although it may not appear a mystery to all of us who dwell in the midst of it, it most assuredly does to most of those who observe us from afar, and especially to those who can congratulate themselves (and they do, almost daily) on living under what they like to call *"responsible* government." They cannot understand, not when they are being entirely frank, first, why we should want to govern ourselves on the basis of the separation of powers and, second, how we are able to do it without making a total mess out of the complicated process of transmuting popular wish into public policy. It is, indeed, a source of never-ending surprise to even our best friends in Canada and England and India that the nation which prides itself on having the most advanced and flexible of economic systems should be governed under the most retarded and rigid of political systems. The sight of an eighteenth century constitution existing in a twentieth century world is enough to amuse them; the recognition that the constitution appears to work with tolerable efficiency leaves them shaking their heads in disbelief.

The purpose of this essay is to probe this mystery, and to probe it at that point of contact—the varied and delicate relations of the President and Congress—where it seems most significant, instructive, and fascinating. To any American who doubts that this relationship is all these things one can only ask, Where were you during the second session of the Eighty-seventh Congress? The hard campaign waged by John F. Kennedy and every last one of his battalions in behalf of tariff reduction, the appeal to executive privilege in the "splendid little war" between Strom Thurmond and Robert J. McNamara (over the censorship of speeches to be given by military men), the collision of personalities and constitutional principles in that other splendid little war between Carl Vinson and the President (over the future of the RS-70, if not of the Constitution)—these were several of the best acts ever staged in a play that has been running for 170 years and will run, let us hope, for at least as many more.

I do not propose to solve the mystery of *why* we govern ourselves as we do, because as a citizen of the United States I deny that this is a mystery at all. I do propose to explore (if not to solve) the mystery of *how* we do it, although this exploration may not take us very far toward the heart of the mystery. As a general rule I agree with Sir Winston Churchill that a little mystery in the prosaic business of government is a Very Good Thing. Always a first-rate political scientist, he was never more insightful than when he acknowledged, some thirty years ago, the "enormous and unquestionably helpful part that humbug plays in the social life of great peoples dwelling in a state of democratic freedom."[1] A constitution without any humbug would be a constitution for either angels or drones, and ours, if nothing else, is a constitution of, by, and for imperfect human beings.

THE POWERS AND FUNCTIONS OF OUR "IRRESPONSIBLE" EXECUTIVE

As a first and essential step toward a sharper understanding of the relationship between the President and Congress, let us take a quick reading of the current dimensions of these great organs of government. In particular, I would call attention to the condition of the Presidency and Congress in terms of five basic qualities of any instrument of constitutional government: power, prestige, independence, responsibility, and support.

The *powers* of the modern presidency (or would it be more exact to say *functions?*) are so numerous, far-ranging, and consequential that it is becoming increasingly difficult for the man who holds this office to bear his burden with anything like the efficiency we have been taught to expect from twentieth century administrators. He is nominated by the Constitution to fill four fairly distinct roles, and no one who watches him go through his daily paces can doubt that each brings a vast accretion of personal and constitutional authority.

He is, first of all, Chief Executive, and as such is held primarily and often exclusively accountable for the efficiency, frugality, loyalty, and ethics of the two and a third million Americans in the national administration. From the Constitution he draws, explicitly or implicitly, the twin powers of appointment and removal, as well as the primordial duty, which no law or plan or change in social circumstance can ever tear from his grasp, to "take care that the laws be faithfully executed." From Congress he has received such remarkable confirmations of his position as the Budget and Accounting Act of 1921, the succession of Reorganization Acts, and section 631 of Title 5 of the United States Code.[2]

[1] Winston Churchill, *My Early Life* (1930) (London, 1959), p. 64.
[2] A deceptively simple grant of authority that reads:

   The President is authorized to prescribe such regulations for the admission of persons into the civil service of the United States as may best promote the efficiency thereof, and ascertain the fitness

The Constitution designates the President specifically as "Commander-in-Chief of the Army and Navy of the United States." In peace and war he serves as the unchallenged, indeed unchallengeable director of the armed might of the nation. In time of peace he raises, trains, supervises, and deploys the forces that Congress is willing to maintain, and he has a great deal to say about the size and makeup of these forces. In time of war he makes all major decisions of strategy (and many of tactics as well), mobilizes the economy for maximum production of the weapons of victory, and draws on the example of Lincoln to institute measures that cut deeply into the liberties of the people.[3] And thanks principally to the nature of war, he has a good deal more to say than does Congress about the manner and timing of the transition from peace to hostility.

He is also, by common consent of Constitution, Congress, custom, and history, our Chief Diplomat; in the still fresh words of John Marshall he is "the sole organ of the nation in its external relations, and its sole representative with foreign nations."[4] He dominates the making of foreign policy; he monopolizes the direction of foreign affairs. If ever there was any question about his primacy in this area, there is no longer; for he is, as we have just noted, Commander-in-Chief, the man who controls and directs the armed might of the United States in a world in which might, real or threatened, is the essence of diplomacy.

The last of the President's constitutional roles finds him serving as a "third house of Congress." Not even the most hard-bitten Republican congressmen can deny that he is a kind of Chief Legislator, a man possessed of a large arsenal of weapons—the veto, the special message, the White House conference, the fireside chat, the bagful of appointments and defense contracts and favors—with which to influence, if never to dominate, the legislative process. While Congress has a wealth of strong and talented men, the complexity of the problems they are asked to solve by a people who assume that all problems are solvable has made external guidance a requisite of effective operation, and the President alone is in a constitutional, political, and practical position to provide such guidance.

---

of each candidate in respect to age, health, character, knowledge, and ability for the branch of service into which he seeks to enter; and for this purpose he may employ suitable persons to conduct such inquiries, and may prescribe their duties, and establish regulations for the conduct of persons who may receive appointment in the civil service.

[3] Ernest R. May, ed., *The Ultimate Decision* (New York: George Braziller, Inc., 1960); Clinton Rossiter, *Constitutional Dictatorship* (Princeton: Princeton University Press, 1948), chaps. 15, 16, 18.

[4] March 7, 1800, *Annals of Congress*, 6th Congr., 1st Sess., 613.

The pressures of history have added at least four subsidiary and yet highly influential tasks—and therefore powers of command and persuasion—to the strictly constitutional burden of the President: first, the leadership of his party, which makes it possible for him to achieve a reasonably cohesive administration and also to make the appeal of fraternal loyalty to roughly half the members of Congress; second, the shaping and expression of what Woodrow Wilson called "the real sentiment and purpose of the country,"[5] that is to say, the service Theodore Roosevelt performed when he used the White House as a "bully pulpit"; third, the many-sided function of acting as the grand protector of "the peace of the United States," under which he can muster troops, experts, food, money, loans, equipment, medical supplies, and moral support to rescue Americans stricken by natural or social disaster; and fourth, the management (within the limits imposed by the facts and ideology of American Capitalism) of the national economy, which calls upon him to take the lead in wielding what President Eisenhower described as the "formidable arsenal of weapons" now at "the disposal" of the national government for "maintaining economic stability."[6]

When one puts all these roles together, then particularizes this total responsibility in terms of the constitutional authority to command, negotiate, veto, appoint, remove, pardon, and supervise and also in terms of the statutory authority to make budgets, reduce tariffs, close banks, and cool off strikes, one is bound to conclude that never in history have free men put so much power in a single office. This is a remarkable display of confidence in the good intentions of one man, a display rendered all the more remarkable by the fact that the man enjoys a kind of *prestige* that is unique among elected heads of government. For he is, by implicit direction of the Constitution and common consent of the people (thanks to the memory of George Washington), the Chief of State in the American system. He is, as it were, a republican king, the figurehead as well as the working head of the government of the United States, "the personal embodiment" (in the words of President Taft) of the "dignity and majesty" of a mighty nation.[7]

If there is much that is trivial about many of the President's activities as Chief of State, there is nothing at all trivial about the role itself. Indeed, no modern President can fail to realize that all his powers are invigorated, even given a new dimension of authority, by the aura of legitimacy and mystery—

[5] Woodrow Wilson, *Constitutional Government in the United States* (New York, 1908), 68.
[6] In his message to Congress accompanying the Economic Report, January 28, 1954, *Congressional Record*, 83rd Congr., 2nd Sess., vol. 100, p. 965.
[7] William Howard Taft, *The Presidency* (New York, 1916), 51.

Sir Winston would be the first to call it "humbug," and do so approvingly—that envelops this office. No one who deals with the President of the United States—whether John McCormack or Barry Goldwater or Curtis LeMay, whether David McDonald or Roger Blough or Cardinal Spellman, whether Nikita Krushchev or Charles De Gaulle or even Drew Pearson—can ever forget that he deals with no ordinary head of government. The Framers of the Constitution, who may not have been quite sure what they were doing,[8] took a momentous step when they fused the dignity of a king and the authority of a prime minister in one elective office.

Remarkable in the way it mingles power and prestige, the Presidency is rendered even more remarkable as an instrument of democratic government by its *independence* of most of the day-to-day, week-to-week checks and pressures to which even the most exalted of prime ministers in parliamentary systems of government must be alert. If we may use the word in a technical sense, the President of the United States is virtually *irresponsible:* he is entirely exempt from votes, even motions of no confidence; he is asked no questions that he is bound to answer; he can look forward confidently, as no prime minister can, to a full term in office. Rarely does the Supreme Court find itself in a mood as well as a position to check or deflect a presidential action;[9] the process of impeachment is now, for all practical and political purposes, a "rusted blunderbuss, that will probably never be taken in the hand again."[10] Even the process of election holds few fears for the resolute and knowing President—the one thing he ought to know about that process is that in an electorate as large as the one he faces (and in which there is only one real alternative to voting for him) the desires of various groups to punish him for wrong behavior have a way of cancelling each other out. In any case he faces this electorate, as President, only once.

The President's unique freedom of action must be exercised, of course, within the institutional and moral boundaries of a democratic government and plural society. Although he may be technically irresponsible, he bears a large burden of responsibility for his actions. His actions have consequences which can be disastrous for his influence and reputation. While his powers are huge, they are of no real effect unless exercised through proper forms

[8] On this interesting point, see John P. Roche, "The Founding Fathers: A Reform Caucus in Action," *American Political Science Review,* LV (1961), 799.

[9] Glendon Schubert, *The Presidency in the Courts* (Minneapolis: University of Minnesota Press, 1957), 3–4; Clinton Rossiter, *The Supreme Court and the Commander in Chief* (Ithaca: Cornell University Press, 1951), 2–10, 126–131.

[10] Henry Jones Ford, *The Rise and Growth of American Politics* (New York, 1898), 288.

and within both constitutional and customary limits. The presidency is nothing if not a constitutional office.

This fact finds overwhelming confirmation in the history of the United States: 170-odd years, 34 Presidents—and still no gross abuse, and no likelihood of a gross abuse, of the confidence of the American people or of the terms of their Constitution. The reasons for the success of the presidency as a constitutional office—and the magnitude of this success can be judged by contrasting it with the failure of almost every constitution ever modeled on our own—are essentially three: first, the screening process of nomination and election that keeps men such as Thaddeus Stevens, Huey Long, and Joseph McCarthy far from the White House, and opens the way only to what Hamilton described as "characters preeminent for ability and virtue";[11] second, the dictates of both public and private morality, which, for a variety of sociological and historical reasons, operate more powerfully on the President than they do upon almost any other person of authority in the United States; third, the vast network of likewise independent centers of power— House, Senate, Supreme Court, parties, regulatory commissions, state governments, corporations, labor unions, foundations, mass media—that sets limits to his striving and keeps him almost always within what Harold Laski called "the range of common expectation,"[12] The President, indeed, is a "lion on a reservation," a man who can "roam widely and do great deeds" as long as he does not try to break out of the pluralistic system of restraints that is the mark of our open society.[13] The system is designed to keep him from going out of bounds, not to paralyze him in the splendid fields that have been set aside for his use. This, not quite incidentally, is why I made a distinction at the outset of these remarks between *function* and *power*. Function can take the form of power only when the President has the acquiescence of most of the other centers of power in our society, particularly of Congress— and the more acquiescent they are, the more genuinely powerful he is.

Finally, a word about what I have labeled *support:* by this, I mean simply the character of the constituency that has elected him and can be prevailed upon to back him in the pursuit of his aspirations. In one sense, of course, his constituency is the whole nation, and he is, as Andrew Jackson long ago

[11] In No. 68 of *The Federalist*, Mentor ed. (New York: New American Library, Inc.; 1961), 414.

[12] Harold Laski, *The American Presidency* (New York: Harper & Row, Publishers, 1940), 37.

[13] Clinton Rossiter, *The American Presidency*, 2nd ed. (New York: Harcourt, Brace & World, Inc., Harvest Books, 1960), 72–73.

insisted, peculiarly entitled to think of himself as the one "direct representative of the American people."[14] In another sense, however, his support is that part of the nation which elected him, and it has become increasingly plain in recent years that, thanks to the imperatives of the electoral system (in particular, the special importance of the large states), his constituency is one in which cities, minority groups, and consumers are given extra weight— whether in the calculations of delegates in the nominating conventions or the calculations of aides in the White House. It is, if we may put it this way, the more restless, problem-plagued, reform-minded classes and groups in his party—and therefore in America—from which the President draws his principal support.

THE FUNCTIONS AND POWERS OF OUR "RESPONSIBLE" LEGISLATURE

When we scrutinize the Congress of the United States in these same terms, we find first of all that it, too, is an instrument of immense *power* for good or ill. During Franklin D. Roosevelt's first term we heard a great deal about the notion of delegated powers. Indeed, it was more than a notion; it was a fact, as the Supreme Court was able to prove in *Schechter Bros. v U.S.* and *U.S. v Butler*.[15] Today, for better or worse, we talk rather differently about Article I Section 8 of the Constitution, because the new and apparently established fact is that the sweep of vast events abroad and the pressures of an industrial civilization at home have blown the restrictive concept of delegated powers into a balloon of immense proportions. Congress, it would seem, now has the constitutional authority (and the implicit blessing of the Supreme Court)[16] to pass laws dealing with just about any problem that appears to be "national" in scope—including problems of agriculture, health, education, morals, civil rights, and urban renewal—without much concern about the admonishing words of Amendment X. The opening words of Article I Section 8 + the war powers + the commerce clause × "necessary and proper" = the full sovereignty of a modern legislature—that, I think, is the equation of congressional authority, real or potential, in modern America.

The powers that Congress brings to the struggle with the President for its fair share of their joint responsibility for shaping the American future are

---

[14] J. D. Richardson, *Messages and Papers of the Presidents* (Washington, 1896), III, 90.
[15] 295 U.S. 495 (1935); 297 U.S. 1 (1936).
[16] See the cases reviewed in *The Constitution of the United States of America: Analysis and Interpretation*, Sen. Doc. 170, 82nd Cong., 2nd sess. (1953), 71–82.

the particular concern of this scrutiny, and one should certainly call attention in passing to the whole range of formal and informal techniques through
which it acts today as a kind of Grand Inquest of the Nation.[17] If the members of Congress, whether gathered together in committees or operating as
lone gladiators, can never quite get at the President himself to demand a
public explanation of this policy or to force a reconsideration of that decision, they can exercise a considerable amount of supervision and control
of even his most powerful lieutenants. If the President does not feel the hot
breath of congressional leaders, then his department heads certainly do.

The cutting edge of the power of Congress, whether the power to hand
the President fifty billion dollars or to make it hard for him to spend it
flexibly, is the pride with which almost all its members contemplate the
past, present, and future of the institution. The Congress of the United States
yields not one inch to the President in point of *prestige*. Although he may be
the Chief of State, the tribune of the people, and the high priest of national
ritual, Congress is the Mirror of the Nation; and in its own opinion it presents a more accurate image of the hopes and fears and needs of the American
people than does even the most alert and dedicated of Presidents.

Almost all Presidents, be it noted, have tended to agree at least halfway
with Congress, and not just because they have had favors to ask. It would be
impossible for any President to deal open-mindedly with Congress without
coming to realize, perhaps more sharply than the rest of us, how much depends upon the skill, courage, and good will of this now quite venerable
body. We may shake our heads over the lapses from dignity that have
marked every session of Congress from the first to the latest, or chuckle over
the slightly ridiculous figures that Herblock or Mauldin uses to represent
the House or Senate, yet one is bound to ask the question, and to ask it
altogether rhetorically (except, perhaps, for the House of Commons—I am
not sure that even this exception should be made): what legislature in the
world is a match for Congress in its claims upon the respect of the nation it
serves? Surely there is no upper house that is remotely comparable to the
Senate, and even the recollection of some few demagogues and mavericks
cannot spoil the sense of awe one must feel in the presence of the history,
authority, and dignity of this body.

Much of the authority and dignity of Congress derives, of course, from its
independence, which is every bit as unique and fateful as the independence of

---

[17] Ernest S. Griffith, *Congress: Its Contemporary Role*, 3rd ed. (New York: New York
University Press, 1961), chap. 5; Charles S. Hyneman, *Bureaucracy in a Democracy* (New
York: Harper & Row, Publishers, 1950), chap. 9.

the President. Let us refix attention on the power of Congress to check or persuade him, and in doing so let us take particular note that the essence of this power is quite simply the untrammeled right to say "no" to his requests for legislation, which includes the untrammeled right of the Senate to say "no" to his requests for confirmation of nominations and treaties. Two points are worth recalling in this connection. First, no important policy, domestic or foreign, can be pursued for long by even the most forceful President unless Congress comes to his support with laws and money. Second, the Constitution makes it impossible for him to force Congress to pass a law or spend money against its will. Ours is almost the only legislature in the world over whose decisions the executive has no final power of persuasion. The President has influence over the legislative process, and the influence can be great, but he has no power—not until Congress presents him, gladly or grudgingly, once in awhile maliciously, with a bill for approval or disapproval. If the members of Congress cannot force him to resign by a vote of no confidence, neither can he send them packing with a proclamation of dissolution. If his term is rigidly fixed, so, too, is theirs. Congress, indeed, is a uniquely independent legislature.

This is not to say that it is free of restraints. To the contrary, Congress is a legislature that bears large responsibility for its decisions and behavior. Apprehension of the next election presses hard upon the political consciousness of most members of Congress; the President's power of veto remains a weapon of immense efficiency; even the Supreme Court's power of judicial review is not quite so rusty from disuse as some observers would have us think. As to the restraints of what we like to call "public opinion," these operate far more immediately upon the minds of all but the most imperious members of Congress than they do upon the most timid of Presidents.

The most consequential restraint of all upon the will of Congress, however, operates internally rather than externally, although little attention is paid to it by those who fuss a good deal about the checks and balances in our system of government. This restraint is quite simply the existence of two equal chambers of the legislature, each of which maintains a committee to range at will through every large area of political concern, each of which has strong men who strike bargains with bureaucrats, each of which must give its assent to a bill before it can be presented to the President for his consideration. If there is no way for the President to force his will upon Congress, there is also no way for one house to force its will upon the other. The sovereign independence that marks the relationship of President and Congress is matched by the sovereign independence that marks the relationship of House and Senate. This is one country in which bicameralism, real as well as nominal, continues to flourish grandly.[18] Not only are the House and Senate very nearly equals in power and prestige; there is no machinery, constitutional or customary, for resolving deadlocks or animosities against the will of either.

Congress draws no less support from the American people than does the President. The important point to remember is that "the people" that elects, sustains, and restrains Congress is not exactly the same "people" with which the President is concerned. For one thing, his constituency is far more of a piece than is the constituency of the House or Senate, which is, after all, a collection of constituencies. For him the American people is more often than not just that: the American people, a society of individuals who share a common interest in the freedom and prosperity of the United States. For Congress, however, it is more often than not a swarm of groups that divide with one another over the spoils of freedom and prosperity. His constituency is, in effect, a nation of citizens, that of Congress a nation of interests.

The natural distinction between the sources of support for President and Congress has been sharpened in recent years by the way in which his constituency seems to be gerrymandered in behalf of the cities and their more restless groups, the constituency of Congress in behalf of the rural areas and their more conservative interests. Whether one good gerrymander deserves another is a question about which we can all dispute with a will, but there can be no disputing that the President is tugged by the imperatives of his nation-wide electorate toward the left, the House of Representatives is tugged by the imperatives of its diverse constituencies toward the right, and the Senate, for reasons too numerous and tangled to unravel here, sits just about on dead center of the American political spectrum.[19] Presidential proposals for legislation in such areas as health, education, and economic growth encounter a good deal less opposition in the Senate than they do in the House—and a good deal more opposition in both than the Administration can cope with comfortably.

EXECUTIVE-LEGISLATIVE RELATIONS: COOPERATION
IN CONTENTION

This has been a perhaps familiar recital of details about President and Congress, yet it has also been a necessary one. Only those who are thoroughly

---

[18] George B. Galloway, *The Legislative Process in Congress* (New York, 1953), 249–254.
[19] Andrew Hacker, "Voice of Ninety Million Americans," *The New York Times Magazine*, March 4, 1962.

familiar with these details can recognize that it is in fact something of a mystery with which we are dealing. Only those who understand the way in which power is set against power, prestige rubs against prestige, independence evokes independence, responsibility overlaps responsibility, and support fails to match support can savor the fascination of the central question: how can such a system work? How can two (three, really) equally proud, unmanageable, often intractable instruments of the popular will ever get together and stay together long enough to bring a major policy to life and move it forcefully on its way to fruition? How, in short, can cooperation ever emerge from this pattern of contention?

Two facts about executive-legislative relations in twentieth century America are worth noting at this juncture. The first is that, although cooperation in pursuit of national purposes is not guaranteed in the Constitution (indeed, is made difficult to achieve), cooperation on a broad and continuing basis is now essential to effective operation of the system. There have been famous periods (and at least one that was infamous) when the conduct of public affairs in the United States was marked by a condition of patent noncooperation—in which the President and Congress spent most of their energies attacking one another instead of the problems of the nation or went their respective ways pretending that the other branch hardly existed. The bitter, protracted, demoralizing struggle between Andrew Johnson and the Fortieth Congress is the most familiar instance of the first kind of noncooperation, the cool and distant relationship between Lincoln and the Thirty-Seventh Congress the most inexplicable example of the second—inexplicable, that is, to modern minds.

Neither savage conflict nor splendid isolation is now a tolerable pattern of executive-legislative relations. The problems of a convulsive world and a runaway technology fall much too thickly upon us. They demand solution, or at least confrontation, and the President who refuses to give a tactful lead to Congress, like the Congress that lets its investigators run riot in the gardens of State, Defense, and Treasury, is a luxury we can no longer afford. Whether Senator Goldwater likes it or not, we have now become a positive state,—a state with 2.3 million civil servants and a $90 billion budget. And this positive state demands an annual outpouring of legislation and a day-to-day practice of efficient administration that can be achieved only if its great political organs work closely and continuously with one another. If the President and Congress were ever again to war openly and massively, or simply to operate in a state of mutual indifference, the American system of divided government would come crashing to the ground.

The second fact is that, a spate of superficial evidence to the contrary, cooperation on this broad and continuing basis is now the normal pattern of operation in most areas of national concern. By and large the President and his lieutenants provide Congress with detailed and tactful guidance, Congress churns out the laws and pours out the dollars that keep the positive state from foundering, and the laws are executed and money spent by men who feel the touch of Congress but are not thrown off stride by it.

It is true, of course, that Congress, especially the House, has been more than usually recalcitrant in the last few years in responding to the pleas and pressures of the President in such areas of national concern as education, health, civil rights, and urban dislocation, but the refusal of Congress to act more decisively in these areas strikes me as a failure of national will rather than a stoppage in our political machinery. The imperatives of American pluralism, indeed the very dictates of our time-tested Constitution, require us to muster a "persistent and undoubted majority" before taking the sort of decisive steps that President Kennedy advocates in beckoning us toward the New Frontier. That kind of majority, I am bound to say, simply does not yet exist in most of those areas in which the ultraconservatives in Congress now seem to be calling the tune. When it does finally emerge, as it will sooner or later in all these areas, it will get its way—and get it largely through processes of cooperation.

This is one of those instances in which our view of reality is distorted by the way in which we gather our information. A fight between President and Congress is news; we read about it avidly. Cooperation between President and Congress, is not news; most of the time we do not get to read about it at all. I do not mean to criticize the political scientists of the United States too harshly—not least because I would have to include myself in the criticism—but I do think that the eyes of teachers and scholars, like the eyes of readers of the daily press, are fixed much too rigidly on the occasional spats between the President and the gentlemen of Congress and much too casually, if at all, on the usual pattern of cooperation.

All things considered, the essence of presidential-congressional relations in the past few years has been harmony rather than dissonance, cooperation rather than dissension, mutual respect rather than mutual mistrust. The American system may not work as smoothly as the British to produce a joint attack of executive and legislature on national problems, but if one probes beneath the surface, one discovers just about as much cooperation as can be expected in a constitutional system designed to prevent action not willed and supported by a thoughtful majority. Once we accept, as accept we must, the notions that this is still an open plural society, that Congress should not be denied the right to be a genuine legislature, and that the President ought not to be given all the laws and dollars he asks for from Congress (and would not know what to do with if he got them), then we will be in a position to recognize the remarkable extent to which this working partnership of equal and independent organs has been carried in recent years.

NEW FACTORS IN THE EQUATION OF COOPERATION

How, then, does this system work, in particular to generate cooperation and to dampen antagonism? To answer this question fully and convincingly is quite impossible. Here is one of those problems in understanding that defies the "science" of political science, that mocks the pretensions of those who claim to know the unknowable and want to measure the immeasurable. One cannot say exactly *how* the American system manages to beget the degree of cooperation it does and must: one can say only that it *does*, and then call attention to several forces and tendencies of vague and variable dimension that have helped to beget it.

The first is the consensus in principle and policy that is the distinguishing mark of American politics. We have had our political differences in America, and there have been times in the past seventy-five years—1896 and 1936 are probably the best-remembered—when it seemed to many sober observers that the class struggle had come at last to these shores. For the most part, however, we have been uniquely exempt from the tensions, hatreds, and unresolved feuds that have made it almost impossible for so civilized a people as the French to govern themselves constitutionally; and despite the accusation of "the radical Right" that at least half of us are traitors, we remain a remarkably united nation in a world full of disunited ones.

The result of all this is that the President and Congress, the political instruments of the nation, are in fundamental, largely unforced agreement on issues that in other countries, and at other times in this country, have divided men hopelessly. To put the matter concretely, not more than two or three eccentric congressmen now look upon the President as a violent political enemy, as a man who might be found sometime on the other side of the barricade in a war of classes or ideologies. It takes a united country to run a divided government, and much of the cooperation that keeps ours running today arises out of the American consensus in such matters as the dictates of ideology, the structure of government, the ownership and control of the economy, and the identity of the enemy. A consensus is by no means an unmixed blessing, for it tends to discourage fresh views and thus to stifle debate on important issues, yet no one can doubt the over-all benevolence

of its influence upon the course of executive-legislative relations in our constitutional system.

A second factor in the equation of cooperation is the political ties that
bind the President to roughly half the members of Congress, and that bind
all but the most secure and factious of them to him. Party government in
the United States, as we have been taught by Professor Schattschneider and
others,[20] is a pallid phenomenon compared with party government in
Britain, Canada, Belgium, and Germany. It nevertheless exists, and there
can be no doubt that it could be a major influence in creating an air of good
will and mutual trust between President and Congress. At the same time,
the fuzzy nature of party divisions and the tolerant sway of party loyalties
make it possible for both the leaders and followers of the opposition in Congress to cooperate with the President on many kinds of issues without sur-
rendering their claims to respectability. When all the pluses and minuses
are cancelled out, the influence of our unique pattern of party politics comes
down rather visibly on the side of cooperation as opposed to dissension.

Another factor is the simple truth that the key element in a good horse-
trade is always present in our system of divided power and shared responsibility: Congress has things the President wants; he has things they want;
each of the principals has goods to buy and sell. If he wants laws, dollars,
confirmations, and expressions of good will (and committees that leave his
chief lieutenants alone), they want loaves, fishes, and acts of friendship (and
lieutenants who acknowledge the right of committees to be informed and to
offer guidance). There is nothing, surely, more conducive to cooperation
than anticipation of the fruits of friendly compromise, and this sense of anticipation, in the White House as well as on Capitol Hill, has much to do with
the mysterious process of creating harmony out of dissonance.

The rules of the game, especially as it is played by the members of Congress, are certainly more favorable to cooperation than they were, say, fifty
years ago. Most of these rules are the product of custom, and custom now
decrees that the President need not confine himself to the points of input and
output on the legislative transmission belt. Rather, he is now expected by
most congressmen, at least, to make detailed recommendations to Congress,
to watch their progress closely on the floor and in committee, and to use
every honorable means within his power to bring about their enactment.
The rules that govern his dealings with the leaders of both parties in both
houses are especially conducive to cooperation. The relations of a Truman
with a Rayburn would have surprised our grandfathers, the relations of an

[20] See *Toward a More Responsible Two-Party System* (New York, 1950), a document produced by the Committee on Political Parties of the American Political Science Association.

Eisenhower with a Johnson would amaze them, the relations of a Kennedy with a Dirksen would stun them into disbelief. Yet the polite and even chummy give-and-take of intensely Democratic President Kennedy and professionally Republican Minority Leader Dirksen seems quite natural to us. Times have changed—and with them, the rules of the game.

Finally, one would want to point, and point with some pride, to the morality that appears to govern the strivings of even the most deeply committed men in American politics. There exists today both in the White House and in Congress a clear recognition that the struggle does have limits, that the game does have rules, and that the first rule reads: "Play to win but not to disgrace or demoralize or destroy." It would be hard to imagine a President who would take delight in a really compliant Congress, hard to imagine a majority of congressmen behaving like the Radical Republicans of 1867–1868. What we are seeing at work today is a general disposition to stay within the bounds of common sense and fair dealing, a disposition sharpened by a rather false but useful memory of the imperious quality of Franklin D. Roosevelt's leadership of Congress during the Hundred Days in 1933 and the first elating months of 1942, and by a rather more true and altogether useful memory of the extent of Senator McCarthy's challenge not merely to the decencies of the Constitution but to the responsibility of the President for the good order of his administration. While the bounds are, like all bounds, by no means unbreachable, they are clearly more visible today than they have been at any time in the past fifty years.

PRESIDENTIAL ASCENDANCY

Consensus, politics, horse-trading, rules, customs, morality—each of these is an important element in the modern pattern of executive-legislative cooperation, yet all of them together are no guarantee that the cooperation will be of the kind that impels men to grapple with problems rather than of the kind that encourages them to stand pat or perhaps to run and hide. Cooperation pure and simple is not enough; Cooperation that moves and shakes, that faces life and takes chances, is the kind we must have in the 1960's.

Such cooperation, I am convinced, is far more of a reality in the American system today than it was only a generation ago, largely because an element has now been added permanently to the pattern we have just been examining: the element of presidential ascendancy. The essence of the situation, the basic reason why the President and Congress work together far more often and readily than they fall out—and work together to get things done—is that he now has a visible edge over Congress in most of their dealings. In the Soviet Union, we have been told, all men are equal, except that some are more "equal" than others. In the American system of government, it can be argued, all branches are equal, except that one is more "equal" than the others. The President of the United States—any President, no matter how modest and moderate a man he may be—is in a position of clear and almost effortless superiority over Congress in the contest for the right to direct the course of the American future. If I may borrow the language and ideas of Stephen Potter[21] (a great student, not only of politics and social behavior, but of life itself), the President is now "one-up" on Congress at all times, and "two-up" if he is disposed to exploit the advantages of his position with tact and vigor.

He is one-up because, if we may think of the governing process in America as a great game, he as executive is usually on the offensive, and Congress as legislature usually on the defensive. His natural posture is that of the active leader, the posture of Congress that of the grudging follower. His great power is essentially positive, the great power of Congress essentially negative. He is a hammer, and hammers are made for striking; Congress is an anvil, and anvils must bear. This has always been true in our constitutional system, and it is doubly true today because of the internal and external pressures under which the system now operates. Action, which is his forte, is at a premium; delay, which is the style of Congress, is at a discount. All over the world, even in the home of parliamentary government, it is a good season for executives and a poor one for legislatures.

The tactical one-upness of the President is most readily apparent in the broad field of "national security," in which he plays the twin roles of Chief Diplomat and Commander-in-Chief. The ingredients of successful diplomacy in time of peace—unity, continuity, dispatch, secrecy, and access to information—have always been properties of his office; none of them has ever been a property of Congress. The ingredient that must be added to the formula in time of cold war—the capacity to threaten or actually use military force— is one that not even the most Coolidge-minded of Republicans would deny the President. And not even the most Stevens-minded Republicans (if there are any still alive) would today presume to give orders to fighting generals. The pace of military technology has laid to eternal rest the pretensions of the famous Joint Committee on the Conduct of the Civil War,[22] just as the

[21] Stephen Potter, *Gamesmanship* (New York, 1948), *Lifemanship* (New York: Holt, Rinehart & Winston, Inc., 1951), and *One-upmanship* (New York: Holt, Rinehart & Winston, Inc., 1952).

[22] W. W. Pierson, "The Committee on the Conduct of the Civil War," *American Historical Review*, XXIII (1918), 550; T. H. Williams, "The Committee on the Conduct of the War," *Journal of the American Military Institute*, III (1939), 139.

pace of events in Asia and Africa has destroyed any lingering hopes of the supporters of the Bricker Amendment.

So long as America plies a diplomacy of involvement, as it must into the indefinite future, Congress can hope to play no more than a delaying, harassing, critical role in this vast area of national security: while it will be, as always, a powerful role, it will also be an essentially negative one. For example, it can make life miserable for a President who even thinks about recognizing Red China, and could make it unendurable for one who decided to go ahead in spite of everything and extend recognition, but it cannot recognize Red China itself, nor could it undo the consequences of a presidential act of recognition. For another example, it can authorize the President to enlarge the Air Force (as it authorized Mr. Truman) or add to the strength of the Marine Corps (as it authorized General Eisenhower) or get on with the development of a supersonic bomber (as it authorized Mr. Kennedy), but it cannot force him (and is reluctant even to "direct" him) to spend the money appropriated for such a purpose.[23] Whatever else we learned in March 1962, we cannot doubt that, while the President must be excessively polite to congressional leaders, he takes no orders from them in the performance of his duties as Commander-in-Chief.[24] The President, it may be added, could have drawn on the authority of Congress itself in a real showdown, for sections 665 (c-2) and 665 (g) of Title 31 of the *United States Code* authorize him, in effect, to "establish reserves in any appropriation"—an astounding yet altogether logical recognition of his permanent one-upness.

PRESIDENTIAL "LIBERALISM" AND CONGRESSIONAL "CONSERVATISM"

One-up on the level of tactics, the President goes two-up on the level of strategy if he is in fact a *modern* President. He is now more likely than Congress to be in touch with what seem to be the great trends of American history, and thus more likely to deal from a position of moral strength.

The United States of America is launched, for better or worse, on four massive courses that have already run an astounding distance in the past thirty years and bid well to run even farther in the next thirty: from diversity toward unity in our national habits and sentiments, from easy acceptance of

---

[23] See the excerpts from the report of the House Armed Services Committee printed in *The New York Times*, March 9, 1962, p. 14.

[24] See the dispatches signalling the termination of "The Battle of the RS-70" in *The New York Times*, March 22, 23, 1962.

discrimination toward at least a rough equality of opportunity for men of all races in our social structure, from a free-swinging capitalism toward a pattern of regulation and welfare in the economy, and from disdainful isolation toward almost frenetic involvement in diplomacy. I do not mean to exaggerate the impact of these four closely related developments upon the American way of life as it was willed to us by Calvin Coolidge and Warren G. Harding, yet the changes of the recent past have been, for a nation as fundamentally conservative as the United States, something almost deserving of the label of "revolution."

The significance of these changes for the American system of government centers upon the indisputable fact that our last four Presidents have been, with no exceptions, purposeful leaders or at least permissive patrons of this long revolution, our last fifteen Congresses, with few exceptions, recalcitrant roadblocks, or at best grudging followers. It is our Presidents, by and large, who have emphasized the power and glory of the nation at the expense of the states, who have hacked away as best they could at the roots of racial and religious discrimination, who have called for new weapons to deal with the problems of an advanced industrial society, and who have taken us adventuring beyond our shores. Even the most conservative of the last four Presidents (and, not at all incidentally, the only one who was a Republican) proved himself more national-minded, more impatient with prejudice, more conscious of the problem of economic growth, and more dedicated to the United Nations and NATO than were the Congresses with which he dealt— certainly more so than the members of his own party in these Congresses.

The causes of this interesting and not yet fully understood situation of what we should not be afraid to call *presidential "liberalism"* and *congressional "conservatism"* are too numerous and complicated for me to probe here, yet I must at least mention certain arrangements, attitudes, or developments in the American system which invite the attention of researchers in political science.[25]

1. The whole complicated process of election, which far too often places men with narrow views and special interests in the seats of power in Congress, yet acts remorselessly to reserve the Presidency for men with broad views and general interests, and thus with a deeper insight into the needs of the national community.

2. The relative immunity of the President from the self-interested pres-

[25] For a pioneering attempt to lay out the dimensions of this cleavage, see Willmoore Kendall, "The Two Majorities," *Midwest Journal of Political Science*, IV (1960), 317.

sures—most of which are, in the nature of our system, "conservative" in character—that beat daily upon all but the most secure members of Congress.

3. The double gerrymander in our electoral system, which asks the President to serve a constituency in which the residents of great cities have the highest visibility, and Congress (especially the House of Representatives) to serve a constituency in which the residents of small towns and rural areas are distinctly over-represented.

4. The sharp contrast between the traditions of the Presidency, which call for strength and action, and the rules and customs of Congress, which place a high premium on caution and compromise.

5. The relative weakness of party government in Congress, which forces the President willy-nilly to assume the responsibility for hard problems that ought in the first instance to be solved by imaginative legislation.

6. The development of a political instinct in the American people, many of whom now seem to expect the President to look out for one set of their interests (the big ones) and their congressman to look out for the other set (the small ones)—and at least some of whom split their tickets accordingly.

7. Finally, the distinction that Andrew Jackson injected forcefully into the American pattern of politics: between the President as the representative of the people-as-community and Congress as the representative of the people-as-interests.

Only a foolhardy political scientist would try to give each of these factors its exact value in this double equation of presidential liberalism and congressional conservatism, yet they all add up to a fact of huge consequence for the historical relationship between the President and the men of Congress, indeed for the course of events: that *he* is clearly more likely than *they* to be ready and willing to take the next and, as it often seems, inevitable steps along the American road. To put the matter as simply and yet dramatically as possible, he is in closer touch with history than they, and that is the one compelling reason for the strategical one-upness that he now enjoys in the American constitutional system. In domestic affairs, he tends to take the broad and progressive point of view; in world affairs, the adventurous and cooperative. In the former, Congress tends to be more parochial and desultory; in the latter, more cautious and nationalistic.

In closer touch with history—that is to say, with the realities of the American future—he seems also to be in closer touch with the objective "right"—that is to say, with the ideals of the American tradition. The truth of this generalization is perhaps most clearly demonstrated in the field of civil liberties, in which each of the last four Presidents has behaved with considerable restraint and has taken at least a few stands in defense of unpopular persons and ideas. By contrast some congressmen have been spoilers of democracy and many more have sat by and, faithful to the rules of the club, have let them get away with it. I do not mean to say that the President's personal virtues are generally superior to the collective virtues of Congress, but I do say that the President of the United States can be counted on to behave tactfully and tolerantly most of the time. On the other hand, the rules and customs of Congress sometimes permit unpleasant and unbridled characters to take undue advantage of their privileged position in legislative debates; and the highly developed pluralism of the committee system sometimes allows a chairman or even a single member to assume unwarranted authority in congressional hearings or investigations. These remarks quite plainly have the character of a value judgment, yet it is the kind of judgment that one can make with the feeling that he is standing squarely on the best American traditions of tolerance and fair play.

THE ROAD AHEAD

These, then, are the outlines of the modern pattern of executive-legislative relationships in the United States; to be more precise, this is the context of law, custom, and historical imperative within which the executive branch works with the legislative to make policies that meet the needs of a high and powerful civilization. If we put the roughly harmonizing forces of consensus, politics, horse-trading, rules, customs, and morality together with the tactical and strategical ascendancy of the President, then thrust this whole complicated pattern of decision-making into the crucible of a world full of tensions and a nation full of rather healthy self-doubts, we may begin to understand why we are getting just about as much harmony between the two great and independent political organs of our federal government as we could expect or perhaps even want in the 1960's. We are getting it because the President's power is now perceptibly greater than the power of Congress, because his prestige is now more solidly based, because his independence is now more real, because his responsibility is now less pressing, and because his support is now of a character to propel him forcefully down the road to the future. Whether the road leads to freedom or serfdom is well worth arguing, but that the President is some years ahead of Congress on the journey along this road can no longer be doubted. It is a fact of huge consequence for the status of the presidency that most of what the Eighty-Seventh Congress refused to give Mr. Kennedy will undoubtedly be given with interest to a successor by, say, the Ninety-Second Congress.

No one can look for long at the antics of this Congress and grimaces of this President without recognizing the persistence of areas of genuine disagreement between them about the policies to be pursued (if not the fundamentals to be honored) in the next decade. Yet a certain amount of dissension, obstinacy, and just plain angry disagreement is, after all, both a sign and a condition of the operations of constitutional democracy. It is a rare political scientist who interprets the dissensions in the British Parliament today—and indeed in the ranks of each of the major parties active in it—over such fateful issues as the pattern of defense or membership in the Common Market as evidence of a bad or badly performing system of government, and perhaps something of the same kind of tolerance should be shown in interpreting the dissensions in our system. We, too, are arguing about some fateful steps, and to ask our system of government to take them smoothly and agreeably would be to ask something of it that no system, certainly no free system, can produce. What one can ask is that, as our disagreements should not be smothered, so they should not be needlessly exacerbated by the cranky operations of an eighteenth century Constitution. As a matter of fact, they are not needlessly exacerbated; ours is more of a twentieth century Constitution than some people seem to realize; and the ongoing dissensions of President and Congress are products of political nature rather than of constitutional art.

All in all, there is a remarkable degree of purposeful cooperation now built into the American system of government. It would surprise the Framers and yet also, upon reflection, make sense to them; and they, wiser men than we, would see that it was perhaps not so much of a mystery after all. They would tell us, I am sure, what the logic of our politics has already told us: that if America fails to do what it has to do at home and abroad in the next generation, it will not be a failure of the American Constitution but of the American character. That Constitution will prove itself equal to any reasonable demand we decide to put upon it.

Suggestions for Further Reading

Binkley, Wilfred E., *President and Congress*, 3rd ed. (New York: Vintage Books, Inc., 1962).

Corwin, Edward S., *The President*, 4th ed. (New York: New York University Press, 1957).

Galloway, George B., *The Legislative Process in Congress* (New York: The Crowell-Collier Publishing Co., 1953).

Griffith, Ernest S., *Congress: Its Contemporary Role*, 3rd ed. (New York: New York University Press, 1961).

Gross, Bertram, *The Legislative Struggle* (New York: McGraw-Hill Book Co., Inc., 1953).

Hyneman, Charles S., *Bureaucracy in a Democracy* (New York: Harper & Row, Publishers, 1950).

Neustadt, Richard E., *Presidential Power* (New York: John Wiley & Sons, Inc., 1960).

Rossiter, Clinton, *The American Presidency*, 2nd ed. (New York: Harcourt, Brace & World, Inc., 1960).

Young, Roland, *The American Congress* (New York: Harper & Row, Publishers, 1958).

CONSTITUTIONAL LIMITATIONS
IN A WORLD OF
CONTINUING CRISIS

Alpheus Thomas Mason

JUDICIAL REVIEW: THE SOBER SECOND THOUGHT
OF THE COMMUNITY

In an observation much quoted, the French aristocrat de Tocqueville noted that "Scarcely any political question arises in the United States which is not resolved sooner or later into a judicial question."[1] Newspaper headlines still illustrate the Frenchman's perceptive identification of what is surely the most peculiar aspect of the American concept of a free society. Almost every Tuesday following the traditional Monday opinion day, *The New York Times* allots generous space to judicial review in action. Whenever government enters any new domain, the natural question is whether the steps taken are constitutionally valid. Hence the inference, especially among lawyers, that

ALPHEUS THOMAS MASON *is Cyrus McCormick Professor of Jurisprudence at Princeton University. A member of the Princeton faculty since 1925, he has written definitive biographies of Justice Brandeis and Chief Justice Stone. The latter,* Harlan Fiske Stone: Pillar of the Law *(1956), won a Liberty and Justice Book Award from the American Library Association. He is author of many books in American political theory and constitutional law, including* Security Through Freedom *(1955),* Free Government in the Making *(1956),* The Supreme Court from Taft to Warren *(1958), and* The Supreme Court: Palladium of Freedom *(1962).*

[1] *Democracy in America*, trans. Francis Bowen (Boston: John Allyn, 1882), I, 357.

the parts of the Constitution deserving most serious consideration are those that limit rather than grant power.

Cases featuring power-hampering provisions are newsworthy. In 1961 five of the nine Justices overruled a state court decision which had accepted as evidence illegally seized material.[2] The full texts of the majority and minority opinions were printed; editorial comment and feature articles covered the case. An act of Congress may be set aside; in 1958, the Court held 5 to 4 that an American does not forfeit his citizenship merely by voting in a foreign election.[3] A state act may fail to pass judicial muster, as in the well-known case of *Pennsylvania v Nelson* (1956),[4] when six of the nine Justices believed that in passing the Smith Act of 1940, outlawing sedition, Congress completely occupied this field, thus invalidating parallel state legislation. Even the President may be caught in the toils of our power-limiting Constitution. In 1952 President Truman seized and operated the steel mills, until stopped by judicial ukase.[5] Each of these cases was front-page news.

Americans have become so accustomed to judicial review—that is, to according nine Supreme Court Justices the final word on controversial legal and political issues—as to take it for granted. The Court is not, however, America's sole power-inhibiting agency. Judicial review is a single cog in the intricate machinery of free government, only one among several constitutional devices obliging government to control itself. The delimiting function of courts is less peculiar than generally supposed. Besides an independent judiciary, enjoying life tenure, the Framers fashioned various contrivances to shackle power. A bicameral Congress with a second chamber of long tenure and indirect election was provided to cool the unruly passions of a more populous House of Representatives; a President, armed with a powerful veto and chosen through a cumbersome mechanism called the Electoral College, guaranteed an election at least one step, and possibly three, removed from popular action. All these devices were calculated to check majority rule. Others have been developed by custom and usage.[6]

From an examination of the record nothing emerges more clearly than the unwavering determination to enthrone, by various institutional arrangements, "the sober second thought of the community." Thus to query the

---

[2] *Mapp v Ohio*, 367 U.S. 643 (1961).
[3] *Perez v Brownell*, 356 U.S. 44 (1958).
[4] 350 U.S. 497 (1956).
[5] *Youngstown Sheet & Tube Co. v Sawyer*, 343 U.S. 579 (1952).
[6] See Herbert W. Horwill, *The Usages of the American Constitution* (London: Oxford University Press, 1925).

Framers' intention to authorize judicial review (and this is still being done[7]) is to cast a shadow over a complex of restrictive principles and procedures of which judicial review is merely the most conspicuous example, and the one least frequently invoked.

The intricate design of our fundamental law is in response to the political puzzle James Madison formulated in the *Federalist*, No. 51:

In framing a government which is to be administered by men over men, the great difficulty lies in this: You must first enable the government to control the governed; and in the next place, oblige it to control itself.[8]

Accordingly, the Constitution both grants and limits authority. Article I lists the powers of Congress; Article II invests executive power in the President; Article III confers the judicial power of the United States on the Supreme Court and on such other courts as Congress may establish. Article I Section 9 sets limits on the national government; Article I Section 10 restricts the states. But the Constitution itself provides no definition of either powers or limitations.

THE CONSTITUTION: INSTRUMENT OF RIGHTS AND LIMITATIONS

In ways both obvious and subtle, the Constitution appears to be an instrument of rights, of limitations, rather than of powers. Congress may not pass an *ex post facto* law or a bill of attainder; it may not tax exports from any state; and it may not—except in great emergencies—suspend the writ of habeas corpus. Amendments I through VIII, the Bill of Rights, contain a longer list of things the national government is powerless to do. The state governments may not enact *ex post facto* laws, coin money, emit bills of credit, or enter into any treaty or alliance with a foreign state.

The Framers of the Constitution sought in other ways to circumscribe government; the principles of separation of powers and of federalism, the due process clauses of the Constitution, and the doctrine of judicial review all manifest their intention to oblige government to control itself. None of these limiting principles is spelled out; they are either implicit in the organization

---

[7] W. M. Crosskey, *Politics and the Constitution in United States History* (Chicago: University of Chicago Press, 1953), II, 1007; Learned Hand, *The Bill of Rights* (Cambridge: Harvard University Press, 1958), p. 7.

[8] *The Federalist*, ed. Max Beloff (Oxford: Basil Blackwell, Ltd., 1948), No. 51, p. 265.

and structure of the Constitution, or, as with judicial review, deducible from its general provisions.

Madison labels this complex system of controls "compound republic":

> . . . *the power surrendered by the people is first divided between two distinct govern-ments [the national government and the states], and then the portion allotted to each subdivided among distinct and separate departments. Hence a double security arises to the rights of the people. The different governments will control each other, at the same time that each will be controlled by itself.*[9]

The Father of the Constitution did not indicate precisely how such controls were to be enforced.

Not only is each government, national and state, bound to restrain itself lest the operations of one encroach upon the domain of the other, but each government must heed the injunction that "no person" may be deprived of life, liberty, or property "without due process of law." The Fifth Amendment limits the national government in this respect; the Fourteenth Amendment controls the states. Under the vague "due process" rubric, the courts consti-tute the ultimate safeguard of individual privilege and governmental prerogative alike. As to all these relations (that of the various organs of the national government to each other, of the states and national govern-ment, and of both these authorities to individual rights) the judiciary func-tions as "the balance wheel of our entire system."[10]

Certain observers find power failures brought on by the application of these limitations hard to understand, especially as they result from the edict of nine men, sometimes only five or six, appointed for life and politically nonresponsible. Without any enforcing authority even remotely comparable to the sword of the Executive or the purse of Congress, the Court can, as in the *Steel Seizure* decision of 1952, bring to heel the President, the labor union, the industrial corporation, and Congress.[11] Here we see the American principle of constitutional limitations in action: restraining Congress, restraining the states, restraining the Executive, restraining majorities—all to prevent wrongdoings of government. At times these judicially imposed restrictions have been carried to extreme lengths, seriously impairing, sometimes defeating, necessary governmental action. The test of consti-

---

[9] *Ibid.*, p. 266.

[10] Woodrow Wilson, *Constitutional Government in the United States* (New York: Columbia University Press, 1917), p. 142.

[11] *The Economist*, May 10, 1952, p. 371.

tutionality threatens to become synonymous with sound policy.[12] "Our constant preoccupation with the constitutionality of legislation rather than its wisdom," Professor Felix Frankfurter noted in 1925, "tends to pre-occupation of the American mind with a false value.[13] Sober critics have sometimes wondered, especially in times of crisis, whether a government so circumscribed, and seemingly misdirected, can survive in an age which calls for power and more power—power to deal with domestic problems of ever-increasing complexity, power to cope with the most baffling international issues, including the threat of Communism. In the present posture of world affairs, prompt political action unparalleled in scope is crucial; government cannot perform the task for which the state exists in the face of obstructive judicial vetoes such as those which hamstrung the Roosevelt Administration during the critical years, 1935–1936.

In spite of a grave economic emergency, Chief Justice Hughes's Court carried judicial usurpation so far that three dissenting Justices protested with unprecedented vigor, and with good reason. In the two terms, 1934 through 1936, a total of twelve congressional statutes fell under the judicial axe. In one case Justice Stone, dissenting, declared that his colleagues had "tortured" the Constitution, transformed judicial *review* into judicial *supremacy*. He charged that the Justices had come to think of courts as the only agencies of government having capacity to govern.[14] Stone echoed the primacy which Chief Justice Marshall had conceded to political restraints.[15] Reiterating the self-abnegating sentiments Chief Justice Waite uttered in 1876,[16] Stone said that "For the removal of unwise laws from the statute books appeal lies not to the courts but to the ballot and to the processes of democratic government."[17] These stern admonitions of 1936 recall James Madison's words in the *Federalist*, No. 51: "A dependence on the people is . . . the primary control on government."[18] In Stone's opinion, as in Madison's, judicial review was merely an auxiliary check.

Justice Sutherland, on the other hand, fearing that the principle of constitutional limitations would be toppled unless the Court persisted in its pre-eminence, challenged: "If the provisions of the Constitution be not up-

---

[12] Justice Frankfurter concurring in *Dennis v United States*, 341 U.S. 494 (1951), 556.
[13] Felix Frankfurter, *Law and Politics* (New York: Harcourt, Brace & World, Inc., 1939), p. 197.
[14] Dissenting in *United States v Butler*, 297 U.S. 1 (1936), 87.
[15] *Gibbons v Ogden*, 9 Wheaton 1 (1824), 197.
[16] *Munn v Illinois*, 94 U.S. 113 (1877), 134.
[17] Dissenting in *United States v Butler*, 297 U.S. 1 (1936), 79.
[18] *Federalist*, No. 51, op. cit., p. 265.

held when they pinch as well as when they comfort, they may as well be abandoned."[19] Justice McReynolds warned that "The adoption of any 'concept of jurisprudence' which permits facile disregard of the Constitution as long interpreted and respected will inevitably lead to its destruction. Then, all rights will be subject to the caprice of the hour; government by stable laws will pass."[20] Justice Roberts predicted that failure to protect a certain domain reserved to the states would make Congress "a parliament of the whole people, subject to no restrictions save such as are self-imposed."[21] On occasion Chief Justice Hughes inferred that the Constitution was a never-changing document, except by recourse to the formal amending process: "If the people desire to give Congress the power to regulate industries within the State, they are at liberty to declare their will in the appropriate manner, but it is not for the Court to amend the Constitution by judicial decision."[22]

By 1936 obscurantist enforcement of constitutional limitations commanded the predictable votes of five, sometimes six, Supreme Court Justices, the effect being to tie "Uncle Sam up in a hard knot."[23] It was precisely this dilemma, this urgent need for the power to govern amid unprecedented economic stress, that prompted President Roosevelt's proposal to increase the Court's membership, and thus break the judicial stranglehold. The significant fact about this abortive presidential foray is that, though the Justices emerged somewhat bloody and bowed, their power remained undiminished. They did not abdicate. Having merely retreated under heavy assault, the Court was still in a position to reassert its "usurpations" any time it saw fit. At long last, the two major power-controls, one political, the other judicial, had been re-ordered. Political restraints had become what Madison in the *Federalist*, No. 51, said they were intended to be—the primary check on government, the judiciary being merely an added safeguard.

For certain Justices any erosion of America's traditional power-killers—separation of powers, federalism, due process of law, judicial review—marked the end of free government. These were not the idle sentiments of alarmists. "The Constitution is gone,"[24] Justice McReynolds exploded in his unaccustomed role of dissenter. The Constitution of McReynolds, Sutherland *et al.* really was gone—their Constitution of about 1895, their Constitution

---

[19] Dissenting in *Home Building & Loan Association v Blaisdell*, 290 U.S. 398 (1934), 483.
[20] Dissenting in *Nebbia v New York*, 291 U.S. 502 (1934), 558–9.
[21] *United States v Butler*, 297 U.S. 1 (1936), 78.
[22] Concurring in *Carter v Carter Coal*, 298 U.S. 238 (1936), 318.
[23] Harlan Fiske Stone to his sister, June 2, 1936. Stone Papers, Library of Congress.
[24] Oral addendum to his dissent in the *Gold Clause Cases*, 294 U.S. 240–381, in *The New York Times*, February 19, 1935, p. 14.

considered, as Justice Sutherland said in a bitter dissent of 1937,[25] as of unchanging meaning—their Constitution regarded essentially as curbing power rather than granting it, their Constitution interpreted as synonymous with Herbert Spencer's *Social Statics.* McReynolds' and Sutherland's Constitution of *rights* had, in the face of unprecedented needs, given way to a Constitution of *powers.*

Teachers of constitutional law were troubled and somewhat confused. In 1940 Thomas Reed Powell wondered about the future of his subject and perhaps of his job:

. . . if the ancient landmarks are no longer stable, what shall be your guide? If what was once high solid ground has now become a lowland marsh, you can no longer trust the ancient maps. . . . The modern judges with their shovels and their dredges may be levelling hills and dredging channels. They have the power and they are exercising it. Sometimes they tell you frankly what they are doing. Sometimes they do not. . . . To the perils of patent change they add the perils of concealed and unacknowledged change.[26]

Pondering the future, Professor Corwin was more relaxed. The Court now seemed "bent upon minimizing its own role in favor of the political forces of the country. . . ."[27] Robert J. Harris also noted how "The transformation of judicial review" had "restored to legislative bodies the freedom to discuss proposals in terms of public policy rather than constitutional law."[28]

Not even those deeply regretting the sudden shifts of judicial doctrine and action were disposed to stem the swiftly-flowing tide of laissez faire for legislatures. American Bar Association President Frank J. Hogan and retired Justice Owen J. Roberts agreed that the new order, long advocated by dissenting Justices Holmes, Brandeis, and Stone, had to be accepted. "Legislative independence and legislative wisdom," Mr. Hogan wrote in 1939, "are now America's sole reliance for the continuance of that security of the blessings of liberty for which the Constitution was framed and the government of the United States created."[29] Justice Roberts noted how the Supreme Court had

---

[25] *West Coast Hotel Co. v Parrish,* 300 U.S. 379 (1937), 400–14.

[26] "Some Aspects of American Constitutional Law," 53 *Harvard Law Review* 529 (1940), 532.

[27] *Constitutional Revolution, Ltd.* (Claremont: Associated Colleges of Claremont, 1941), p. 113.

[28] "The Decline of Judicial Review," 10 *Journal of Politics* 1 (1948), 16.

[29] "Shifts in Constitutional Doctrine," 64 *Reports of the American Bar Association* (1939), 498–500.

limited and surrendered the role the Constitution intended to confer on it. Vox populi, vox Dei *was not the theory on which the charter was drawn. The sharp divisions of powers intended has become blurred; . . . doctrines announced as corollaries to express grants of power to the Congress have more and more circumscribed the pristine powers of the States, which were intended to be preserved to them by the Constitution. . . .*[30]

Yet the Justice recognized that continued judicial resistance "might have resulted in even more radical changes."

Mr. Hogan and Justice Roberts had misread history. For James Madison, John Marshall, and a host of Supreme Court Justices, including the most eminent, political restraints had always been our primary reliance against governmental wrongdoing. James Bradley Thayer had enunciated the classic doctrine of judicial self-restraint:

The checking and cutting down of legislative power, by numerous detailed prohibitions in the constitution, cannot be accomplished without making the government petty and incompetent. . . . Under no system can the power of courts go far to save a people from ruin; our chief protection lies elsewhere.[31]

In 1937 the judiciary surrendered its self-acquired pre-eminence. Though it had not abdicated, judicial veto of congressional acts was destined once again to become an inconspicuous phase of the Court's work. Between 1790 and 1857 only two congressional statutes were set aside. Between 1857 and 1937, the Court disallowed 69 acts of Congress, many of major importance. Since 1937 only six acts, all of relatively minor significance, have failed to win judicial endorsement.[32] Does this sharp drop in the number of judicial negatives mean that in a world of continuing crisis the most distinctive feature of American politics—constitutional limitations—has fallen into innocuous desuetude? May one infer that a political system in which power is checked, divided, and balanced cannot survive in a world constantly faced with the dread of paralyzing economic crisis, of devastating thermonuclear

---

[30] *The Court and the Constitution* (Cambridge: Harvard University Press, 1951), pp. 95, 62.

[31] James Bradley Thayer, "The American Doctrine of Constitutional Law," 7 *Harvard Law Review* 129 (1893), p. 156.

[32] The cases are: *Tot v United States,* 319 U.S. 463 (1943); *United States v Lovett,* 328 U.S. 303 (1946); *United States v Cardiff,* 344 U.S. 174 (1952); *Toth v Quarles,* 350 U.S. 11 (1955); *Perez v Brownell,* 356 U.S. 44 (1958); and *Reid v Covert,* 354 U.S. 1 (1957) and *Kinsella v United States ex rel. Singleton,* 361 U.S. 234 (1960). The last two cases dealt with different aspects of the same statute so that seven cases affected only six congressional acts.

war? Answers to these questions are suggested by what happened, under the stress of economic collapse, to certain of our most effective brakes on government: separation of powers, dual federalism, due process of law, and judicial review itself. In comparatively recent years—down to 1936—the Court had used all these shackles to defeat urgent government action. Since 1937 all have been eroded in the face of rising demand for the power to govern. Writing in 1943, Justice Jackson declared that "the laissez-faire concept or principle of non-interference, at least as to economic affairs, has withered, and social advancements are increasingly sought . . . through expanded and strengthened governmental controls."[33] Since the Constitution embodies no "particular *economic* theory," social democracy was not precluded. Still to be determined was whether Holmes' suggestion of 1919, that the Constitution embodies a particular *political* theory, would be enforced as the law of the land.

JUDICIAL RESTRAINT AND NEW LIMITATIONS
IN WORLD WAR II

At the very moment the Court yielded its protection of economic interests, the Justices entered upon a period marked by creative decisions, recalling the judicial statesmanship of Chief Justice Marshall. New areas of constitutional interpretation, new-old subjects of judicial guardianship, new constitutional limitations emerged. Leading this judicial break-through, as was natural for the Justice who had spearheaded opposition to the idea of a static, unchanging Constitution, was Harlan Fiske Stone. In an obscure case of 1938,[34] he proclaimed the new dispensation tentatively, unobtrusively—using a footnote as the vehicle of his prognostications. Implicit in its three paragraphs are closely related doctrines—judicial self-restraint, political restraints, and preferred freedoms. All have roots in the past, but they remained largely undefined. In the body of the opinion, Stone suggested that the Court would not go so far as to say that no economic legislation would ever thereafter violate the Constitution. He merely suggested that in this area political restraints—the ballot box and election returns—would normally provide adequate protection. In cases involving the so-called preferred freedoms, however—speech, thought and religion—judicial self-restraint, the usual presumption of constitutionality, may not be appropriate. Legislation

---

[33] *West Virginia State Board of Education v Barnette*, 319 U.S. 624 (1943), 640.
[34] *United States v Carolene Products Co.*, 304 U.S. 144 (1938), 152.

restricting the political processes of discussion, debate, dissent, voting, now the primary reliance for repeal of undesirable legislation, may impose on the Court a correspondingly larger responsibility. Stone referred specifically to statutes directed at particular religions, or national or racial minorities. The Court must subject such restrictive legislation to "more searching judicial inquiry," because the very processes which the Framers thought of as furnishing the primary control on government are themselves curtailed. In other words, if the political processes are in fact to operate as the primary check on government, it logically follows that the Court must assume a larger responsibility for the unimpeded, uncorrupted functioning of that process.

In this historic footnote, Justice Stone laid the groundwork for doctrinal disputes destined to divide the Justices in ways far more subtle than those separating them during the embattled years prior to 1937. Noting the changes wrought by the Court as reconstituted in 1941, Walton Hamilton and George Braden observed:

A few years ago a bench headed by . . . Chief Justice [Hughes] read "liberty of contract" out of the due process clause and promptly read freedom of speech into its place. The current bench . . . has in effect set up a presumption of unconstitutionality against all legislation which on its face strikes at freedom of speech, press, assembly, or religion.[35]

In 1950, another student of the Court, surveying its work since 1937, concluded that the Justices had shifted their scrutiny and protection to other fields—to "the privileges of picketers, prisoners, proselyters, publicans (in the Scriptural sense), and pigmented portions of the population."[36] Constitutional limitations were still viable.

Shortly after Chief Justice Stone had adumbrated and won judicial guardianship of those rights which constitute "the very essence of a scheme of ordered liberty,"[37] the Court's positive duty to protect them ran headlong into the inexorable demands of a nation at war. Following the sneak attack on Pearl Harbor, General J. L. De Witt, military commander of the Western Defense Command, issued a proclamation, pursuant to a Presidential Order ratified by congressional statute, establishing a curfew for all alien Japanese, Germans, and Italians, and all persons of Japanese ancestry resident within

[35] Walton H. Hamilton and George D. Braden, "The Special Competence of the Supreme Court," 50 *Yale Law Journal* 1319 (1941), 1349.

[36] Edward Dumbauld, "Judicial Review and Popular Sovereignty," 99 *University of Pennsylvania Law Review* 197 (1950), 201.

[37] *Palko v Connecticut*, 302 U.S. 319 (1937), 325.

specified military zones on the west coast. One-hundred-and-twelve thousand persons of Japanese ancestry, two-thirds of them United States citizens by birth, were removed from their homes to assembly centers and then to relocation centers. These restrictions on Japanese residents of the Pacific states were justified in military orders as necessary to protect Army and Navy facilities, as well as industries and public utilities, from sabotage in the event of a Japanese invasion of the mainland. The nation was in the grip of fear.

Were a citizen's rights to live peaceably in his own home, to go and come as he might choose, to pursue an occupation undisturbed, any less expendable than freedom of speech and religion? Was an Army General's estimate of the situation immune to "searching judicial inquiry"? Answers to these questions were forthcoming early in 1943.

In *Hirabayashi v United States*[38] an American citizen had disobeyed both the curfew edict and an order to report to an assembly center preparatory to evacuation. With great caution the Justices, looking only at the validity of General De Witt's order establishing the curfew, refused to consider the detention order. Though such drastic invasion of the rights of United States citizens was unprecedented, Chief Justice Stone required only that "those charged with the responsibility of our national defense have reasonable ground for believing that the threat is real." This test, while giving great latitude to military discretion, was also designed to keep the door ajar for judicial intervention. The question before the Court, said Stone, "is not one of Congressional power to delegate to the President the promulgation of the Executive Order, but whether, *acting in cooperation*, Congress and the Executive have constitutional power to impose the curfew restriction here complained of."

Reaction to the *Hirabayashi* decision was predominantly unfavorable. Civil rights had been circumscribed. The curfew for Japanese citizens had been sustained, as one writer saw it, "because the Court found that it had 'some relation' to the winning of the war, because the Court would not 'sit in review of the wisdom' of administrative action, because the Court could not say that the Government 'did not have some ground for believing' the curfew was necessary."[39] In this and in other cases of this genre, the Supreme Court had been somewhat in the position of a private on guard duty accosting the commanding general without his pass. Just as constitutional limitations withered in the face of government effort to meet the problems growing out

[38] 320 U.S. 81 (1943).
[39] Morton Grodzins, *Americans Betrayed, Politics and the Japanese Evacuation* (Chicago: University of Chicago Press, 1948), p. 353.

of economic depression, so the unprecedented demands of World War II witnessed the erosion of safeguards normally accorded civil rights.

In light of this and other decisions, it is clear that in wartime the Constitution tips the scales in favor of authority and thus furnishes adequate power for any emergency. War subsumes to its purposes the entire Constitution and all organs of government, including the Supreme Court. In time of international conflict or civil strife the power-generating provision is that designating the President as the Commander-in-Chief. Presidential authority may be delegated by Congress, or rest more securely on the doctrine of inherent powers.[40]

But the war power, great as it is, is not unlimited. The Constitution assumes that the President, as a politically responsible civilian executive, will exert an overriding supervision of the military. In time of war the stakes are high. The two political branches abjure strict interpretation; power failure might mean death for some individuals or defeat for the nation. Clearly, the Justices do not wish to obstruct prosecution of the war. But they must not completely ignore those rights that constitute the very basis of any system of ordered liberty. Lincoln's poignant dilemma confronts them: "It has long been a grave question whether any government, not too strong for the liberties of its people, can be strong enough to maintain its existence in great emergencies."[41] In the circumstances, it is understandable that the judges will avoid the risk of rendering it too weak.

For Chief Justice Warren, these World War II decisions, "demonstrate dramatically that there are some circumstances in which the court will, in effect, conclude that it is simply not in a position to reject descriptions by the Executive of the degree of military necessity." But, he added, "if judicial review is to constitute a meaningful restraint upon unwarranted encroachments upon freedom in the name of military necessity, situations in which the judiciary refrains from examining the merit of the claim of necessity must be kept to an absolute minimum." The present Chief Justice is acutely aware that, "In times of stress, the Court is not only vulnerable . . . to the emotions of our people, but also to action by Congress in restricting what that body may consider judicial interference with the needs of security and defense."[42] Writing in 1947 after the shooting war had ended and before the

---

[40] Edward S. Corwin, *The President: Office and Powers, 1787–1957* (New York: New York University Press, 1957), p. 261.

[41] "Response to a Serenade," November 10, 1864, in John G. Nicolay and John Hay, eds., *Complete Works of Abraham Lincoln* (New York: Francis D. Tandy, 1905), X, 263.

[42] Earl Warren, "The Bill of Rights and the Military," 37 *New York University Law Review*, 181 (1962), 192, 193.

cold war had really begun, Professor Corwin commented that "our participation in World War II, far from cutting athwart the prevalent trend in
constitutional interpretation in peacetime, has simply intensified, extended
and accelerated it, so that we cannot reasonably expect any pronounced
reaction from most of the war's results for constitutional law."[43]

JUDICIAL BEHAVIOR IN THE COLD WAR

Eclipse of constitutional limitations in the period of cold war is reflected in
attribution to Congress of indefinite legislative power; concession to the
President of power to initiate national legislation for enlarged social objectives; the right of Congress to delegate power *ad libitum* to the President;
and recognition of presidential prerogative—power to act in the public
interest without a law and even in contradiction of it. Under the quiescent
leadership of Chief Justice Fred M. Vinson, the Court seldom challenged
these propositions. By 1957, however, it was clear that the judicial back-
track of 1937 had been less complete than generally supposed.

In 1953 Earl Warren, Thomas E. Dewey's running mate in 1948, became
the Court's titular head. Warren's appointment coincided with the early years
of Eisenhower's moderate Republicanism. Into the serenity of Washington's
political life, the new Chief Justice promptly introduced judicial dynamism.
He brought to the Court a conviction that "the heart of any constitution
consists of its Bill of Rights" and a belief that the Court is under special
responsibility to enforce its mandates.[44] "Our Judges," he announced in
1955, "are not monks or scientists, but participants in the living stream of
our national life.[45]

On May 17, 1954, within a few months of Warren's appointment, his
Court unanimously outlawed racial segregation in the public schools.[46] Cold
war tensions were mounting. Racial discrimination was not only creating
domestic unrest but also projecting a highly unfavorable image of America
to the entire world. As in 1940, when the Court ruled against Jehovah's
Witnesses and upheld Pennsylvania's flag salute in the public schools, the
Court may have felt, as Justice Frankfurter then said, that it was necessary
"to make the adjustment that we have to make within the framework of

---

[43] Edward S. Corwin, *Total War and the Constitution* (New York: Knopf, 1947), p. 179.
[44] Address to the Legislative Joint Interim Committee on Constitutional Revision and
its Advisory Committees, October 29, 1947. Reprinted in *The Public Papers of Chief Justice
Warren*, ed. by Henry M. Christman (New York: Simon and Schuster, Inc., 1959), p. 7.
[45] Earl Warren, "The Law and Future," 52 *Fortune* 106 (November, 1955), 107.
[46] *Brown v Board of Education of Topeka*, 347 U.S. 483 (1954).

present circumstances and those that are clearly ahead of us."[47] Both decisions reflect considerations not unrelated to the crises in which they were reached. In the *Flag Salute* case, constitutional limitations were waived in deference to the proposition that "national unity is the basis of national security." In the desegregation case, constitutional limitations were enforced and a half-century-old precedent sacrificed on the altar of national security.

Nor was the judicial order to integrate "with all deliberate speed" the only example of Chief Justice Warren's assertion of constitutional limitations. In June 1957 the Court, despite the pressures growing out of the Cold War, proceeded to take on the task of safeguarding civil rights generally. At a single sitting—June 17, 1957—the Court had a field day. It upheld the right of anyone to preach the overthrow of government, as long as the preaching is limited to "abstract principle" and does not openly advocate specific action. It limited the power of congressional committees to make investigations and to require witnesses to testify. It circumscribed the power of states to require witnesses to testify in investigations of subversvie activities. It restricted the power of officials to discharge government employees. Revival of constitutional limitations had occurred earlier in the term, when the Justices held that reports of the Federal Bureau of Investigation and other government agencies must be made available to defendants in criminal trials if the persons who made the reports are called as witnesses. In another case, the Court had ruled that past Communist connection, or suspected connection, is not sufficient cause for a state to refuse an admission to the bar.[48] These decisions, all reached by a narrow majority, have not remained unqualified. Subsequent rulings make it clear that a new majority, also narrow, is reluctant to challenge Congress' attempt to cope with subversion.[49]

---

[47] Felix Frankfurter to Harlan F. Stone, May 27, 1940. Quoted in A. T. Mason, *Security Through Freedom* (1955), p. 219. On June 2, 1940, a Gallup Poll recorded that 65 per cent of the American people expected Germany to invade the United States. "This country," the *New Republic* of June 24, 1940, noted, "is now in the grip of a war hysteria; we are in great danger of adopting Hitler's philosophy in the effort to oppose Hitler's legions. When the Supreme Court says in effect that we must imperil religious liberty in the interest of the American State, which is worth preserving because it guarantees religious liberty, it comes dangerously close to being a victim of hysteria" (pp. 843–44).

[48] *Yates v United States*, 354 U.S. 298; *Watkins v United States*, 354 U.S. 178; *Sweezy v New Hampshire*, 354 U.S. 234; *Service v Dulles*, 354 U.S. 363; *Jencks v United States*, 353 U.S. 657 (1957); *Schware v Board of Bar Examiners*, 353 U.S. 232 (1957); *Konigsberg v State Bar*, 353 U.S. 252 (1957).

[49] See *Barenblatt v United States*, 360 U.S. 109 (1959); *Uphaus v Wyman*, 324 U.S. 388 (1960); *Wilkinson v United States*, 365 U.S. 399 (1961); *Braden v United States*, 365 U.S. 431 (1961); *Communist Party v Subversive Activities Control Board*, 367 U.S. 1 (1961); *Scales v United States*, 367 U.S. 203 (1961).

Taking into account this uncertain balance, Chief Justice Warren, speaking in 1962, assayed the security-through-freedom theme:

Some believe that these cases may be disposed of by the Court balancing the security of the Nation against the freedom of the individual litigant. If these are the appropriate weights to put in the scales, it is not surprising that the balance is usually struck against the individual. If balance we must, I wonder whether on the individual's side we might not also place the importance of our survival as a free nation. The issue, as I see it, is not the individual against society; it is rather the wise accommodation of the necessities of physical survival with the requirements of spiritual survival.[50]

Following closely on the heels of the 1957 decisions, the familiar clamor of judicial usurpation was heard. The Court had once again ignored, as in 1935–1936, the salutary self-restraint doctrine. Drastic measures to restrict the Court's power and jurisdiction were introduced in Congress. Individual Justices were singled out for impeachment. Nor was the attack confined to the lunatic fringe. In August 1958, the chief justices of 36 states issued a report expressing grave doubt as to whether we have a government of laws and not of men. The next year a committee of the American Bar Association charged that the Warren Court's decisions encouraged the march of Communism. The shock stimulated by these power-crippling decisions was the more intense in coming so quickly after Chief Justice Vinson's judicial passivism. The Court had been a tame tabby for so many years that some observers were surprised to discover that it still had power, teeth, and muscle.[51]

The Court is as sharply divided now as in the years immediately preceding 1937. Five-to-four rulings have once again become familiar. The divisive issues include freedom of speech and belief, and the right of association. As in 1937, the principle of constitutional limitations is at stake. Frankfurter and Whittaker (both now retired), Clark, Harlan, Stewart and their successors have been inclined to pay greater deference to presumption of constitutionality, and, in any conflict between public power and individual rights, to strike the balance in favor of the former. For this judicial bloc, the Court's role is relatively narrow. The minority of four—Warren, Douglas, Black, and Brennan—has tended to accord speech, press, and religion a relatively higher rank among our constitutional values and to take a broader view of the Court's role in protecting them. How President Kennedy's recent appointees, Byron White and Arthur Goldberg, will affect this uncertain balance remains to be seen.

[50] Warren, "The Bill of Rights and the Military," *op. cit.*, p. 200.
[51] John P. Frank, *Marble Palace* (New York: Alfred A. Knopf, Inc., 1958), p. vii.

Chief Justice Warren proclaims the continuing vitality of constitutional limitations. "Our Constitution and Nation are one," he declared on February 1, 1962.

Neither can exist without the other. It is with this thought in mind that we should gauge the claims of those who assert that national security requires what our Constitution appears to condemn. . . . I am one who believes firmly that the Court must be vigilant against neglect of the requirements of our Bill of Rights and the personal rights that document was intended to guarantee for all time.[52]

More often than not, however, Supreme Court Justices have not followed this course during times of stress.

"The dominant lesson of our history," John P. Frank has noted, "is that courts love liberty most when it is under pressure least."[53] Our wartime experiences indicate that constitutional limitations are not completely viable when the national interest is at stake. A Constitution cannot limit a nation's needs. This is one of the few propositions on which Madison, Hamilton and Thomas Jefferson could unite. Writing in the *Federalist*, No. 23, Hamilton declared that power to provide for common defense, preservation of the public peace or superintendence of our intercourse with foreign countries "ought to exist without limitations because it is impossible to foresee or to define the extent and variety of national exigencies, and the correspondent extent and variety of the means which may be necessary to satisfy them." "It is vain," Madison wrote in the *Federalist*, No. 41, "to oppose constitutional barriers to the impulse of self-preservation." With no authorization from either Congress or the people, President Jefferson consummated the Louisiana Purchase. He knew that this was an exercise of power beyond the bounds of the Constitution, and said so. "The laws of necessity, of self-preservation, of saving our country when in danger, are of higher obligation." "To lose our country by a scrupulous adherence to written law," he explained, "would be to lose the law itself, with life, liberty, property and all those who are enjoying them with us; thus absurdly sacrificing the end to the means."[54] John Quincy Adams stated the classic theory:

. . . in the authority given to Congress by the Constitution of the United States to declare war, all the powers incidental to war are, by necessary implication, conferred

---

[52] Warren, "The Bill of Rights and the Military," *op. cit.*, pp. 200, 201–02.

[53] John P. Frank, "Review and Basic Liberties," in Edmond Cahn, ed., *Supreme Court and Supreme Law* (Bloomington: Indiana University Press, 1954), p. 114.

[54] Paul L. Ford, ed., *The Works of Thomas Jefferson* (New York: G. P. Putnam's Sons, 1905), XI, 146.

upon the government of the United States. Now the powers incidental to war are derived, not from internal municipal sources, but from the laws and usages of nations . . . . There are, then, . . . in the authority of Congress and of the Executive, two classes of powers, altogether different in their nature, and often incompatible with each other—the war power and the peace power. The peace power is limited by regulations and restricted by provisions prescribed within the constitution itself. The war power is limited only by the laws and the usages of nations. This power is tremendous: it is strictly constitutional, but it breaks down every barrier so anxiously erected for the protection of liberty, of property and of life.[55]

But no emergency, however serious, justifies complete disregard of constitutional limitations. "Every breach of the fundamental laws," Hamilton wrote in the *Federalist*, No. 25, "though dictated by necessity, impairs that sacred reverence which ought to be maintained in the breast of rulers towards the constitution of a country, and forms a precedent for other breaches where the same plea of necessity does not exist at all, or is less urgent and palpable." Judicial decisions illustrate the Court's sensitiveness to this danger. The presidential order convening the military tribunal in the *German Saboteurs* case purported to close all access to the civil courts.[56] But Chief Justice Stone, speaking for a unanimous bench, was at great pains to demonstrate that the law of the land still governed, no matter what the President proclaimed. In the *Steel Seizure* case, a similar process of inspecting the President's passport was gone through, and here the "plea of necessity" was not considered "urgent and palpable."[57] Though future Presidents may hesitate to enter this debatable territory, judicial intervention in the Steel Seizure case, under the doctrine of separation of powers, may be the exception that proves the rule—at least in times of great emergencies.

THE COURT'S PECULIAR RESPONSIBILITY

Just as the President and Congress supply the dynamics of government, so the political check remains the primary control. Accented thereby is the Court's peculiar responsibility for enforcing the limitations provided in the Bill of Rights and those absorbed into the Fourteenth Amendment. The political process must be kept uncorrupted and accessible to all on an equal basis. On occasion, a narrow majority of the present Supreme Court, led by

[55] Speech in House of Representatives, May 25, 1836. *Register of Debates in Congress* (Washington: Gales & Seaton, 1836), XII, 4037–8.
[56] *Ex parte Richard Quirin*, 317 U.S. 1 (1942).
[57] *Youngstown Sheet & Tube Co. v Sawyer*, 343 U.S. 579 (1952).

the Chief Justice, has rendered decisions carrying the implication that the judiciary may block the will of the majority in the name of minorities without jeopardizing our security. It is apparently believed that such action may even serve to promote it.

This stand is in accord with the position taken during the formative years of our history. Then, the youthful Republic surrounded, as Jefferson said, "with nations who feel power and forget right"[58] recognized that free discussion must be maintained. Thus the Founding Fathers erected specific constitutional barriers protecting the right to differ, to oppose, and to dissent. Nor were they unaware that a nation, confronted with security threats, would be tempted "to fling away freedom at the first disturbance" before discovering how "freedom itself serves to promote" it.[59] Jefferson argued that freedom makes ours "the strongest government on earth. . . . I believe it the only one where every man," he wrote, "at the call of the law, would fly to the standard of the law; and would meet invasions of public order as his own personal concern."[60]

Security and freedom are not necessarily at cross purposes. At some point—and this is the core of the problem—the two values coincide. Differences as to when and where that point is reached are unending. The search for it is a domain appropriate for judges. Through war and in peace, some of our most eminent jurists, in principle, have been on freedom's side.

Justice Holmes "thought that the Judge should not be too rigidly bound to the tenet of judicial self-restraint in cases involving civil liberties."[61] During World War I and its frenzied Red Scare aftermath, Holmes began to suspect that Americans had grown so accustomed to the enjoyment of the Bill of Rights "that we forget that they had to be fought for and may have to be fought for again." Believing that the Bill of Rights "could not be kept unless we were willing to fight for them," he was inclined to "stand by them."[62]

---

[58] Quoted in Julian P. Boyd, "The Fear of Ideas," address commemorating the 175th anniversary of the Virginia Bill of Rights. *The American Scholar*, Autumn, 1952, p. 417.

[59] The words of Alexis de Tocqueville. Quoted by Henry Steele Commager, *The New York Times Magazine*, December 15, 1935, p. 15. Compare Hamilton, *Federalist*, No. 8, p. 32.

[60] First Inaugural, in *Inaugural Addresses of the Presidents of the United States from George Washington 1789 to Harry S. Truman 1949*, 82nd Cong., 2nd Sess., House Doc., No. 540, p. 12.

[61] H. F. Stone to Clinton L. Rossiter, April 12, 1941. Stone Papers, Library of Congress. Justice Frankfurter reinforces this view, declaring that Justice Holmes "was far more ready to find legislative invasion where free inquiry was involved than in the debatable area of economics." Felix Frankfurter, *Mr. Justice Holmes and the Supreme Court* (Cambridge: Harvard University Press, 1938), p. 51, and see pp. 49–63 *passim*.

[62] August 25, 1923; May 12, 1919. M. D. Howe, ed., *Holmes-Laski Letters* (Cambridge: Harvard University Press, 1953), I, 529–30, 203.

Holmes thought that political restraints usually provide adequate safeguards against arbitrary social and economic legislation. In the *Abrams* case of 1919, however, he subscribed to the belief that "the ultimate good desired is better reached by free trade in ideas." This, he said, is "the theory of our Constitution."[63]

Brandeis also went back to the formative years. He traced the wide range accorded "freedom to think as you will and to speak as you think" to those "who won our independence," to men who believed "that this should be a fundamental principle of the American government."[64] In 1937, the year of the dramatic judicial about-face, Justice Cardozo spelled out the hierarchy of values that inspired eighteenth century exponents of a Bill of Rights. "We reach a different plane of social and moral values," he wrote, "when we pass to the privileges and immunities that have been taken over from the earlier articles of the federal Bill of Rights and brought within the Fourteenth Amendment by a process of absorption." As for freedom of thought and speech, Cardozo added, "it is the matrix, the indispensable condition, of nearly every other form of freedom."[65]

Chief Justice Hughes insisted that, in times of crisis particularly, the Constitution's provisions for peaceful change must be enforced lest resort to violent remedies be encouraged. In his address of 1939, commemorating the one-hundred-fiftieth anniversary of the First Congress, he referred to the Bill of Rights as establishing barriers "against the abuses threatened by gusts of passion and prejudice which in misguided zeal would destroy the basic interests of democracy. We protect the fundamental rights of minorities, in order to save democratic government from destroying itself by the excess of its own power. . . ."[66]

The Court's function is not to determine what decisions can be made by the political process, but to prevent the mechanism from breaking down. Judicial hands-off in economic matters (unless the political processes are impeded or threatened) is perfectly consistent with judicial activism to maintain the integrity and effective operation of the process itself. The genius of our system, which Hamilton identified as "vibrations of power," is thereby preserved.[67] This means more than separated and balanced organs

[63] Dissenting in *Abrams v United States*, 250 U.S. 616 (1919), 630.

[64] Concurring in *Whitney v California*, 274 U.S. 357 (1927), 375.

[65] *Palko v Connecticut*, 302 U.S. 319 (1937), 326, 327.

[66] Proceedings at the ceremony in commemoration of the 150th anniversary of the Commencement of the First Congress of the United States. 76th Cong., 1st Sess., House Doc. No. 212, March 4, 1939, p. 32.

[67] Alexander Hamilton to Rufus King, June 3, 1802. Henry Cabot Lodge, ed., *The Works of Alexander Hamilton* (New York: G. P. Putnam's Sons, 1904), X, 439.

of government, more than swinging, pendulum-like, from right to left, from action to inaction. Also required is such tension as will discourage any political or social group from daring to bid for total or permanent power. Government must maintain order without losing the incalculable advantage that stems from the factions and pulls inherent in a free society.

Conflict has been and is endemic. Divergence of opinion does not necessarily hinder advance toward national security. Political struggle may yield a heightened, better informed view of the public interest and a strengthened determination to take positive steps in promoting it. The real peril now, as always, is that at some point in the quest for freedom and for security, we become so weighted down with the responsibilities freedom inevitably entails, so troubled by domestic turmoil verging on chaos, so fearful of external aggression and internal subversion, as to yield to the lure no free society can rationally pursue—the status-quo phantom.

VOTING AND THE CRUCIAL PRELIMINARIES

Voting is only the end result of the political process, of course. Whether in war or in peace, maintenance of constitutional limitations in this area is vital.[68] When on grounds of race, color, or creed minority groups are permanently kept from exercising the right to vote, the democratic process is obviously obstructed. But the Court has not always acted to keep the electoral process pure and unimpeded. While insisting that each individual otherwise qualified has the right to cast his ballot, the Justices have been hesitant about insisting that each vote count equally. A glaring inequity in our electoral system, by which certain groups are permanently kept from full participation, has resulted from the unwillingness of state legislatures to reapportion election districts to conform with the actual distribution of population. The voter in a district of rapid population growth has a much smaller voice in elections than the voter from the district of steady or declining population. When this system works, as it often does, to give certain areas having less than a majority of the population permanent control over the state legislature, or over the state's congressional delegation, the practical result is a proportionate disenfranchisement of those in the rest of the state.

---

[68] During the Civil War, when it was suggested that the Presidential election be bypassed, Lincoln responded: ". . . the election was a necessity. We cannot have free government without elections; and if the rebellion could force us to forego or postpone a national election, it might fairly claim to have already conquered and ruined us." (Speech of November 10, 1864. Nicolay and Hay, eds., *Complete Works of Abraham Lincoln*, X, 263.)

On March 26, 1962, amid continuing world crisis, the Court took a notable step in making rotten boroughs subject to judicial correction. Constitutional limitations, formerly unenforced, were asserted. In the Tennessee re-apportionment case, the Court held for the first time that a voter whose franchise is diluted by unfair, unequal, or discriminatory apportionment of legislative seats may seek relief in the federal courts.[69] A colloquy between Justices Frankfurter and Clark illustrates a basic divergence. Both agreed that political checks on government are primary. Frankfurter insisted that they are the sole restraint:

> *Disregard of inherent limits in the effective exercise of the Court's "judicial Power" presages the futility of judicial intervention in the essentially political conflict of forces by which the relation between population and representation has time out of mind been and now is determined. It may well impair the Court's position as the ultimate organ of "the supreme Law of the Land."*

Frankfurter insisted that "Appeal must be to an informed, civically militant electorate," to "an aroused popular conscience that sears the conscience of the people's representatives." Responding to Frankfurter's plea for reliance on a procedure patently helpless to provide a remedy, Justice Clark observed:

> *I would not consider intervention by this Court into so delicate a field if there were any other relief available to the people of Tennessee. But the majority of the people of Tennessee have no "practical opportunities for exerting their political weight at the polls" . . . . Tennessee has an "informed, civically militant electorate" and an "aroused popular conscience," but it does not sear "the conscience of the people's representatives."*

With the triumph of Justice Clark's realistic argument for the assertion of judicial responsibility, the American ideal of political equality came a step closer to realization. By enforcing constitutional limitations, the Court functioned as an instrument of democracy and of majority rule.

But effective political action through voting would be impossible if the climate of opinion were such as to discourage free and effective interchange of ideas. Without equal opportunity to utilize the crucial preliminaries— speech, press, assembly, petition—the idea of government by the consent of

---

[69] *Baker v Carr*, 369 U. S 186 (1962).

the governed becomes an empty declamation. Majorities—and this is a key point in democratic theory—are in flux. Tomorrow's majority may have a different composition as well as different goals. Defense of the political rights of minorities thus becomes, not the antithesis of majority rule, but its very foundation. The majority must leave open to minorities the political channels by which it can be replaced when it is no longer able to command popular support. The alternative is violent overthrow—revolution. By protecting the integrity and unimpeded operation of the entire process by which majorities are formed, judicial review becomes a surrogate for revolution and contributes positively to the preservation of democracy.

Our system of government was framed by men who believed that the only security worth having is built on freedom. In response to urgent promptings from various state ratifying conventions, the first Congress proposed the Bill of Rights. Contemporary leaders—including Madison, Jefferson, and Hamilton—regarded independent tribunals of justice as the peculiar guardians of those rights. Judicial intervention in behalf of the right to dissent, to differ, and to oppose is essential to the continuance of free government; it is indeed its most distinctive hallmark. No opposition means no democracy. Constitutional limitations are not only relevant, but urgent. In a turbulent world, stalked by fear in all quarters, the Supreme Court must keep aflame the torch of freedom forged by our ancestors in the crucible of revolution.

Suggestions for Further Reading

Black, Hugo L., "Absolutes, Courts, and the Bill of Rights," 35 *New York University Law Review* 865 (1960).

Corwin, Edward S., *Constitutional Revolution, Ltd.* (Claremont, California: Associated Colleges of Claremont, 1941).

——, *The President: Office and Powers* (New York: New York University Press, 1957), Chapter VI.

——, *Total War and the Constitution* (New York: Alfred A. Knopf, Inc., 1947).

Douglas, William O., *Columbia Law Alumni Bulletin*, December 1958.

Givens, Richard A., "Chief Justice Stone and the Developing Functions of Judicial Review," 47 *Virginia Law Review* 1321 (1961).

Mason, Alpheus Thomas, *Harlan Fiske Stone: Pillar of the Law* (New York: The Viking Press, Inc., 1956), Chapters 39, 40, 41, 46, and 47.

McCloskey, Robert, *The American Supreme Court* (Chicago: University of Chicago Press, 1960).

Rossiter, Clinton, *Constitutional Dictatorship* (Princeton, New Jersey: Princeton University Press, 1948).

Schwartz, Bernard, *The Supreme Court: Constitutional Revolution in Retrospect* (New York: The Ronald Press Company, 1957).

Warren, Earl, "The Bill of Rights and the Military," 37 *New York University Law Review* 181 (1962).

LOCAL STRENGTH IN THE AMERICAN FEDERAL SYSTEM
The Mobilization of Public-Private Influence

Morton Grodzins

THE MIXTURE OF PUBLIC AND PRIVATE BUSINESS

Local and state governments have great strength in the American federal system. Constitutional arrangements are one source of that strength. The distribution of power within political parties is an even more important source.[1] Measures of centralization which are constitutionally possible are politically impossible. Decisions made by the central government—to establish a federal airport program, for example—may be decentralizing decisions: the principal gainers in power are state and local, not national, institutions.

MORTON GRODZINS, *Professor of Political Science at the University of Chicago, has served in a consultative or directive capacity for various public-private groups, among them the Council of State Governments, Public Administration Clearing House, Hoover Commission, National Manpower Council, President's Commission on National Goals, Advisory Commission on Intergovernmental Relations, and U.S. Department of Agriculture. His essay is a product of the Federalism Workshop of the University of Chicago, which he now directs. Supported by funds from the Ford Foundation and the Social Science Research Council, the Workshop conducts research into intergovernmental relations. Among his numerous publications are* Americans Betrayed *(1949),* The Loyal and the Disloyal *(1956), and* Government and Housing in Metropolitan Areas *(with E. C. Banfield, 1958).*

---

[1] Morton Grodzins, "The Federal System," in *Goals for Americans* (Englewood Cliffs, N.J.: Prentice-Hall, Inc., 1960).

The importance and influence of the central government have vastly increased in consequence of the nation's new importance in world politics. National defense expenditures for goods and services averaged more than $43 billion annually between 1956 and 1960, some 11 per cent of the gross national product and almost 90 per cent of all federal expenditures for goods and services. Outside the defense area, national influence has blossomed as a result of Supreme Court decisions, particularly those concerning school desegregation and the apportionment of seats in the state legislatures. The size of the defense budget and the decisions of the Supreme Court are precisely those areas of governance farthest removed from the influence of domestic politics. But where political forces are free to act, the fear of the federal octopus is not supported by the facts. To give only one example, federal expenditures for civilian functions, expressed as a percentage of the gross national product, have *decreased* by more than 50 per cent in the last thirty years. State-local expenditures have remained almost constant (though they also show a slight decline) by this measure.[2] And state-local expenditures for civilian functions during the recent years have been roughly six times central government expenditures for those purposes.

This essay is concerned with one facet of state-local strength in the federal system: the mobilization of public-private influence at the local level for the purpose of influencing national programs. Interest group theory, in the literature of political science, assigns an important role to voluntary groups. The aggregate of group interests, it is argued, becomes national policy and, indeed, the national interest.[3] But voluntary groups do not only influence governments for their own private interests. The literature largely overlooks the fact that they also work on behalf of governments.

It should come as no surprise that private and public purposes often become completely intertwined; or that a public function in one place may be private in another; or that in a given community there may be an easy substitution of public and private responsibilities. Not more than four centuries ago in Europe even tax collecting and the armed forces were in private hands. Within the memory of living men, aid for the indigent in the United States was thought of as almost exclusively a matter of charity, a private virtue and a private responsibility.

---

[2] See Jacob Cohen and Morton Grodzins, "How Much Economic Sharing in American Federalism?" (Unpublished mimeographed paper, 1962.)

[3] Arthur F. Bentley, *The Process of Government* (Chicago: University of Chicago Press, 1908); David B. Truman, *The Governmental Process* (New York: Alfred A. Knopf, Inc., 1951); E. Pendleton Herring, *The Politics of Democracy* (New York: W. W. Norton & Company, Inc., 1940).

Some confusion exists in distinguishing the public from the private sphere even for central portions of both. But a determination is in most cases possible. The manufacturer of steel who has important government contracts, for example, may convince both himself and others that his first concern is the national defense. In some larger sense, especially during crises which threaten the fate of the nation, the public concern of the industrialist can be taken at its face value. Nevertheless, for most of the group in noncrisis periods (and for some even in crisis), private ends have primacy. Profits, dividends to stockholders, and responsibilities to employees are paramount values. Similarly, officers of the Department of Defense have many obligations to the private sector of the economy. Their programs are carried out with the advice of business advisory groups, and they must always be sensitive, for economic as well as political reasons, to the need for balancing defense purchases among large and small businesses and among the various regions of the nation. But their primary business is the public business of maintaining the nation's armed strength. The mixture of the public and private in these "pure" cases suggests that the distinction becomes greatly blurred in cases that are not so pure. This is so. At the local level, private groups perform public functions, and public offices are used for private purposes.

PRIVATE GROUPS DOING PUBLIC BUSINESS

The mixture of public and private spheres can be seen with great clarity on the local scene. Local influence on national programs is exercised by bringing to bear on national officers the combined weight of the public and private sectors. Where the public-private linkage is strong and where its strength is utilized, local influence over federal activities on the local scene is maximized.

Private groups are involved, and often play a dominant role, in a wide assortment of public, local activities. Private schools, including parochial schools, are an obvious example of the substitution of private for public services. Here public and private facilities exist in parallel, performing roughly identical tasks. In other cases, private contributions are used to initiate, enlarge, or enrich the public program. The recreation program of a small Arizona town exemplifies this relationship. The Rotary Club was the principal force behind a drive to secure federal land for a large mountain park, and Rotary funds were used in payment for the land conveyed to the city. The city swimming pool was secured through the joint efforts of the

Lions, Rotary, and other civic groups, and the same cooperation was responsible for building a Scout Lodge on city-owned land.[4]

In still other cases there are complete amalgams of the public and private spheres. The private groups retain their separate, legal identities but become institutionalized as a unified arm of the government. Many health and welfare departments take this form. To cite only one example, a number of Michigan counties operate public health services through city-county Visiting Nurse Association departments. The Visiting Nurse Association is a private organization deriving its income from private donations and the Community Chest. It maintains its private character, but it has become an integral part of the official health department. Similar amalgamations can be found over a wide range of activities. Fire departments in many small towns are operated by private volunteer organizations, with equipment frequently furnished out of public funds. Hospitals in the largest cities provide services to indigent patients through a combination of public funds, medical association cooperation, private university staffing, aid from women's clubs, and donations of time and skill by private practitioners. Local libraries, museums, and parks often represent the same combination of public and private resources.

In many cases the private groups make important public decisions, later ratified by public bodies. An observer in an Arkansas town remarked that the local Chamber of Commerce handled "virtually all new projects" for the city. "Anything that must be tested before the city council will formally risk committing itself is handled through the Chamber." Once a program is proved worthy of official city acceptance, it is taken off the Chamber's hands. Paul Ylvisaker has said that in Mankato, Minnesota (the largest community in Blue Earth County), the Chamber of Commerce, the Junior Chamber, the Builders' Exchange, and the Manufacturers and Wholesalers Association constituted an "economic legislature." "Here are staged the preliminary, and in many cases the decisive, debates on such issues as whether the commercial zone of the city is to extend more than a block and a half up from Front

---

[4] The examples could be multiplied indefinitely. In many places individual businessmen have an important role in recreational programs. In a Georgia city the basketball leagues are sponsored by one of the largest businesses; Little League baseball groups by the local bank, a mill, and the Rotary Club; teenage baseball by the Veterans of Foreign Wars, and teenage dances by the Women's Club, utilizing the American Legion clubhouse. The town stadium was built by an ad hoc group drawing membership from many civic and business groups. The town square and the courthouse yard were landscaped and maintained by the Women's Club, and plans for new parks in the city were made by a private utility company.

Street, whether and at what expense the state's postwar planning council should be invited to conduct a local economic survey, whether certain business practices are to be condoned. . . ."[5]

In a number of areas private organizations performing public services directly assume important intergovernmental responsibilities. Welfare activities of veterans' organizations provide a case in point. Each of the veterans' groups maintains a nationwide network of "service officers" whose function is to aid veterans to qualify for federal and state benefits. Where the veterans' groups are strongly organized, their service officers are very active indeed. Under these circumstances an officer of a private club in effect acts as the local representative of a vast federal (and a more modest state) welfare program, and simultaneously represents local constituents in pressing their claims before federal and state administrators. This is an important adjunct to the more widely publicized lobbying activities of the veterans' groups.

For example, the American Legion service officer of a small town in DuBois County, Indiana, has done this work for more than twelve years. He is a specialist in veterans' benefits, a private public servant of experience and competence. His aim is to be certain that veterans in his community make maximum use of the special services available to them. These have included a state bonus and federal pension, disability compensation, aid to widows and orphans, and funds for hospitalization, medical appliances, educational training, insurance, and burial. The officer does not consider it desirable to forward claims for every veteran who comes to him for aid. He feels free on the basis of his experience to tell inquirers that their claims will not be allowed and to advise them not to prepare formal applications. In so doing he exercises greater discretion than many government field officials usually do.

The service officer estimates that he spends a minimum of ten hours a week on his social welfare activities. He has in a decade's work processed more than 2300 claims and interviewed more than 3000 veterans or their widows—an impressive record of services rendered. A considerable private bureaucracy at central points is needed to handle business of this volume, and the Indiana Department of the American Legion has fifteen full-time people in the Indianapolis office working on veterans' benefit problems. Moreover, the Legion places its own personnel in the Washington office of the Veterans Administration to act as expediters and as liaison persons between the public and the private bureaucracies.

The other veterans' organizations maintain parallel national networks for

---

[5] Paul N. Ylvisaker, *Intergovernmental Relations at the Grass Roots* (Minneapolis: University of Minnesota Press, 1956), p. 49.

the private administration of the public welfare services. In DuBois County the Veterans of Foreign Wars and the Disabled American Veterans are active. The effectiveness of American Legion service officers in the county has led the other groups to refer their "cases" to the Legion. In difficult matters, nevertheless, the VFW service officer will take an active role in soliciting aid from the local congressman. In other places the rivalry of the service organizations in the public welfare field precludes this sort of co-operation.

The collaboration in DuBois County among the private organizations engaged in veterans' welfare work is matched by collaboration between private and public officers. No local government in the county has any official responsibility for veterans' affairs despite the fact that Indiana, like many other states, makes it possible to spend county funds for a veterans' service officer. The post has not been filled in DuBois County, partly because of the efficiency of the Legion services and partly because cooperation between the private veterans' groups does not extend to an agreement on who should be named to the official post. The county, therefore, does not duplicate Legion veterans' activities. But the Legion service officer and county welfare workers nevertheless find themselves working on many common problems. The exchange of information, and referral of persons by one service to the other, is continuous, easy, and informal. The cooperative circle extends beyond the specialized boundaries of welfare activities. For example, the mayor of one of the towns in the county, acting as municipal judge, became irked at the continued necessity of sending a mentally deficient veteran to the county jail (usually at the request of the veteran's wife). The mayor-judge requested that the veterans' service office find some way to help. Once an application to the Veterans Administration was filed by the service officer on behalf of the veteran, the mayor continued his good offices by writing to the local congressman to insure, as he put it, that the application received "fast and fair treatment."[6]

PUBLIC BUSINESS FOR PRIVATE GAIN

In many cases where private groups perform public business, private advantage is apparent. The service functions of the American Legion are clearly aimed at bringing advantages to Legion members and, by no means

[6] Discussion of the welfare activities of the veterans' organizations in DuBois County is based upon the field notes of Douglas St. Angelo. See his unpublished doctoral dissertation, *Local Impact Upon Federal Programs*, University of Chicago, Department of Political Science, 1960.

incidentally, at strengthening the Legion itself. Sponsorship by the Farm Bureau of extension service activities is a well known example of a similar amalgamation of public and private purposes. And when a Chamber of Commerce assumes leadership for a local function, it is often possible to see in the short or long run some special advantage to the business groups concerned. Nevertheless it is important to distinguish these cases from those in which private business firms perform public services directly for private gain. Here the profit is immediate and the result of contractual obligations assumed by the local government in return for service received.

All localities at one time or another must take advantage of the special skills and competences of engineering and legal firms, planning and survey organizations, and private specialists in public finance and other fields. In the larger local governments—New York and Chicago, for example—the scale of operations is large, specialization is possible, and experts are employed within the government on a full-time basis. Specialists under contract are utilized as an adjunct to the official administrative group.

For the smaller local governments many special competences are not available at all within the official staffs. This personnel gap is often filled by professional associations of government workers. Organizations such as the American Municipal Association, the International Association of City Managers, and the Federation of Tax Administrators are an important source of technical assistance and advice over a wide range of activities. Private nationwide organizations, such as the National Board of Fire Underwriters, may play the same role.[7] And in all states, official state agencies supply technical aid to localities over a variety of fields. The University of Arkansas, for example, serves as a technical advisor to localities applying to the federal government for urban planning grants. The University also provides personnel for utilizing grants once they are received by local governments. In a number of states—North Carolina, Tennessee, New Jersey, and New York are good examples—a considerable range of services is offered local governments by state agencies. In a very large number of cases, however, localities turn to private organizations for technical services, another incidental demonstration of the easy substitution of the private for the public. Frequently private firms do not simply furnish an adjunct to local skills; rather, they constitute the local government's total specialized staff.

---

[7] The National Board of Fire Underwriters is a unique private organization doing public business. Through its activities in establishing fire insurance rates, it is in effect a tax levying body. Later publications of the University of Chicago's Federalism Workshop will analyze the various roles of voluntary professional associations in the American government.

A convenient example is provided by Casa Grande, Arizona, a desert town of fewer than 10,000 population, on one of the main highways between Phoenix and Tucson. In Casa Grande a private engineering firm has in effect become the city's planning and construction agency and simultaneously one of its chief avenues of influence in shaping national and state programs to local purposes. The process by which Casa Grande secured its sewage treatment plant illustrates how this relationship operates. Casa Grande built a badly needed sewage plant by obtaining a construction grant from the United States Public Health Service and by receiving a loan, covered by a special bond issue, from the Housing and Home Finance Agency. The private engineering firm was responsible for negotiating both the grant and the loan.

The possibility in the first place that Casa Grande was eligible for this federal aid was made known to city officials by a leading engineering firm. In its original contract with the city the engineering company agreed to perform necessary field surveys; prepare plans, specifications, bidding and contract documents; provide a complete inspection for all work done under the project; and, most important, prepare a project application for the proposed work for submittal to the state Department of Health and the United States Public Health Service. Once the contract was approved by the mayor and city council of Casa Grande, the entire task of securing the sewage disposal plant for the city was in the hands of the private company, although city officers were kept fully informed and were called upon occasionally for aid.

The engineering firm was in direct contact with the state and federal agencies concerned. It submitted directly to the State Department of Health the elaborate federal form justifying the grant-in-aid to the city. The state agency had only to certify that the project was constructed in accordance with state approved plans and specifications, and transmit the application to the regional office of the United States Public Health Service. After state approval of the application was secured, the firm continued direct negotiation with the officers of the Public Health Service. Well before official word concerning the grant was received by the city, an officer of the company was able to inform the city manager that he had been advised unofficially that the federal grant had been approved.[8]

---

[8] Federal officials were scrupulous in dealing with the city through the State Department of Health. When a medical officer of the Public Health Service, for example, desired further information on the sewage disposal plant, he sent his inquiry to the State Health Department, which submitted it to the city manager of Casa Grande, who in turn transmitted the inquiry to the engineering firm. The firm was less formal. It replied directly to the state, keeping the city informed through a carbon copy of the response. Officers

The Public Health Service grant could not be completed until arrangements were made for financing the city's share of the sewage plant's cost. While managing the grant application for the sewage plant itself, officers of the engineering firm simultaneously steered the local money-raising effort. They did this by securing aid from another federal program, administered by the Housing and Home Finance Agency, and by mobilizing further private assistance for the city. This assistance was provided by an investment securities firm which acted as fiscal agents of the city in the issuance of the sewage approvement bonds, and by a law firm which gave the necessary legal advice for the proposed bond elections. The engineering company recommended both the legal and the investment companies to city officers.

Just as the private engineering firm had previously taken full responsibility for justifying the Public Health grant, so it supplied all technical information to the Housing and Home Finance Agency. The city's only role was to have the mayor fix his signature to the loan application form. A technical assessment of the city's financial ability to service the loan was at the same time provided the federal agency by the investment securities firm. Once the preliminary loan application had been approved by the Housing and Home Finance Agency, the engineering firm completed the final application and sent it directly to the federal agency, a copy being sent to Casa Grande. This was a technical document, more than forty pages in length. Officers of the engineering and investment firms visited the Housing and Home Finance Agency in order to work out an arrangement for the bond purchase. When officers of the engineering firm were informally given notice that the Public Health Service had approved the basic grant, they pushed hard by wire and telephone for quick approval of the bond arrangement so that there would be no possibility of the grant being lost because of delays in the bond financing.

The private firms were also active on the local scene, managing all arrangements for the necessary special bond election. For example, the investment securities firm supplied the city with all the needed forms, including poll lists, tally lists, challenge lists, and signs warning that electioneering could not take place too near the polling place. The attorneys supplied the city council with the actual text of the bond resolution and provided the mayor with the text for his official announcement of the bond election. When the special election issue was approved, the bond attorneys (in cooperation with the engineering firm) provided all the technical information needed to support

---

of the engineering firm followed this up by a direct visit to the field office of the federal agency.

the offering and call for bids; and the engineering firm (in cooperation with the investment company) drafted the city ordinance establishing a sewer-rate schedule to provide income for the repayment of the bonds. Finally the investment security firm supplied the Housing and Home Finance Agency with all the relevant technical information needed by that agency before it could approve purchase of the city's bonds; and the private firms collaboratively then produced a long list of documents that were required by the Housing Agency before the actual purchase of the bonds could take place.[9]

This sort of service to localities by private firms is exceedingly widespread, although existing data do not make it possible to provide exact calculations of its importance in comparison with projects managed by localities themselves. The engineering firm which handled Casa Grande's affairs was one of the largest in Arizona, and a major fraction of its business was with state and local governments. Similar firms exist in other states, some highly specialized in school or road matters, some having wider scope. In Chicago a private engineering and consulting firm has had primary responsibility for constructing the mammoth airport facilities at O'Hare Field. In Arkansas, private organizations give cities and towns precisely the same sort of services described for Casa Grande in Arizona.

A number of private engineering and construction firms have departments whose sole responsibility is to encourage local governments to take advantage of existing state and national programs. In some places this service extends to bringing together citizens for the formation of special ad hoc governments to improve electrical, road, drainage, irrigation or other services. The private firms are then able to solicit funds and perform work for the very governments they helped to establish.

PUBLIC OFFICERS AND THE PUBLIC-PRIVATE MIXTURE

Private, quasi-governmental, and governmental areas shade so imperceptibly into each other that even public officials cannot distinguish among them. Local officers believe they are serving public purposes when promoting private interests. At least they find it convenient to act as if they did; and in

[9] In effect, the Housing and Home Finance Agency asked the city (through its private consultants) to supply justification for the sewage disposal plant very much like the original justification that was necessary for the Public Health Service. In addition there was required a classification of laborers and mechanics, their minimum hourly rates, certification by trade unions that the prevailing wage rates were being met, complete plans and contract documents for construction, and the actual forms for contract advertisements, instruction to bidders, forms of the contract, forms of the bid bond, forms of performance and payment bond, and a long list of additional technical data.

many cases they would not be returned to office if they tried to draw sharp lines of separation.

Simple cases of public support for private and quasi-public activities are those in which public funds are involved. The budget of a county or a city, for example, may contain appropriations for a humane society, a children's aid group, a tourist association, a Chamber of Commerce, a 4-H Club, a soldiers' burial fund, a family operated museum, a poultry society, and an agricultural fair.[10] A step removed from the cases of outright donations are those in which departments of a local government (or officers of those departments) are enrolled as active members of private or quasi-private organizations. Chambers of Commerce benefit frequently from this type of relationship.

The activities of locally elected officers, like the "case work" of congressmen and senators, often illustrate the public-private mixture. The mayor of Chicago traveled to Washington in February 1959 with a pocketful of problems to present to federal officers. He wanted increased aid for public housing, and he wanted the federal government to provide insurance on home mortgages for persons displaced by slum clearance projects. But his primary aim was to seek from defense department officials top priority for new defense contracts for the Ford Motor Company's aircraft engine factory in Chicago. The mayor explained that he wanted to obtain additional work for the Ford plant because layoffs there had resulted from cutbacks in defense spending.[11] His concern was not with what the cutbacks were doing to the nation's defense, over which he could have no comprehensive view, but rather with the unfortunate effects they were having on employment in Chicago.

Similarly, local prosperity and not national defense was the primary issue when Mayor George Christopher of San Francisco was charged by a political rival with having lost a valuable naval installation for the city. The mayor, his critic said, was "at fault for not sending a lobbyist to Washington, D.C., as we asked him to do. . . ." The mayor's response was to indicate that he would be his own lobbyist. He released a letter he had written to the senior senator from California in which he asked for a conference with "the highest officials of the Department of Defense" to discuss the city's future as a defense center. He said he would try to work out "a formula for the equitable distribution of shipbuilding and ship repair, along with other defense facilities, in this highly important strategic area."[12]

---

[10] State budgets, as well as the federal government's, are used for analagous purposes.
[11] *Chicago Sun Times*, February 4, 1959.
[12] *San Francisco Chronicle*, January 13, 1959. But on February 4, 1959, it was announced that San Francisco was sending a full-time lobbyist to Washington, D.C.

These are typical examples of public officers laboring for mixed public-private purposes. In such circumstances the private interests concerned, of course, collaborate. Energies are merged for a common end that can be designated either public or private, depending only upon the perspective from which it is viewed. For example, when it became known in Borger, Texas, shortly before World War II, that the federal government was expanding facilities to produce synthetic rubber, city officials and the managers of the city's largest industries were at one in believing that it would be wholly desirable to locate a new rubber manufacturing plant near Borger. The city was in an advantageous position because it was located close to a deposit of natural gas, a principal ingredient of synthetic rubber, and because a basic industrial complex, including large refineries, was already located nearby. Yet a number of other oil and natural gas centers were competing for the synthetic rubber factories, and it was by no means certain that one would be located in or near Borger. Officials of the city, civic club leaders, and businessmen joined forces to fight for the plant. In the words of the city manager, "all of us worked like the devil, and [Senator] Tom Connally worked right along with us." The city manager, in company with officers of the petroleum corporation which would operate the plant, made a number of trips to Washington. City officials realized that their work benefited the petroleum company. Then and afterward, they were also sure that success in locating the plant near their town was of first civic importance. "It brought us some problems, but it also brought us a lot of new residences and a lot of our prosperity."

The extreme case of the public-private mixture occurs when a single person cannot tell at a given moment whether he performs a public or a private service. In Texas a number of cities have official Boards of City Development. Board members in Borger were appointed automatically by the city council on the nomination of the local Chamber of Commerce, and the secretary of the Chamber was automatically named manager of the Board of City Development. In this way fifteen leading businessmen of the city were given official advisory posts in the city government. Moreover, the Chamber of Commerce in 1958 received half its total budget by a direct subvention from the city in the form of an appropriation to the official Board of Development. It was hard to say whether the city paid the Chamber to do the city's work, whether the city paid for the private activities of the Chamber, or whether the Chamber made a contribution of labor and time to the city for public purposes.

All three were true, and they were true of many individual actions by many persons. The Chamber, for example, was responsible through its paid staff for developing the sidewalk and sewer programs of the city. Sidewalks were built only if 50 per cent of the homeowners on a given block agreed to pay the cost, at which time all owners could be assessed. Chamber staff members drummed up the needed support. Even more significantly, a given individual simultaneously represented the private Chamber of Commerce and the public Development Board in matters involving the state and federal governments. Representations were made (before federal agencies) to increase postal services and to extend airline services and (before state agencies) to build a colosseum just outside the city limits. In all such matters, a community spokesman truthfully could say that he represented both the Chamber and the city; if pressed, he could not distinguish one role from the other. It was even impossible to determine at any given moment whether a representative of Borger was spending private or public funds. The Chamber secretary and Development Board manager explained:

I go to Washington to testify before the Civil Aeronautics Board as a representative of this city. I don't know until I come back whether my trip will be charged to Chamber [private] or Development Board [public] funds. What difference does it make? They are used for the same purpose. I see which of the funds has more liquid cash in it. Then I charge my trip to the one that can take the item most easily.

THE PUBLIC ROLE OF PRIVATE GROUPS

The dependence of local governments upon civic organizations for the performance of public functions is in some cases the simple result of official caution or official ineptitude.[13] And the incentive of private firms is clear: it is profit. What is less simple and less clear is more important for understanding the operation of the American system of government.

First, the sponsorship of public activities by civic and social groups provides the local community the means for trying out politically what otherwise might not be tried at all. If private sponsorship proves successful, the public body often assumes responsibility with minimum risk of political penalty.

Second, private civic sponsorship also gives the people of a community a sense of molding activities to their own specifications. This is particularly true in large national programs, like that of veterans' welfare services: one can go to his friend at the grocery store or the freight office and there find personal aid in matters involving complicated forms and distant Washington

---

[13] This accounts for the important role played by the Community Club in the upstate New York community of Springdale, according to Arthur J. Vidich and Joseph Bensman, *Small Town in Mass Society* (Princeton: Princeton University Press, 1958), pp. 130–31.

offices. The services of government are thus translated into very human and very personal terms.

Third, the network of public services maintained by private groups represents in some measure savings to public treasuries. A clear case is the failure of DuBois County to appoint an official veterans' service officer. It is true for many other private-public services. The Community Chest budget of any large city may include *lagniappe* items such as summer camps that might be deemed inappropriate for public treasuries in some (but not all) local communities. But such private budgets contain many items—hospital and welfare services, for example—that would undoubtedly become charges against a public budget if they were not supported by privately-collected funds.[14]

Fourth, from the private side, the public-private mixture plays an important legitimating role. For civic groups it provides purpose and status. For individuals it rectifies what in other circumstances might be deemed improper. A businessman seeking special consideration from a federal agency may have less need for aggressiveness when he can in truth say he is also performing a public service. But if he must be demanding, he can be so with relative impunity when accompanied by city officials who argue that what the businessman wants is what the city needs.

Fifth, the firms for profit supply the expertise and sophistication needed for the planning and execution of large and complex governmental programs. They are a supplementary arm of local governments—like state agencies in some programs, like professional associations in others—that make it possible for localities to deal expertly and aggressively with the state and federal governments. "What the engineering firm did for us on the sewage disposal system," said the city manager of Casa Grande, "We could not possibly have done for ourselves." From this point of view the private firms are substitutes for the civil servants and other professional workers of larger governments. They aid in balancing the scale of power, particularly the power of knowledge and of specialization, between small and large local governments and between units of the federal system.

Sixth, the specialized knowledge is also utilized as a means of communication. The *Federal Contributions* manual of the Civil Defense Administration is a large and cumbersome set of regulations, resembling a big-city phone

---

[14] It may be true that the total *social* cost would be less for the same services if they were entirely supported by public funds and entirely administered by public officials. This might, for example, reduce costs of duplicating personnel for both fund raising and administration. Assuming this to be true does not negate the point made in the text. Year to year budgetary savings for public bodies are not inconsistent with larger total public-private costs.

book in size, and reads partly like a legal, partly like an engineering text. City officials, especially those in smaller places, have neither the time nor the skill to make full use of it. Salesmen for electronic manufacturing firms are of first importance in bringing possible federal contributions to the notice of local officers.[15] The private engineering firm serving Casa Grande was assiduous in pointing out forms of federal and state aid to local officers in Arizona. Municipal officials of Casa Grande were informed in the first place by that firm of the existence and availability of a number of federal grants from which the city has profited. Other firms in other fields in other states perform the same communications function.

Seventh, knowledge and specialization, given impetus by the desire for profit, are powers of persuasion. The typical contract provides no payment to the private firm unless the grant applied for is received, the bonds are sold, or the facility is built. Considerable investments, especially investments of time, are made in the early stages of any federal contract, and these investments have to be protected by a high percentage of successes. This is a strong spur to the private firm to render rapid and professionally competent work that will stand the scrutiny of federal inspection. It also enlists the private firms in campaigns for winning approval of local proposals. The process is a simple and natural one. It is abetted by the easy professional ties that exist between federal and private lawyers, engineers, school specialists, and financial experts. They talk the same language. A phone call or a cocktail conversation can settle in a few moments a problem that might go unsolved for months if it followed the official channel from federal to state to local officer to private consultant and then back up the chain.

Finally and most importantly, the civic groups, local officials and firms-for-profit come together at this point of persuasion. Working as a single unit for a single purpose they utilize all possible avenues for fostering the local program. They can speak with the voice of the Chamber of Commerce at one moment, the Rotary at another, the City Council at a third, the expert engineer at a fourth. They can present their cause at a congressional hearing,

---

[15] A city manager of a small midwestern town told an interviewer that he had received a two-way radio system from the CAA "by courtesy of the General Electric Company." The manager said that "the GE salesman told me about the program and filled in all the forms." The interviewer noticed that the radio was made by the Motorola Company. "Sure," said the manager, "that poor GE fellow did all the work and was then underbid by Motorola. But it was still his idea." During World War II the Office of Price Administration carried on an elaborate information program to keep butchers informed of rationing and price changes. But a study revealed that butchers hardly ever utilized the official publications. They acted upon information received from their wholesalers.

a public meeting, or an administrative conference; and although the cause is one, the local voices are varied for maximum effectiveness. If a congressman needs persuading, a friend of the congressman will phone or wire him. If a conference in a senator's office will expedite matters, someone in the nexus of public-civic-private relationships can be found to make such a conference possible and effective.

In sum, the public activities of civic groups and business firms strengthen the position of local governments, especially small local governments, *vis-à-vis* the state and federal governments. As the local government's equivalent of a professional, specialized civil service, the firms-for-profit play the principal role. As a powerful lobbying aid at all administrative and legislative points, the civic and social groups are most prominent.

THE STRENGTH OF THE MOBILIZED COMMUNITY FRONT

The mobilized locality is very strong indeed. A single small city can win significant concessions from both state and federal officials in establishing personnel standards for the administration of public assistance programs. Local insistence not only maintained in office a person formally without qualifications for his job; it also led to the alteration of state merit standards in order to qualify the unqualified local incumbent, as well as to the approval of this change by federal officials.[16]

When a federal agency decided for economy reasons to close a field office in a city of 49,000, local officials and businessmen mobilized in protest. They were able to bring together for a final conference an assistant secretary of one of the great federal departments, four congressmen and spokesmen for three others, and spokesmen for two senators. The decision was made to keep the office open.[17] When it was announced that a link of the national highway system was to run through Hillcrest, an unincorporated suburb of Binghamton in upper New York State, residents of the community first asked themselves in despair, "What chance do we have against the State Department of Public Works and the United States Bureau of Public Roads?" They discovered that their chances were very good indeed. The local citizens established a protest group that included representatives of the Rotary and the Kiwanis, a number of churches, the American Legion, the PTA, the

---

[16] See Paul N. Ylvisaker, "The Battle of Blue Earth County," in Harold Stein, ed., *Public Administration and Policy Development* (New York: Harcourt, Brace & World, Inc., 1952), pp. 89–106.

[17] Field notes of Kenneth E. Gray, Washington, D.C. February 1958.

Town Board, the Board of Education, the Children's Home, several garden clubs, and a general community association. Leaders of this group were soon in touch with the local congressmen, the state senator, the appropriate state and district engineering officers, civil defense authorities, local planning boards, and other officials. "We kept Albany and the Washington Bureau of Public Roads and our legislators at all levels apprised of what we were doing." When their request that the highway be built at another place was initially rejected, the group simply redoubled its efforts. An impartial expert was employed, the local congressmen and both New York senators were again contacted, and over a thousand signatures, telegrams, and letters appealed to Governor Harriman. The state senator arranged a meeting between community leaders and the Superintendent of the State Department of Public Works. Subsequently, a new routing of the highway was established.[18]

Many more examples could be given. The mobilized community—in which the private and public spheres act as one—is potent far beyond numbers. It takes full advantage of the openness of the political system, operating through diverse channels and hitting many points of the legislative-administrative process. In short, it makes use of what I have called "multiple crack."[19] The mobilized community capitalizes on the regard of the legislative member for the local constituency, a regard that must be maintained if the legislator is to remain in office. It can be obdurate and badger an administrative official, knowing that the local congressmen are watchdogs of any administrative affront to local interests.

VARIATIONS IN LOCAL INFLUENCE

Evidence of the strength of the mobilized locality in influencing state and federal programs is of course no evidence of absolute local control over those programs. Full consideration of limitations on, and variations in, local power would have to consider that local strength in national affairs varies markedly from program to program. Local control over the many projects of the United States Army Corps of Engineers is maximized by virtue of the Corps' definition of its mission, its relationship to Congress, and its procedures for determining what to do. Though local influence is not inconsiderable with respect to foreign policy, the nature and extent of that influence is of a

---

[18] Polly Traeger, "Extinction by Thruway: The Fight to Save a Town," *Harper's Magazine*, December 1958, pp. 61–71.

[19] Morton Grodzins, "American Political Parties and the American System," *Western Political Quarterly*, Vol. XIII, No. 4 (December 1960), pp. 974–998.

different and lesser order than is true with respect to most domestic areas.[20] Furthermore, some localities have greater power than others in state and federal legislatures (here rural local governments have an advantage); some places have greater influence than others in the election of chief executives (the big cities are at a relative advantage in affecting the presidency, and urban areas in general are becoming more powerful in governors' offices); and certain kinds of cities have natural alliances with national interest groups (for example, the NAACP and Chicago's mayor are not likely to take opposite stands on any major issue). The effectiveness of any particular city in promoting or opposing a given federal action is likely to be affected by such larger considerations.

On the other hand, the issue of party is not likely to be controlling. A mobilized community, by definition, is one in which public-private proponents from both parties are involved. Aid from congressmen and senators follows as a matter of course. If the community majority and a crucial congressman or senator are of the same party (and faction), the city's cause may be aided. But party congruence is by no means necessary. A congressman is likely to work very hard for a community in which he does not have a majority of votes; he sees an opportunity to win new friends. So partisanship gives way before community programs that cut across party lines, a process made easier by the relative lack of definition in party lines.

The degree of community mobilization produces the chief variations in local influence on federal programs. Where local leaders are skillful in producing community consensus, where they understand the political resources of the united public-private front, where they can exploit the sensitivity to local demands by national legislators and administrators, localities have maximum power. Success is easier where there is substantial social and political homogeneity. Again, this gives advantage to the smaller and more rural places where, if actual homogeneity does not exist, dissidents at least are not likely to be noisy. Larger urban places suffer in this game because of their lack of consensus (the urban masses, it turns out, are not a mass but a highly differentiated social structure). When a community loses in a contest of strength with a federal agency, it often turns out, on closer inspection, that the community is splintered. Such a situation not only decreases its strength but gives federal officials an opportunity to reward friendly factions and punish unfriendly ones. An apparent local defeat is, therefore, often a victory

[20] With respect to foreign policy, see Dennis Palumbo, "The States in American Foreign Policy," unpublished doctoral dissertation, Department of Political Science, University of Chicago, 1960.

for one local group. Where local groups are united and determined, defeat is unlikely.

CONCLUSIONS

This essay has attempted to show some of the many overlaps between public and private spheres at the local level and demonstrate the importance of the public-private linkage in giving strength to local governments in their relationships with the federal government. There are three concluding observations.

First, the power of the mobilized community (or group of communities) is the power of those who feel strongly about a given matter and are willing to work for it. Yet the widespread understanding among localities that the system may operate to their special advantage cuts in two directions. On the one hand, acting upon that understanding often gives them what they want. On the other hand, it sets up numerous competing influence sources. If every individual locality, and every group of localities, and every group of officers serving localities were well organized to exercise influence on national programs, the influence of any single place or group would thereby be diminished. Special privileges are readily available only if the knowledge and skill necessary to achieve them are relatively limited. Widespread sensitivity to what localities may accomplish with respect to federal programs means, in effect, that the special influence of one locality or one group of localities is continuously checked by the influence of others. The wealth of the nation is such that accommodations to many special requests are possible. At the very least, attempts to satisfy competing special interests have the effect of freeing the hands of those who have broader views. The competition of special interests makes it easier to assert and implement a more general interest.

Second, local communities, even assuming maximum skill in mobilizing the public-private spheres, do not always win. But they are full and powerful partners in the process of decision-making. In most programs at most times some group of localities (or a single one) exercises a substantial influence. The fact of local influence has more meaning to the local leaders concerned than the fact of federal financing or general federal rule-making. From this perspective many federal programs may be considered local programs. The sense of substantial participation and the fact of substantial influence are everywhere apparent.

Finally, the data illustrate the falsity of the rhetoric of local-federal conflict. Though local communities gird themselves to mold federal programs to their desires, federal agencies are themselves organized to make this process an easy one. The two planes of government are not adversaries. They serve the same people for the same ends. If local advantage occasionally means national disadvantage, the congruence of advantages is far more frequent. (There is even a national interest in the pork barrel.) "Victory" for the locality, among those most concerned, is rarely conceived as national "defeat." The Public Health Service did not grant funds grudgingly to Casa Grande for a sewage disposal plant. National and local officers toasted each other when Chicago's application for a large urban renewal program was approved by the Housing and Home Finance Agency.

The traditionally described three-level American government is in fact telescoped on the community. From the point of view of the local consumer of governmental products, the American system of government is not a pyramid, but a range of services sometimes supplementary and sometimes duplicative but rarely alternative. No logic can distinguish between the local character of government's services and the non-local character of another's.[21] The federal government has built city halls for many cities and has paid for tearing down slums in others. It provides for the health of new mothers. It draws plans for the best land use for a poor farmer and supplies funds for the construction of a vast manufacturing plant to a multimillion-dollar corporation. It constructs schools here and libraries there. It aids one community in drawing up a city plan, supplies a second with funds to build a sewer, gives a park to a third, and provides expert advice to the police chief of a fourth when the hardware store is robbed. Federal activities of this sort are as close to the citizen as any activities of the states and localities, however closeness may be defined. They are also close to local citizens because, by the process of public-private mobilization, they are substantially controlled by those citizens. The typical situation is one in which all governments participate in given activities. To deny the local character of federal activities one would be forced to deny the local character of local governments. Closeness to the citizen is an attribute of all American governments. Local is as local does.

Suggestions for Further Reading

On relationships between the public and private:

Foss, Phillip, *Politics and Grass* (Seattle: University of Washington Press, 1960).

[21] See Morton Grodzins, "Issues of Centralization and Decentralization in the American Federal System," in a forthcoming volume ed. by Robert Goldwin (Chicago: Rand McNally & Co., 1963).

Garceau, Oliver, *The Political Life of the American Medical Association* (Cambridge, Massachusetts: Harvard University Press, 1941).

McConnell, Grant, *The Decline of Agrarian Democracy* (Berkeley, California: University of California Press, 1953).

Selznick, Philip, *TVA and the Grass Roots* (Berkeley, California: University of California Press, 1953).

Truman, David B., *The Governmental Process: Political Interests and Public Opinion* (New York: Alfred A. Knopf, Inc., 1951).

On the American federal system:

Anderson, William, *The Nation and the States, Rivals or Partners?* (Minneapolis, Minnesota: University of Minnesota Press, 1955).

Elazar, Daniel J., *The American Partnership: Intergovernmental Cooperation in Nineteenth Century American Federalism* (Chicago: University of Chicago Press, 1962).

Grodzins, Morton, "The Federal System," in *Goals for Americans* (The President's Commission on National Goals) (Englewood Cliffs, N. J.: Prentice-Hall, Inc., 1960).

Macmahon, Arthur W., ed., *Federalism, Mature and Emergent* (New York: Doubleday & Company, Inc., 1955).

THE EVOLUTION OF UNITED STATES FOREIGN ECONOMIC POLICY

Arthur Smithies

ECONOMIC POLICY IN AMERICAN FOREIGN POLICY

One of the striking facts of the postwar world is that economic policy has become a major instrument of the foreign policy of the United States and all other major countries of the world. The frightfulness of nuclear weapons has led the contestants to seek additional methods for conducting the cold war, and economic policy has assumed an increasingly important role. The United States realized that the Free World would be endangered unless its members have good prospects of economic improvement. The Communist Bloc, on the other hand, attempts to persuade the uncommitted countries that communism offers the only solution to their economic problems. Even if there were no ideological conflict between communism and capitalism, the advent of more than fifty newly independent countries on the world scene, most of which are poor and underdeveloped, would bring economic questions

ARTHUR SMITHIES *has been Professor of Economics at Harvard University since 1949, Nathaniel Ropes Professor since 1957. During World War II, he was Chief of the Economic Bureau in the U.S. Bureau of the Budget; subsequently Director of the Fiscal and Trade Policy Division of the Economic Cooperation Administration and Economic Adviser for the Office of Defense Mobilization. He was also a member of the secretariat both at Bretton Woods where the International Bank was established and at San Francisco where the United Nations Charter was written. He is author of* The Budgetary Process in the United States *(1954) and a frequent contributor to professional journals.*

to the forefront of international politics. Finally it is hoped that economic unification may help to avoid the political chaos in Europe that has produced two world wars.

The use of economic measures as an instrument of foreign policy is a new preoccupation for the United States. On some occasions in the past, it may have attempted to secure economic advantages through its political influence abroad. But in general its policy was one of economic isolation.

Up to World War I, the abundant resources of the country were cultivated under the shelter of a high protective tariff. Foreign capital was far less important than domestic accumulation. The main resource obtained from the rest of the world was the indispensable flow of skilled and unskilled immigrants from Europe. Foreign trade was of minor importance; after the Civil War, the United States actually ceased to be an important mercantile maritime power.

After World War I, although we badly needed a foreign economic policy, we continued to do without one. High protection was still the gospel. But at the same time we became a large private commercial lender to Europe. Our unwillingness to accept imports meant, in effect, that Europe had to borrow in the United States to pay for the goods it needed and to repay past loans. Probably nothing could have averted the worldwide impact of the American depression of the Thirties, but the lack of a coherent foreign economic policy hastened its spread, and helped to deprive Europe of any real prosperity in the 1920's.

During the 1930's, our policies were still inadequate and contradictory. Devaluation of the dollar in 1933 may have helped our own recovery, but it did so by "exporting" unemployment to other countries. We did not import as much as we exported; and other countries had to pay us in gold. At the same time nationals in other countries were sending their capital here because of uncertainties in Europe. Consequently most of the world's gold stock found its way to Fort Knox—to the embarrassment of the United States and the rest of the world.

In 1934, however, the Trade Agreements Act was passed. This reversed in principle the high protection policy of the past, and set the pattern for the future. The Act was due almost entirely to the fervent beliefs of Cordell Hull and a small group of disciples, and ran counter to the general policies of economic isolation of the Roosevelt Administration. Reciprocal tariff reductions during the 1930's were substantial, but outside the United States they were easily offset by other forms of import restriction. However, the United States had committed itself to a principle from which it has never receded, and which it now proposes to extend.

During World War II, Allied policy makers realized the need, in the post-war world, for national and international policies that were less chaotic and haphazard than those that had bedeviled the world in the past. In 1944, the Bretton Woods Conference, including both Russia and China, set up the International Monetary Fund and the International Bank for Reconstruction and Development, the one to stabilize currencies and the other to provide long-term loans in equal measure to countries devastated by war and to underdeveloped countries. Far from the roar of guns and politics, one felt that rural New Hampshire had delivered the solution to the problems of the postwar world. But it was not to be. Although both institutions have flourished, the hope of cooperation with Russia was soon dispelled and they are but one component of the economic arrangements of the Free World.

Together with Bretton Woods, the United States proposed an International Trade Organization that would embody the spirit of the Trade Agreements Act and negotiate worldwide reduction of trade banners on a multilateral basis. Owing to congressional resistance, this grand vision failed to materialize. Instead the General Agreement on Tariffs and Trade provided for multilateral reduction under the authority of the Trade Agreements Act. Negotiations under the GATT have converted the United States from a high tariff to a low tariff country and its industry is less highly protected than that of Western Europe.

Realization of the hopes expressed in the Bretton Woods Agreements was to be delayed. The happy illusion that there was to be one postwar world was rapidly dissipated, and the economic dislocations of the Free World proved to be far more serious than they had appeared in New Hampshire. The British loan in 1945, emergency aid to France and Italy, financial support for Germany and the Marshall Plan in 1947 all testified to the fact that Europe could not earn the dollars required to pay for the imports needed for economic recovery. In fact, during the Marshall Plan period, the belief became widespread that the competitive position of the United States was so strong that the dollar shortage would last indefinitely.

The outbreak of the Korean War and the imminence of the communist threat to Western Europe, made apparent by the conquest of Czechoslovakia, ushered in the period of military aid both to the NATO alliance and to the countries on the periphery of the Communist Bloc throughout the world. The provision of weapons as military assistance had to be accompanied by further economic assistance from the United States.

Meanwhile colonial empires were dissolving; and every newly independent country adopted economic development as its slogan, as a successor to liberation. The deliberate procedures of the International Bank have been far from sufficient to cope with the problem of economic development assistance. Beginning with President Truman's Point Four in 1951, countries on both sides of the Iron Curtain and the United Nations have been preoccupied in major and controversial ways with the problem of development aid. Until recently the United States addressed its attention mainly to the Far East and South Asia. The problems of the new countries of Africa are new, complex and bewildering. Meanwhile we have discovered to our chagrin that we cannot take Latin America for granted. At the present time the United States is providing development assistance, including technical help, public grants and loans, and agricultural commodities to about fifty countries. President Kennedy has announced that the 1960's is to be the Decade of Development.

With respect to the Communist Bloc, our policy has been one of dis-association. The United States maintains a complete embargo on trade with Communist China. Since 1947 we have restricted or eliminated exports of items of strategic importance to the Soviet Union and have attempted, with indifferent success, to persuade our Western allies to do likewise. Over the years our early, broad conceptions of "strategic importance" have been considerably narrowed, so that now prohibitions are confirmed to items that have a fairly direct military significance. Nevertheless United States trade with Russia remains far more restricted than that of its Western allies. But while our direct relations with the Communist Bloc remain remote, we are competing with them incessantly for the underdeveloped countries. It is largely by using economic means to win those areas to Communist allegiance that Mr. Khrushchev hopes "to bury us."

The area of signal and striking success of U.S. foreign economic policy has been Western Europe. While European recovery has been chiefly due to the regenerative forces within Europe, those forces could hardly have come into play without the Marshall Plan. Not only did the plan provide needed resources for Europe, but it helped sow the first seeds of European economic unity, and to introduce Europe to American concepts of productivity. But even if the United States had something to do with the conception of the Common Market, it did not foresee the outcome. An area that we had grown accustomed to regard as a poor relation is rapidly becoming an economic entity as powerful and as productive as the United States itself. Needless to say, Europe, with the exceptions of Greece, Turkey and Spain, is no longer in need of American aid. On the contrary, the Six have become aid-providing countries themselves. The Atlantic Community has ceased to be divided into currency areas and is rapidly becoming a vast single region of economic competition.

Partly as a result of the extent and pace of European recovery, the international economic position of the United States has changed profoundly. The shortage of dollars which a few years ago was believed to be enduring has disappeared. Instead the United States is finding difficulty in earning enough foreign currencies to provide for the payments it has to make abroad on public and private account. For the first time in its history, it finds that its freedom of economic action is constrained by the need to keep its balance of payments in order. At the same time the United States remains aware that the way in which it conducts its own economic affairs can profoundly influence any international economic arrangements. For international order to exist, national and international policies must be harmonized.

This capsule account of American economic foreign policy reveals an unmistakable trend away from economic isolation and indifference towards a positive desire to extend and preserve the area of economic freedom according to the principles of Adam Smith and Cordell Hull. But it also reveals recognition of the fact that liberal trading policies alone will not alleviate the desperate poverty that still afflicts hundreds of millions of people. Finally, United States policy is based on the premise that half the world is not free and is unlikely to be for the indefinite future. In the economic, as well as the political and military areas, the facts of competitive coexistence must be faced.

Foreign economic policy, therefore, cannot be discussed in terms of pursuit of a single clearcut objective. Rather, a number of interrelated policies must be simultaneously carried out. The subject must therefore be discussed in terms of its major components. These are policies with respect to Western Europe; with respect to the underdeveloped countries; with respect to the Communist Bloc, and with respect to the United States economy itself, with particular reference to the balance of payments.

THE UNITED STATES AND WESTERN EUROPE

The Common market of the Six is already an accomplished fact. The process of economic unification has already gone so far that the member countries and their citizens have acquired compelling interests in its continued success. It has borne out the hopes of the early post-war planners that close economic cooperation can precede political agreement, and can itself lead in the direction of political unity. The other European countries feel that they have little choice but to join the Six. Their hopes for establishing a rival free trade area were doomed from the outset. The United Kingdom with understandable anguish has decided that its future lies more with Europe than with the

Commonwealth and Empire. There is now a good prospect that the whole of Western Europe will be surrounded by a common external tariff. The crucial outstanding question is whether that tariff will be high or low.

The administration of the United States has decided that the interests of the United States and the rest of the world demand that the Common Market tariff be low, even at the cost of extensive reductions in United States tariffs. If the President's proposals are substantially enacted, not only will low tariffs prevail between the United States and Europe, but between both areas and the rest of the world.

Without question both areas can benefit by an extension of reciprocal trade. But in the process of bargaining, European restrictions need to be reduced more than American. The United States has already become a low tariff country. On the other hand, European countries retain many restrictions on trade (such as import quotas) besides tariffs. Ironically, they were encouraged by the United States to economize on dollar imports during the Marshall Plan period. Rather than provide them with more dollars with which to buy our goods during the period of stringency, we encouraged them to protect themselves against our goods. This was a penny-wise decision whose consequences we are now striving to reverse.

Beneficial though a vast trading area is, Europe and the United States are each large enough to provide economies of scale. There can be little doubt that both regions can attain great prosperity with the present degree or with a greater degree of separation from each other. In fact, both have. Contrary to most of the arguments advanced for the trade program, I do not believe that the economic benefits of direct trade between the two regions is its most important aspect. To say this is not to disparage the program, but merely to emphasize its most important aspects.

For the Free World as a whole it is of the utmost importance that the countries in Latin America, Africa, Asia and Oceania have access to the markets of the West. At the present time both the United States and, to a greater extent, Europe severely restrict imports of primary products on which many underdeveloped countries depend for their livelihood. Inability to earn export income has meant increasing reliance on direct economic aid to pay for needed imports. But direct aid does not provide employment for millions of workers who depend on the export industries.

The underdeveloped countries, however, depend not only on exports of primary products, but their future progress depends heavily on their being able to expand industrial exports as well. For instance, India's future in the free world, and its eventual independence of aid, depends on its ability to pay for its imports by exporting the products of its new industries to Free World markets.

Of critical importance in this connection is Japan, which is far from under-developed, but whose economic situation is precarious. Its economic survival and its continued alignment with the West depend on its ability to export industrial commodities to the United States, and Europe. Because a combi-nation of low wages and high technical efficiency make it a formidable competitor, nearly every Western country formally or informally discrimi-nates against Japanese exports. If the West resorts to high rather than low tariff policies, the discrimination will become more severe. In that event, it is virtually certain that Japan will be driven to close economic association with the Communist Bloc—not from choice, but as a matter of practical necessity.

A vital feature of trade negotiations between the United States and Europe is that tariff reductions be generalized to cover the entire Free World. In my opinion, that is their most important economic purpose. Generalization on a most-favored-nation basis is the declared intent of the United States, and it is essential that Europe take the same point of view. But the task will not be easy, especially since agriculture protection has a demonstrated ability to withstand assaults upon it.

A second point concerning the importance of trade concerns its political effects. Does free trade between regions facilitate or impede political co-operation? Free trade within Europe seems to be driving the European countries towards closer political association. They realize that the survival of the Common Market demands harmonization of domestic economic policies. Economic cooperation can lead to greater cohesiveness in other aspects of political life. Against this point of view the aphorism that good fences make good neighbors may be invoked. Even taken literally this may not be true of Berlin. Moreover the analogy of a tariff with a fence is a false one. Trade barriers represent a state of active rivalry rather than passive separation. Can close political cooperation exist under these circumstances? I pose these matters as questions rather than assertions. The answers to them may be of critical importance from the point of view of the political unity of the Atlantic community and the whole free world.

The growth and strength of the European economy requires further revisions of American policy—which are already under way—with respect to the provision of development aid and collective defense. It is and should be a cardinal point of U.S. policy that Europe is an equal partner with it in sup-porting and promoting economic development and other international programs. Quite apart from the question of economic cost, the European countries have political interests in economic development identical with those of the United States. It is their responsibility more than ours to lay the ghosts of the colonial period.

The increasing strength of the European economy also calls for revision of collective defense arrangements. The original NATO system was devised in 1950 when Europe had not fully recovered and was still short of dollars. The United States therefore provided many military items free, extended economic aid to enable European countries to support their forces, and encouraged military production in Europe in order to economize on "dollar" equipment. Though economic aid to Europe has now ceased, there is still substantial aid to Europe in the form of weapons. It is now time to consider removing remaining vestiges of the NATO economic arrangements and to regard the United States as a main source of supply of military equipment, for cash payment. Important steps in this direction have already been taken; Germany is making large purchases of weapons in the United States.

The idea of European purchase in the United States is offensive both to military and to pacifist sentiment. The military like military assistance because they doubt whether European countries will purchase enough; and they also like to have an outlet for United States weapons that have become obsolescent from the point of view of U.S. forces themselves. Those who fear the momentum of the arms race object on the grounds that the United States should not become dependent on export of arms to balance its international payments. To do so would create still another obstacle to disarmament.

These objections have weight, but the arguments on the other side are also impressive. From the strictly economic standpoint, the United States is the most efficient arsenal in the Free World, insofar as advanced technological weapons are concerned. In recent years, it has devoted more research and development to the military sector, while Europe has built up its civilian industries. The orthodox principles of international trade suggest that arms from the United States should be traded for civilian goods from Europe.

Furthermore, economic burden-sharing may improve the political health of the Western Alliance. NATO never seems to have functioned as a true partnership. Europeans in one mood seem to believe that they are being endangered in order to defend the United States; in another, that the United States will not defend them at risk of serious damage to itself. The establishment of a more equal economic partnership may help but no more than help to resolve these difficulties.

I have tried to show that the trade negotiations between the United States and Europe have much wider implication than the negotiation of reciprocal trading benefits between two trading partners. If they are to be fruitful, they must imply the establishment of a liberal multilateral trading system throughout the entire Free World. Such a system, inevitably, carries with it changes in international political relationships. For it to be successful it also imposes limitation on the freedom of the parties with respect to their domestic policies.

THE UNITED STATES AND ECONOMICALLY
UNDERDEVELOPED COUNTRIES

The promotion of economic development throughout the world has become a major component of foreign economic policy with bewildering suddenness. Of the two billion people outside the Communist Bloc about half a billion live in rich industrial countries, the rest in countries whose state of economic well-being is extraordinarily low by Western standards. Poverty is not new in the world. But fifty countries demanding economic improvement with nationalistic fervor, and blaming the West for their present plight—not without a modicum of justice—is a new phenomenon, one which has erupted since 1950. At the end of World War II, Latin America was the only major independent underdeveloped area.

The voice of the underdeveloped countries comes through more clearly than it otherwise might because we believe that many of them may choose the Communist alternative unless they can see a promising economic future in the Free World. Others may see their best prospects for the future in posing as so-called neutrals, playing one side against the other. Still others may allow their anti-colonial passions to preclude rational judgment.

(I shall henceforth use the initials EUC to denote "economically under-developed country." National sensitivities object to "underdeveloped" since many of them possess cultures and religions that do not deserve that designation. Consequently the words "emerging," "developing," or "less developed" are frequently used. The sad fact is that in many cases signs of emergence or development are few. Surely no one should object to calling countries whose incomes per head are one-tenth or less that of the United States "economically underdeveloped.")

Everyone will agree that economic aid has not worked miracles. Few of the EUC's can see ahead a clear road to economic improvement. Few of them are unequivocally committed to the Free World. Ten years of experience has furnished legitimate grounds for doubt and skepticism.

The United States embarked on aid to the EUC's in the first flush of the

Marshall Plan success, and hopefully assumed that a similar success could be achieved by similar methods. Or perhaps we made that assumption because there was no other one to make. In any event it was wrong. Europe, after all, was the cradle of industrialization. It possessed skilled management, skilled labor, technical ability, capital equipment, and an economic organization that was only temporarily dislocated by the war. Moreover the desire for economic success motivated not only the leaders of countries but the entire populations. Even wartime destruction and dislocation seems to have worked to their advantage. They were able to make a fresh economic start and to break away from the restrictions that had been hampering economic life. It is hard to believe that the Common Market would have come into being but for World War II.

After the Napoleonic wars Malthus pointed out how rapidly a vigorous population can repair losses of physical equipment. With respect to the EUC's, we have tended to accept the view that injections of physical equipment would infuse vigor and enterprise into the population. That was the doctrine on which the International Bank was set up, the doctrine of orthodox economics—a doctrine, incidentally, to which Malthus did not subscribe.

The last decade has taught us that orthodoxy was wrong in this respect. It is now realized that economic development depends on the human factor more than anything else. Consequently the emphasis has shifted not only to technical training, but to general education and public health measures. The hope is that a literate and a healthy population will make use of the tools that are provided in the form of aid, but, more importantly, will acquire the Western spirit of accumulation, and will provide themselves with tools from their own resources.

The slogan of the Decade of Development is that the United States will help those countries who are prepared to help themselves; in other words, to create the conditions that made the Marshall Plan a success. One example of self-help is land reform designed to get the land out of the hands of large and indolent landowners into the hands of an energetic and productive peasantry. Another example is tax reform that is both fair and yields revenue for development undertakings. A third is elimination of governmental corruption and extravagance.

From the Far East to Latin America, application of these simple ideas has been more difficult than their proponents thought. In countries on the rim of communist empires, opportunities for experiment are limited. We do not dare withdraw support from established regimes since the only organized alternative is a communist regime, which might not be corrupt but would not be on our side. Force of necessity may leave us with dubious clients.

One hopeful sign in Asia is the enterprise of the local military who, with no encouragement from the United States, have taken over the governments of Pakistan and South Korea. We may have to recognize that democracy is the privilege of the well-to-do and the literate and requires the support of a well-organized and efficient bureaucracy. In many newly independent countries the military are the only group with the ability and the integrity to conduct public affairs. Our recognition of military regimes implies not general approval of military governments, but realization that, like other forms of government, they can be malignant or benign. Even though not democratic they are not separated from the democracies of the Free World by the ideological gulf that separates us from communism.

Land reform may be the biggest hurdle that the Alliance for Progress has to clear. The owner of the hacienda is not a capitalist accumulator. As the classical economists pointed out, he is an employer of unproductive labor interested in continuing his opulent existence in the style to which he has become accustomed. His primary interests are neither to obtain maximum agricultural production from his land, nor to save and invest in industrial expansion. In conditions of modern uncertainty his savings are more likely to seek a safe haven abroad.

The difficulty in Latin America is that the landlords frequently exercise a controlling influence on government and they are understandably reluctant to legislate their own expropriation. Our hope is that the Alliance for Progress, supported by American aid, can bring to political power the liberal enterprising middle class who can overthrow the dominant landlord influence. To accomplish this change is far from a matter of simple economics or financial support. Meanwhile Cuba offers what appears to many of the impatient and dispossessed to be a more direct and attractive alternative.

One of the problems that bedevils Latin America is inflation. The standard cure for inflation is for governments to reduce expenditures and increase the severity of taxation. This remedy has recently been applied in British Guiana and in Argentina. In British Guiana an austerity budget recommended by a British economist was adopted by the Jagan government. A revolution ensued that ended the short-lived hopes of the first Marxist government on the South American continent and brought about a resumption of British authority. Economic austerity thus may have had beneficial consequences, but they were hardly those that were intended.

About 1960 Argentina adopted a program recommended by the International Monetary Fund to reverse the extravagances of Peron. The intervening period has been one of economic stagnation. At the same time its neighbor Brazil has been enjoying spectacular economic growth accompanied by equally spectacular inflation. In March 1962 the Frondizi government fell. While the relations of cause and effect are not as clear as they are in British Guiana, it is evident that the path of economic virtue can be hard for a liberal and well-intentioned government.

I give these examples not to suggest that the prescription of the Decade for Development is wrong. Economic development must depend basically on the efforts of the countries themselves. Economic aid will be wasted and misused if such efforts are not made. There is a record of successes as well as of failures. But an awareness of the difficulties is a necessary protection against disillusionment.

Perhaps the greatest difficulty remains to be mentioned, the population explosion. Because of the general reluctance of governments even to mention the matter, no independent writer would lose any opportunity to emphasize it. The facts are as widely known as they are ignored. If present rates of population increase are continued, the population of the EUC's taken together will double before the end of the century. That is a matter of arithmetic. To find out the period in which a number will double at compound interest, divide 72 by the rate of increase. An annual rate of increase of 2 per cent is commonplace in the EUC's. In some of the Latin American countries the rate is more than 3 per cent. A 2 per cent rate of increase means doubling in 36 years. During the last 10 years, the Indian population increased by as much as the entire population of the United Kingdom. Egypt already has twice the population of Holland and the same fertile land area.

Some population increase helps economic development and the increase in per capita incomes. Some of the EUC's are far short of the populations needed to exploit their natural resources effectively. But virtually all economists agree that the over-all increase in the EUC's is too high, from the point of view of raising living standards.

It is generally proclaimed that reduction of the economic disparities between the West and the EUC's is necessary for a stable and peaceful world. There can be little doubt that present rates of population increase will help to perpetuate those discrepancies.

The EUC's are thoroughly aware of the situation. Japan has adopted an effective and forthright birth control policy, without which its recent prosperity could not have been achieved. India has announced birth control to be its official policy, but so far that policy has hardly impinged on the procreative habits of 400 million people. Most if not all the remaining EUC's do not even have a policy.

The response of the United States so far has been to regard population increase as an argument for providing more aid, especially in the form of agricultural commodities. Relieving hunger appeals to basic humanitarian instincts and also helps to get rid of unwanted food surpluses. Looking at the matter brutally, we convert surplus wheat at home into surplus population abroad.

Perhaps that is the right policy. If a country can see some future other than Malthusian disaster, it may become less fatalistic in its attitudes. Individuals who see the prospect of economic improvement may learn to prefer further improvement to more children. Reduction of infantile mortality may lead parents to believe they need fewer children for economic security. But should the western governments remain silent on the population problem itself? Should they not at least express their willingness, upon request, to provide technical help in setting up programs and in conducting research in birth control methods? The political sensitivity of the subject may make it a suitable field of activity for the great private foundations of the United States. But the natural caution of the institutions makes it unlikely that they will act in the face of a completely passive attitude on the part of governments.

Western policy toward the EUC's is of course severely constrained by the apparent availability of the communist alternative and the active efforts of Russia and Communist China to promote it. In the ideological contest for the EUC's, the communists have some decided advantages. Whatever they have done within the borders of the Bloc, they were not the colonial powers that until recently ruled most of the EUC's; China can pose as a country that experienced the evils of imperialism but enjoyed few of its benefits. The Opium War is still recorded in the history books. Consequently they are able to keep alive the memory of the imperialist past of the West and to cast suspicion on present interventions, however well-intentioned and necessary.

Furthermore, communism seems to offer a quick and direct solution to the problems of development. Landlords can be expropriated, workers can be made to work by coercion, cajolery or appeals to their devotion to the state. Wages can be kept low and the economic surplus applied to industrialization. Economic progress will be rapid, and what if freedom is sacrificed for a generation, especially when for many the only visible freedom is freedom to starve. Russian industrial and technical success has been spectacular, but, after all, Russia is itself a Western country. The event that bemused the EUC's was China's "Great Leap Forward."

Fortunately for the West, neither Russia nor China has been able to cope with the obstinate peasant. He will not work in the manner prescribed, or, if he does, he is unwilling to turn over the produce of his toil to the state. Moreover, some of the communist countries have become disenchanted with central planning and control. Yugoslavia, for instance, is moving toward decentralization to such a degree that, in many respects, its economic decision-making is hard to distinguish from that of the United States. Finally the dissension between Russia and China may give pause to countries that feel inclined to join the Bloc. I do not mean to imply that choice of the communist alternative by EUC's is not still a threat to the West. But that threat does not seem quite so menacing as it was only three years ago. But it would be rash to assume that the EUC's are committed to find a "Western" solution to their development problems.

The United States and other Western countries for their part are committed to assist the EUC's to develop as free economies. This, of course, does not mean that we expect them to model their economics or their institutions on those of the United States. Forms of government and economic institutions must be adapted to local circumstances. The state must probably play a more prominent part in economic life than we would like to see. Democracy may not flower quickly. Freedom, however, does not lose its meaning because of such variations in national life. It retains definite meaning so long as the alternative of communist dictatorship exists. We espouse freedom in our own interest. But we can with equal sincerity espouse it in the interest of the countries themselves.

The commitment to aid a country involves a degree of involvement in its internal affairs that is contrary to the best traditions of correct diplomacy. Development does depend on the efforts a country makes for itself. The provision has shown that to attain the desired results, a positive influence must be exerted by aid-providing countries. This requires a degree of subtlety, firmness, and tact to which we are not entirely accustomed.

To avoid such relationships, the International Bank was restricted to financing specific development projects. Money could be paid out as the projects progressed and relationships between the Bank and the borrowing countries could be kept on a business rather than on a political basis. So it was hoped and believed. But the Bank itself has discovered that it cannot remain within the refuge of this restricted approach. The worthwhileness of a dam or a power plant depends on the economic state of the country. If its economy is stagnant or deteriorating, the project itself can be worthless. Consequently the Bank has had to satisfy itself that the country concerned is pursuing sound general economic policies, as part of its appraisal of the merits of particular projects.

Development policies, however, include matters outside the economic field, even broadly conceived. Education, health, land tenure and the very structure of government are involved. How can the United States or any other Western country use its influence? One possibility is to make the provision of aid strictly conditional on the accomplishment of reform. But then a difficult dilemma can easily arise: if the country fails to reform, it is in greater need of aid than if it does. Do we then cut off aid in the hope that making matters worse will eventually make them better? But making matters worse may mean permanent loss of the country to the free world. In such circumstances we usually submit as gracefully as we can; and it would have been better not to have adopted the firm and rigid tone in the first place. Success is more likely to result than the threat of sanctions. A country's prospects, policies, and intentions can be taken into account before an aid commitment is made, but commitments already made probably have to be carried out, even though conditions are not fulfilled.

The problem would be simplified by a selective rather than a wholesale approach to the provision of development aid and advice. If it were feasible, there would be much to be said for centering attention on a few countries whose prospects are good or whose strategic position is important. Success in a number of countries could stimulate others to follow their example. Meanwhile, aid to other countries would be confined to specific projects or grants of agricultural commodities. But such an approach may be no more than an academic pipe dream. One can imagine the consequences of selecting particular members of the Alliance for Progress for preferential treatment. At the present time, the U.S. seems committed to sponsoring the development of all countries that request our help, and most of them do.

However tactfully and skillfully the arts of persuasion are practiced, the relationship between providers and receivers of aid is likely to be difficult. In view of the colonial past, the United States is bound to be charged by the Left with imperialistic designs and sinister intentions. As a specific case in point, most economists would agree that private foreign investment has a useful role to play in economic development. But the United States immediately becomes suspect if it tries to persuade a country that its policies with respect to private investment are unduly restrictive. The United States government also has trouble with its own nationals when it tries to convince them that some restrictions on private foreign investment are warranted.

Some of these difficulties may be reduced or avoided by an international approach to aid. The International Bank is an intermediary between lending and borrowing countries. The Bank sells its bonds to citizens of lending countries and makes loans to governments of private businesses in the borrowing countries. United Nations Technical Assistance and its Special Fund have provided aid on a strictly international basis. But no national government has yet been prepared to entrust large capital funds to the United Nations or its agencies, and there is little likelihood that this attitude will change.

There is thus room for more informal international arrangements, such as the consortium of countries that consolidate their aid to India into a single program. Similar arrangements may be useful elsewhere. In Africa in particular the consortium idea seems promising. Relations between many of the newly independent countries and their former rulers will undoubtedly be strained. Yet the former colonial powers should be major providers of both aid and technical assistance. Countries such as the United States, Japan, Canada, and Australia that have had no previous history in Africa could usefully join in cooperative provision of aid. Undoubtedly Algeria will soon become a large-scale claimant for aid, and the merits of a collective approach to its provision are too evident to require further comment.

The Alliance for Progress attempts to ease the diplomatic problem of the United States by creating a consortium of receivers rather than providers of aid. It thus corresponds with the Office for European Economic Cooperation (OEEC) of the Marshall Plan. The difficulty with this kind of arrangement is that the members of the receiving consortium are extremely reluctant to make hard decisions in respect to each other. The United States never succeeded in persuading OEEC to allocate the amounts of aid that were available. The normal reaction of such a consortium is to please all its members by asking for more. Whether the Alliance for Progress can work differently remains to be seen.

This discursive account of the substantive and diplomatic aspects of the relations of the West with the EUC's should at least demonstrate that the subject is still full of unsolved problems. Despite the intensive and ardent research of the last ten years, we are still far from our theory of how rapid development can be achieved in countries that have fallen behind in the economic race. The historical record of development relates to the countries that have succeeded; to derive from their experience the remedy for underdevelopment is full of hazard. It is like deriving a theory of abnormal psychology from the study of normal human beings; perhaps development itself is the abnormality. So far, the majority of the human race has not participated in it extensively. In view of such uncertainties, both our prescriptions and our procedures must remain flexible and should be revised in the light of experience. Both the West and the EUC's are in the midst of a complicated and difficult learning process.

THE FREE WORLD AND THE COMMUNIST BLOC

Relations with the Communist Bloc impinge on every aspect of the foreign economic policy. In some ways economic measures can be used as positive instruments in the cold war. In the main, however, the expansionist and possibly disruptive economic activities of the Bloc call for defensive actions on the part of the West, in the sense that we want countries now in the Free World to avoid economic entanglements with the Bloc, that will have adverse political consequences.

A prime example of positive action is aid to Yugoslavia. To provide both military and economic aid has been the policy of successive United States administrations, but the policy has aroused considerable criticism. In my opinion, it is a valid objective of American policy to reduce the monolithic character of the Communist Bloc. On the other hand, we are not interested in strengthening any Communist power. A balance must be struck between these conflicting interests. As in the case of most foreign policy questions no simple dogma provides the right answer. In the Yugoslavian case, I see no reason to disagree with official policy.

An interesting issue has recently arisen with respect to the provision of surplus wheat to relieve mass starvation in Communist China. Should the United States follow the example of Canada and sell wheat to China; should it allow its citizens to do so; or should it even make grants of wheat as it does to other countries? All these questions have been officially answered in the negative. Perhaps that answer is right but the question is, nevertheless, complicated.

If the agricultural crisis is likely to bring about the downfall of the communist government, the argument against sending food is compelling. Harsh though such a decision may seem, it is no more destructive of human life than use of military force, which we are prepared to consider rationally. On the other hand, failure to provide food may make the Chinese government even more intransigent, if that is possible. One possibility is that the United States should supervise distribution throughout China. In this way humane instincts can be combined with political advantage.

In the independent EUC's, the West has to face the fact that the Bloc is an active competitor in the provision of foreign aid, and in the competition they have several advantages. In the first place they can adopt a selective approach, and concentrate their aid on countries such as India, Indonesia, Afghanistan, and Cuba, which are of strategic importance to them. They can afford to be selective because there is little danger that countries will become irrevocably committed to the West if they are not provided with Communist aid. And they welcome economic deterioration in countries that do not join the Bloc. The West does not feel it can afford these attitudes.

For the same reason, Bloc aid to any particular EUC can be provided on a selective basis. A steel mill, a hospital or a highway can be constructed; the Bloc can get the credit for it, and does not have to assume any responsibility for the development of the country as a whole. That can wait until the country decides to commit itself to Communism.

Finally, as stressed above, Russia and China are able to pose as the enemies of imperialism, and to align themselves with "the forces of liberation."

The Western countries have to accept the Bloc as competitors in the provision of aid. Their own purposes would be frustrated if they attempted to make refusal of communist aid a condition for receiving aid from the West. Such a course would inevitably give rise to vehement and successful charges of imperialism. The reply of the West must be a demonstration that Western methods of development are feasible. They can operate with the confidence that countries are likely to prefer success in the Free World to a future under communist authority.

With respect both to Western Europe and the EUC's, Bloc trading arrangements can present a definite political threat. If an independent country becomes committed to the Bloc as a dominant market for its exports, it inevitably becomes vulnerable to political blackmail. Instances of blackmail have already occurred in the cases of Iceland and Finland. The same problem arises in connection with Cuba. The trade embargo imposed by the United States is a gamble. If it brings about the downfall of the Cuban government, U.S. policy objectives will have been furthered. If it does not, it means that Cuba becomes tied to the Bloc by bonds of economic as well as political interest.

The favorite economic instrument of Bloc trade is the bilateral agreement which is essentially a barter agreement. Countries receive claims to goods rather than gold in exchange for their exports. One useful Western move would be to persuade Free World countries to sell to the Bloc only for gold or convertible currencies. This should insure that countries will not have to make political concessions in order to get imports in exchange for their exports. It would not, however, provide them with markets for their exports.

It is of the utmost importance that countries in the free world have export opportunities outside the Bloc. This emphasizes the need to reduce trade restrictions not only for the purpose of economic advantage, but also as a defensive measure in the cold war. But removal of trade restrictions may not be all that is needed. Suppose there is a slump in the world market for coffee, and the Russians undertake to buy the Brazilian coffee crop. That presents the West with a serious dilemma. It can accept the fact and the extension of Russian political influence that is likely to go with the transaction. Or various schemes of commodity stabilization can be considered. Every economist shudders at the prospect of international application of the type of policy that has burdened the United States with unwanted agricultural surpluses; and no international scheme has been devised that will insure against this consequence.

So far the Bloc countries do not appear to have made deliberate attempts to dislocate the trade of the Free World by "dumping." Such dislocation as they have caused has probably resulted from accident or bad administration rather than design. The reason is that those countries so far have been poor. They have needed all the imports they can obtain in exchange for their exports, and have not been able to afford to throw their goods on world markets merely to create political disturbance. But this will not always be the case. Russia in particular may soon be in a position to afford the luxury of dumping. China, although poor, may begin to engage in disruptive trading operations.

If the Bloc, as it grows in economic strength, pursues a disruptive trading policy on a large scale, liberal trade in the West may be far from enough. One can imagine conditions where the Western countries would virtually have to nationalize their own foreign trade in order to make adequate countermoves. These ominous possibilities have hardly been mentioned in policy discussions in the West. One can only hope that it is unduly alarmist to bring them to anyone's attention.

Finally the United States has to consider its general policy of restriction of East-West trade, especially in view of the fact that some of its major allies and closest neighbors do not share its point of view. Our general policy of restriction, and our complete embargo on trade with China, may have slowed down economic growth. On the other hand, it may simply have led them to greater efforts to grow in strength by imposing hardships on their populations or we may have merely diverted them to rely on European suppliers.

In the case of Russia there is no convincing evidence that our policies have been effective, even in the field of military weapons. Is there any possibility that a political *détente* may be made easier by increased trade? The United States supports that argument in connection with its relations with Europe. It could conceivably be valid with respect to the Communist Bloc.

THE UNITED STATES IN THE WORLD ECONOMY

One of the important lessons of the Great Depression was that no international system can withstand violent fluctuations in the domestic economies
of its leading members. This applies to the liberal multilateral world the
United States is trying to achieve. A major depression originating either in
the U.S. or in the Common Market can spread rapidly to the rest of the
world; the primary producing countries would likely be the worst sufferers.
Under such conditions, any international system would break down. The
immediate pressure of unemployment and underproduction would lead
countries to seek quick relief. This implies resort to policies of autarchy, of
which Germany in the 1930's was the leading example. But Germany was
not alone—in smaller measure, the United States followed the same line.

The only remedy for this kind of breakdown is domestic policies that will
avoid severe depressions. Purely international measures can do no more
than mitigate the spread of mild recessions. Fortunately this lesson has been
learned. The United Nations Charter contains a pledge on the part of all
countries to maintain full employment. This pledge was inserted on the
initiative of the small countries, notably Australia and New Zealand, who
feared that the war would be followed by another full-scale depression in the
United States. Such a depression has not occurred, and the United States has
learned its lesson in large measure. It possesses the fiscal and monetary
instruments needed for the purpose and knows how to use them. Perhaps
our major task, in this respect, is to convince the Common Market also to
become depression-proof. So far it has succeeded in the context of expanding
world demand. However, more does need to be done at home. Our constitutional system sometimes works well by good luck as much as good management. Various measures are needed to make the response to the onset of
recession more prompt, orderly and automatic. But, from the national and
international points of view, these are of minor importance compared with
the political revolution that exists to avoid a repetition of the 1930's.

So far the problem of the postwar world has been inflation rather than
depression. Inflation has resulted from the world wide demand for goods for
defense, economic development and also in part from the fact that high
employment has been maintained and the quest for higher living standards
has proceeded without serious interruption. If prices rise in all countries at
the same rate, international balance need not be disturbed. But this does not
always happen.

Continuing inflation in a major country can seriously impair international economic order. A country that inflates faster than its trading partners is almost certain to get into payment difficulties. As its prices increase, its products cease to be competitive with foreign products; its earnings abroad decline; and its payments abroad increase. The brunt of the adjustment is borne initially by loss of reserves. But that cannot go on indefinitely. If inflation continues, the country is forced to take measures to increase its receipts or reduce its payments abroad. Such measures can include export subsidies, direct import controls, tariff increases, exchange controls, reduction of government expenditures abroad, and, usually as a final resort, devaluation. This means that, in one way or another, agreements to liberalize trade are broken or escape clauses are invoked. The atmosphere becomes even less favorable for achieving further liberalization. The control of domestic inflation is therefore an international imperative.

The balance of payments difficulties now confronted by the United States arise basically from the fact that its competitive position in world markets, including its own, has declined. This is due mainly to the fact that as Europe and Japan gained in productive strength the United States has experienced more inflation than has occurred in those areas. The symptoms of the consequent lack of balance has been the outflow of gold and the increase in foreign holdings of dollars, which are readily convertible into gold. The state of the balance of payments has become a major preoccupation of policy makers; of equal importance, perhaps, with the level of unemployment.

The payments situation has had a direct effect on foreign policy operations. It has led to a close scrutiny of all government expenditures abroad for defense and foreign aid purposes. It has also led to the tying of the bulk of foreign aid expenditures to American goods. This is itself a violation of the liberal trading policies we are espousing. The United States should be in a position to provide aid in unrestricted dollars, with confidence that the recipients will want to spend those dollars on American products.

The United States, with its frequent assertions that it is the richest and strongest country in the world, is placed in an invidious and undignified position when it has to confess publicly that its foreign policy is constrained by its ability to spend one or two extra billions abroad—out of a total national product of more than $500 billion.

To conduct a successful foreign policy, the United States must have the freedom to spend abroad the amounts required to make that policy effective. This means that it must earn from exporting more than it spends on imports. Its ability to do that depends essentially on domestic policy, and the great outstanding problem is the control of inflation. This point needs little emphasis today. The President in April 1962 brought to bear the full weight of his authority to reverse a moderate price increase in steel. The main basis for his action was the damaging effect of a price increase on the international position of the United States. It is very doubtful whether he would have felt justified in taking such dramatic action on domestic grounds alone.

International and domestic policies are thus inextricably interwoven. Sharp divergences among internal polices of trading partners can cause the breakdown of any international system. The United States is now attempting to make partnership with Western Europe the core of its foreign economic policy. This will require more than mere agreement to reduce trade barriers. The continued success of the partnership will require substantial harmonization of domestic policies. Within the Common Market, the Six have agreed to accept the authority of a supranational executive. To evoke adequate techniques for harmonization throughout the Atlantic Community in the years ahead will be an intricate and challenging task for statesmanship.

Suggestions for Further Reading

Bowie, Robert R., and Theodore Geiger, *The European Economic Community and the United States,* Joint Economic Committee Print, 87th Congress, 1st Session (Washington, 1961).

Foreign Aid Program. Compilation of Studies for U.S. Senate: Senate Doc. No. 52, 85th Congress, 1st Session (Washington, 1957).

Harris, Seymour, ed., *The Dollar in Crisis* (New York: Harcourt, Brace & World, Inc., 1961).

Herter, Christian A., and William A. Clayton, *A New Look at Foreign Policy,* Joint Economic Committee Print, 87th Congress, 1st Session (Washington, 1961).

Kene, Peter B., *United States Commercial Policy: A Program for the 1960's,* Joint Economic Committee Print, 87th Congress, 1st Session (Washington, 1961).

Love, Alec N., and Desmond Donnelly, *Trade With Communist Countries* (New York: The Macmillan Company, 1961).

Mikesell, R. F., and Robert Loring Allen, *Economic Policies Toward Less Developed Countries,* Joint Committee Print, 87th Congress, 1st Session (Washington, 1961).

Millikin, Max F., and Donald L. M. Blackmer, eds., *The Emerging Nations: Their Growth and the U.S. Policy* (Boston: Little, Brown & Co., 1961).

Research and Policy Committee, Committee for Economic Development, *The International Position of the Dollar,* Joint Economic Committee Print, 87th Congress, 1st Session (Washington, 1961).

Viner, Jacob, *The Customs Union Issue* (New York: Carnegie Endowment for International Peace, 1950).

SPECTRUM  BOOKS

S-1   THE CAUSES OF THE CIVIL WAR, edited by Kenneth M. Stampp
S-2   IMMIGRATION AS A FACTOR IN AMERICAN HISTORY, edited by Oscar Handlin
S-3   PSYCHOANALYSIS AND PSYCHOTHERAPY: 36 SYSTEMS, Robert A. Harper
S-4   FALLACY: THE COUNTERFEIT OF ARGUMENT, W. Ward Fearnside and William B. Holther
S-5   THE GREAT DEBATE: OUR SCHOOLS IN CRISIS, edited by C. Winfield Scott, Clyde M. Hill, and Hobert W. Burns
S-6   FREEDOM AND CULTURE, Dorothy Lee
S-7   UNDERSTANDING TODAY'S THEATRE, Edward A. Wright
S-8   GOLDEN AGES OF THE THEATER, Kenneth Macgowan and William Melnitz
S-9   THE SEARCH FOR AMERICA,* edited by Huston Smith
S-10   THE GREAT DEPRESSION, edited by David A. Shannon
S-11   WHAT PRICE ECONOMIC GROWTH?* edited by Klaus Knorr and William J. Baumol
S-12   SCARCITY AND EVIL,* Vivian Charles Walsh
S-13   JUSTICE AND SOCIAL POLICY, Frederick Olafson
S-14   CONSTRUCTIVE ETHICS, T. V. Smith and William Debbins
S-15   LONELINESS,* Clark E. Moustakas
S-16   KNOWLEDGE: ITS VALUES AND LIMITS,* Gustave Weigel, S.J., and Arthur G. Madden
S-17   THE EDUCATION OF TEACHERS,* G. K. Hodenfield and T. M. Stinnett
S-18   LITERATURE, POPULAR CULTURE, AND SOCIETY, Leo Lowenthal
S-19   PARADOX AND PROMISE: ESSAYS ON AMERICAN LIFE AND EDUCATION,* Harry S. Broudy
S-20   RELIGION IN AMERICA: PAST AND PRESENT, Clifton E. Olmstead
S-21   RELIGION AND THE KNOWLEDGE OF GOD,* Gustave Weigel, S.J., and Arthur G. Madden
S-22   INTUITION AND SCIENCE, Mario Bunge
S-23   REVOLUTION, EVOLUTION, AND THE ECONOMIC ORDER,* Allen M. Sievers
S-24   AN ANATOMY FOR CONFORMITY,* Edward L. Walker and Roger Heyns
S-25   SCIENCE AND THE NATION,* J. Stefan Dupré and Sanford A. Lakoff
S-26   POLITICS IN AFRICA: PROSPECTS SOUTH OF THE SAHARA,* Herbert J. Spiro
S-27   THE FIRST RUSSIAN REVOLUTION: ITS IMPACT ON ASIA,* Ivar Spector
S-28   MASTERY OF THE METROPOLIS,* Webb S. Fiser
S-29   JOHANN SEBASTIAN BACH: AN INTRODUCTION TO HIS LIFE AND WORK,* Russell H. Miles
S-30   IN DEFENSE OF YOUTH,* Earl C. Kelley
S-31   HEROES, VILLAINS, AND FOOLS: THE CHANGING AMERICAN CHARACTER,* Orrin E. Klapp
S-32   COMMUNIST CHINA'S STRATEGY IN THE NUCLEAR ERA,* Alice Langley Hsieh
S-33   SOCIOLOGISM AND EXISTENTIALISM,* Edward A. Tiryakian

*Also available in limited clothbound edition.

S-34   PHILOSOPHY OF SCIENCE: THE LINK BETWEEN SCIENCE AND PHILOSOPHY, Philipp Frank

S-35   FREE WILL: A BOOK OF READINGS, edited by Sidney Morgenbesser and James J. Walsh

S-36   NINE MODERN MORALISTS,* Paul Ramsey

S-37   THE IMPORTANCE OF LANGUAGE, edited by Max Black

S-38   SOCIAL JUSTICE,* edited by Richard B. Brandt

S-39   EXISTENTIALISM AS PHILOSOPHY, Fernando Molina

S-40   TRUTH, MYTH, AND SYMBOL, edited by Thomas J. J. Altizer, William A. Beardslee, and J. Harvey Young

S-41   GOVERNMENT AND POLITICS OF THE MIDDLE EAST,* Maurice Harari

S-42   ART AND EXISTENTIALISM,* Arturo B. Fallico

S-43   THE PHILOSOPHY OF MIND, edited by V. C. Chappell

S-44   THE AMERICAN LABOR MOVEMENT, edited by Leon Litwack

S-45   DISCRIMINATION,* Wallace Mendelson

S-46   MAN'S DISCOVERY OF HIS PAST,* edited by Robert F. Heizer

S-47   LOUIS SULLIVAN: AN ARCHITECT IN AMERICAN THOUGHT,* Sherman Paul

S-48   THE FAITH TO DOUBT,* M. Holmes Hartshorne

S-49   UNDERSTANDING OTHER CULTURES,* Ina Corinne Brown

S-50   CLASS IN SUBURBIA,* William M. Dobriner

S-51   A GUIDE TO THE WORLD'S RELIGIONS,* David G. Bradley

S-52   PSYCHOTHERAPY IN OUR SOCIETY,* Theron Alexander

S-53   POSITIVE PROTESTANTISM: A RETURN TO FIRST PRINCIPLES, Hugh T. Kerr

S-54   CONTINUING CRISIS IN AMERICAN POLITICS,* edited by Marian D. Irish

S-55   THE NEGRO LEADERSHIP CLASS,* Daniel C. Thompson

S-56   THE NATURE OF SCIENTIFIC THOUGHT,* Marshall Walker

S-57   PSYCHOANALYSIS AND HISTORY,* edited by Bruce Mazlish

S-58   THE PROBLEM OF RELIGIOUS KNOWLEDGE,* William T. Blackstone

S-59   SLAVERY DEFENDED: THE VIEWS OF THE OLD SOUTH,* edited by Eric L. McKitrick

S-60   FIVE HISTORIANS LOOK AT COMMUNISM,* edited by Henry F. May

S-61   THE BOLSHEVIK TRADITION: LENIN, STALIN, KHRUSHCHEV,* Robert H. McNeal

S-62   LENIN, STALIN, KHRUSHCHEV: VOICES OF THE BOLSHEVIK TRADITION,* edited by Robert H. McNeal

S-63   THE SHAPING OF MODERN THOUGHT, Crane Brinton

The American Assembly Series

S-AA-1   THE FEDERAL GOVERNMENT AND HIGHER EDUCATION,* edited by Douglas M. Knight

S-AA-2   THE SECRETARY OF STATE,* edited by Don K. Price

S-AA-3   GOALS FOR AMERICANS: THE REPORT OF THE PRESIDENT'S COMMISSION ON NATIONAL GOALS

S-AA-4   ARMS CONTROL: ISSUES FOR THE PUBLIC,* edited by Louis Henkin

S-AA-5   OUTER SPACE,* edited by Lincoln P. Bloomfield

* Also available in limited clothbound edition.

S-AA-6 THE UNITED STATES AND THE FAR EAST (Second Edition), edited by
        Willard L. Thorp
S-AA-7 AUTOMATION AND TECHNOLOGICAL CHANGE,* edited by John T. Dunlop
S-AA-8 CULTURAL AFFAIRS AND FOREIGN RELATIONS,* edited by Robert Blum

Classics in History Series

S-CH-1 FRONTIER AND SECTION: SELECTED ESSAYS OF FREDERICK JACKSON TURNER,*
        Introduction and Notes by Ray Allen Billington
S-CH-2 DRIFT AND MASTERY: AN ATTEMPT TO DIAGNOSE THE CURRENT UNREST,
        Walter Lippmann, *Introduction and Notes by William E. Leuchten-
        burg*
S-CH-3 THE NEW NATIONALISM, Theodore Roosevelt, *Introduction and Notes
        by William E. Leuchtenburg*
S-CH-4 THE NEW FREEDOM: A CALL FOR THE EMANCIPATION OF THE GENEROUS
        ENERGIES OF A PEOPLE, Woodrow Wilson, *Introduction and Notes
        by William E. Leuchtenburg*
S-CH-5 EMPIRE AND NATION: JOHN DICKINSON'S "LETTERS FROM A FARMER IN
        PENNSYLVANIA" AND RICHARD HENRY LEE'S "LETTERS FROM THE
        FEDERAL FARMER," * *Introduction by Forrest McDonald*
S-CH-6 THE SUPREME COURT AND THE CONSTITUTION,* Charles A. Beard, *Intro-
        duction by Alan F. Westin*
S-CH-7 SOCIAL DARWINISM: SELECTED ESSAYS OF WILLIAM GRAHAM SUMNER,*
        Introduction by Stowe Persons
S-CH-8 WEALTH AGAINST COMMONWEALTH, Henry D. Lloyd,* *Introduction by
        Thomas C. Cochran*

Science and Technology Series

S-ST-1 THE ATOM AND ITS NUCLEUS, George Gamow
S-ST-2 ROCKET DEVELOPMENT,* Robert H. Goddard
S-ST-3 STARS AND GALAXIES: BIRTH, AGEING, AND DEATH IN THE UNIVERSE,*
        edited by Thornton Page

* Also available in limited clothbound edition.

Twentieth Century Views*

S-TC-1   CAMUS, edited by Germaine Brée

S-TC-2   T. S. ELIOT, edited by Hugh Kenner

S-TC-3   ROBERT FROST, edited by James M. Cox

S-TC-4   PROUST, edited by René Girard

S-TC-5   WHITMAN, edited by Roy Harvey Pearce

S-TC-6   SINCLAIR LEWIS, edited by Mark Schorer

S-TC-7   STENDHAL, edited by Victor Brombert

S-TC-8   HEMINGWAY, edited by Robert P. Weeks

S-TC-9   FIELDING, edited by Ronald Paulson

S-TC-10   THOREAU, edited by Sherman Paul

S-TC-11   BRECHT, edited by Peter Demetz

S-TC-12   EMERSON, edited by Milton R. Konvitz and Stephen E. Whicher

S-TC-13   MELVILLE, edited by Richard Chase

S-TC-14   LORCA, edited by Manuel Duran

S-TC-15   HOMER, edited by George Steiner and Robert Fagles

S-TC-16   DOSTOEVSKY, edited by René Wellek

S-TC-17   KAFKA, edited by Ronald Gray

S-TC-18   BAUDELAIRE, edited by Henri Peyre

S-TC-19   JOHN DONNE, edited by Helen Gardner

S-TC-20   EDITH WHARTON, edited by Irving Howe

S-TC-21   SARTRE, edited by Edith Kern

S-TC-22   BEN JONSON, edited by Jonas A. Barish

S-TC-23   YEATS, edited by John Unterecker

S-TC-24   D. H. LAWRENCE, edited by Mark Spilka

S-TC-25   HARDY, edited by Albert J. Guerard

S-TC-26   JANE AUSTEN, edited by Ian Watt

S-TC-27   F. SCOTT FITZGERALD, edited by Arthur Mizener

S-TC-28   EMILY DICKINSON, edited by Richard B. Sewall

S-TC-29   EZRA POUND, edited by Walter Sutton

S-TC-30   MARK TWAIN, edited by Henry Nash Smith

* Also available in limited clothbound edition.

May 15, 1970